BIG SCREEN
BOSTON

BIG SCREEN
BOSTON

From Mystery Street to The Departed and Beyond

■ □ ■ □ ■

PAUL SHERMAN

BLACK BARS
PUBLISHING

Big Screen Boston:
From Mystery Street to The Departed and Beyond

COVER DESIGN BY DAVID YOUNT, JR.

ISBN-13: 978-0-9776397-4-8
ISBN-10: 0-9776397-4-6

Library of Congress Control Number: 2007909889

Printed in the U.S.A.

Black Bars Publishing
P.O. Box 448
Malden, MA 02148

www.BigScreenBoston.com

Big Screen Boston is a registered trademark of Paul Sherman.
All Rights Reserved.

Publisher's Cataloging-in-Publication
(Provided by Quality Books, Inc.)

    Sherman, Paul, 1960-
      Big screen Boston : from Mystery street to The
    departed and beyond / Paul Sherman.
      p. cm.
      Includes index.
      LCCN 2007909889
      ISBN-13: 978-0-9776397-4-8
      ISBN-10: 0-9776397-4-6

      1. Motion picture industry--Massachusetts--Boston--
    History. 2. Motion picture locations--Massachusetts--
    Boston. 3. Motion pictures--Reviews. 4. Boston (Mass.)
    --In motion pictures.   I. Title.

    PN1993.5.U751S487 2008   384'.8'0974461
                QBI07-600340

9 8 7 6 5 4 3 2 1

CONTENTS

To the blinking stars on the ceiling of the Oriental Theater,

the Jimmy Rushing songs playing between movies at the Park Square Cinema,

the curtains at the Coolidge Corner Theater,

the balcony at the Brattle Theater...

And, most of all, to Sue.

Introduction:
This is Boston, Not L.A.

People get the wrong idea of Boston. I'm on the road, they go, 'We love that show *Cheers*. And we really think *St. Elsewhere* is great. Is Boston like that?' And I go, 'No. Did you see *The Boston Strangler*? That's Boston.'
                                        —Lenny Clarke joke, circa 1984

The cover of the February 1977 issue of *Boston* magazine says it all: "Why Hollywood Hates Boston." Inside, Michael Blowen and Gary Grossman's article catalogues the bizarre misadventures often awaiting Hollywood productions that dare to film in Greater Boston: Otto Preminger being dragged into court for desecration over a harmless scene he filmed in a Braintree cemetery for 1970's *Tell Me That You Love Me, Junie Moon* (he beat the rap); Norman Jewison getting a big thumbs up from Mayor Kevin White to use the city as a backdrop for 1968's lush *The Thomas Crown Affair*, then almost being shut down by a lone beat cop who claimed to know nothing about the movie; and Beacon Hill politicians acting characteristically slowly to establish a Massachusetts film commission, initially doing it on the cheap in the mid-1970s while other states were properly funding such offices and reaping the revenue-generating benefits.

The amazing thing about the article is its date. It's shortly *before* the production of *The Brink's Job*, the ultimate in troubled Boston productions. Not only did *Brink's* add to the lore of Boston moviemaking horror stories—for instance, one day the production paid a North End resident to remove an air conditioner, since the movie is set in the early 1950s; the next day, everyone on the block had an air conditioner, or a box painted *to look like one*, in his or her window, and collected, too. But what happened on *The Brink's Job* went beyond the inconvenient and the costly. Armed robbers stole film footage and tried to ransom it (not realizing the negative was the valuable item, not the developed film). Later, the federal government also charged several local Teamsters with extorting money from five Massachusetts productions, *The Brink's Job* among them.

The more things have changed, the more they've usually stayed the same between Boston and Hollywood (you could have updated the names in the *Boston* story in 1987 and 1997, and much of it still would have read eerily true). For the movie studios, Boston is usually a place to *sell* movies, not a place to *make* movies. Unpredictable weather, separation from families, high labor costs and the lure of less-expensive Canada or North Carolina locations have all conspired to make Boston a rare destination for Hollywood over the years. If producers want to make a movie in the Northeast, they'll usually do so in New York, where crews are more experienced, actors are more comfortable and locations are much more familiar and dramatically recognizable to international moviegoers.

Such a situation will never completely disappear. The original *The Parent Trap* puts Hayley Mills and Maureen O'Hara "in" the Public Garden, thanks to back projection that plays behind them as they speak their lines on a Los Angeles soundstage. Forty years later, *Legally Blonde* includes an aerial shot of the Zakim Bridge with a Volkswagen crossing it, then cuts to Reese Witherspoon in the same model car, filmed 2500 miles away from Cambridge, where her character is supposed to be arriving at Harvard Law School. The more things change...

Still, things are really on the upswing. A new Massachusetts Film Office is up and running after a five-year absence. The MFO had been defunded out of existence in 2002, becoming a political hot potato after getting trapped in the middle of the ongoing feud between Boston Teamsters and Hollywood (with shades of 1978, the Feds had stepped up their investigation into the Boston Teamsters' conduct with film productions). Tax incentives passed by the legislature now also sweeten the pot for movie productions big and small, and 2007 saw an unprecedented level of filmmaking in Greater Boston.

Just as importantly, heavy hitters Clint Eastwood and Martin Scorsese visited Boston to make, respectively, *Mystic River* and *The Departed*: Eastwood inspired by Bostonian Dennis Lehane's novel and Scorsese by Boston-born screenwriter William Monahan's reworking of the Hong Kong thriller *Infernal Affairs*. Each gritty tale was a hit and an award winner, *The Departed* grabbing an unexpected Best Picture Oscar. You might say it took a remake of a Hong Kong thriller directed by a moviemaker from New York—where much of *The Departed* was filmed—to, at long last, put Boston on the cinematic map. But that's not entirely true. Hollywood may come and go, but Boston's own filmmakers have built the city into a viable movie locale.

■□■□■

Long ago, mainstream movies rarely shot anywhere outside of California or New York. Transportation wasn't so convenient then, and lugging the hefty tools of commercial filmmaking to Massachusetts—even only from New York—was something few dared to do. The 1922 silent whaling melodrama *Down to the Sea in Ships*, featuring footage shot in and around New Bedford, is a rare instance in which the area offered moviemakers something they felt they couldn't recreate elsewhere. Other movies, including the 1915 version of *Vanity Fair* and 1935's *Ah, Wilderness*, mixed in local footage to add a New England flavor, but these films were few and far between.

Like Philadelphia or St. Louis, Boston just wasn't a place for Hollywood to even semi-regularly visit. The 1940s *Boston Blackie* series, about a safecracker turned crimefighter, isn't even set in Boston, let alone shot here, despite the hero's name. Instead, Boston was usually just a sort of shorthand in scripts. If you wanted to let an audience immediately know a character was prim, stuck-up and/or from old money—a sourpuss!—you just made him or her from Boston. Such movies as Frank Capra's *Here Comes the Groom* and John Ford's *Donovan's Reef* are just two that clung to the Boston cliché. The puritanical clichés have lingered, mostly as elements in TV series such as *Banacek*, *Cheers* and *Boston Legal* over the years.

Location shooting became easier and even trendy following World War II. The first features shot primarily in Boston resulted from the success of New York and Los Angeles post-war docudramas such as *The House on 92nd Street* that reveled in real locations and topical stories. Boston got its first real taste of big-screen glory in *Mystery Street*, in which Harvard forensic scientists help police solve a Cape Cod murder, and *Walk East on Beacon!*, a rather hysterical anti-Communist screed made by *House on 92nd Street* producer Louis de Rochemont, a Chelsea native.

Visits by Hollywood were infrequent and rather random through the 1950s and much of the 1960s: The light crime drama *Six Bridges to Cross* (1955) shot here because it's loosely based on the same famous heist as *The Brink's Job*, the heavier *Home Before Dark* (1958) because the novel upon which it's based is set in a fictional New England coastal town, the big-budget epic *The Cardinal* (1963) because some of it occurs in the city and the comedy *Never Too Late* (1965) because it takes place in a traditional small town. Such movies filmed only a portion of their action locally, from a handful of scenes to roughly half of their story. The rest was usually done back in Los Angeles. In 1970's *Tell Me That You Love Me, Junie Moon*, palm-tree-filled San Diego is even supposed to pass for a Cape Ann resort—despite the fact that the movie is full of actual North Shore locales.

It wasn't until the late 1960s and 1970s when movies that came to Boston tended to shoot most of their scenes in the area. The original Steve McQueen version of *The Thomas Crown Affair*, written by Brookline lawyer Alan Trustman, offers a fantastically glamorous panorama of the area, while *Charly*, also from 1968, contrasts the Cliff Robertson title character's blue-collar neighborhood with Boston's prim medical-academic elite. That medical-academic world is a favorite backdrop of such 1970s and 1980s movies as *The Paper Chase*, *Coma* and *The Verdict*, but as the number of Boston movies increased, so did the city's screen personality. The best movie ever made in Boston, the decidedly unglamorous *The Friends of Eddie Coyle*—based on the work of yet another Hub writer, the late George V. Higgins—is as far from the elites as you can get. I don't think Robert Mitchum's Eddie Coyle would know what to do at a college or a hospital, unless he was stealing something.

■□■□■

Boston might have been a periodic pit stop for Hollywood by the 1970s, but feature filmmaking that really reflected the city didn't emerge until two local traditions, documentary filmmaking and theater companies, intersected.

Boston had long been a hot spot for both. Many of the country's most innovative non-fiction filmmakers had ties to the area. Albert and David Maysles (*Salesman*, *Gimme Shelter*) grew up in Brookline and Dorchester; lawyer turned filmmaker Frederick Wiseman (*Titicut Follies*) was based here; and such directors as Richard Leacock, Ed Pincus, Alfred Guzzetti and Richard Rogers were teaching locally.

Boston was one of the homes of "direct cinema" non-fiction filmmaking, a style that frowned upon narration and other overt forms of audience manipulation. These filmmakers went out into the world and shot "fly on the wall" style, and for this they needed stripped-down, portable equipment, much of which they developed themselves. Boston's documentary films were also often politically motivated, with an eye toward focusing on the disenfranchised and issues of the day. There was a Boston chapter of the activist film collective Newsreel,

Henry Hampton formed his production company Blackside in 1968 (it would eventually make the definitive civil-rights chronicle *Eyes on the Prize* in the late 1980s) and WGBH supplied a substantial amount of documentary programming to PBS.

So, in the 1970s, Boston did not have many people who knew how to shoot and edit a polished, "professional" feature film. But it did have many who knew how to make documentaries.

Meanwhile, David Wheeler's Theater Company of Boston was ambitiously staging plays in the area, with such actors as Al Pacino, Robert De Niro, Dustin Hoffman, Blythe Danner, John Cazale, Stockard Channing and Lance Henriksen appearing in its productions. So, too, did Jan Egleson, a young actor who'd begun directing for the company. Egleson had had a small part in *The Friends of Eddie Coyle* as a soldier selling stolen guns; technical problems necessitated the reshooting of his scene, and he took the extra time on the set to observe the logistics of moviemaking.

"The transition was just a natural step from doing theater to doing film," he says, years later. It wasn't until a few years after *Eddie Coyle* that he'd have the inspiration. During the run of one Theater Company of Boston production, *The Medal of Honor Rag*, he had pondered filming a performance for posterity. But that never happened. Then Egleson and his wife, actress (and future casting agent) Patty Collinge, volunteered to teach drama at The Group School, an alternative Cambridge school for working-class kids.

"A lot of the kids were great actors, they were naturals," Egleson recalls. "Their stories were fascinating, and their experiences were different from what you could see in mainstream films. So we took the stories that the kids told and wove them into a script and worked with them as actors. And we used the technique of documentary guys who were here: we used their lightweight equipment, we shot on the street with available light."

The result was *Billy in the Lowlands*, among the first homegrown feature films and the most ambitious yet (James A. Pike's 1966 teen picture *Feelin' Good* and Dick Bartlett's daffy 1971 comedy *Ruby* predate it). With Henry Tomaszewski as the feisty anti-hero, *Billy* is no-frills filmmaking that challenges audiences to invest themselves in characters who are just scraping by in life, if that, and to find drama in the everyday world around them. *Billy* is certainly not for all audiences—not escapist enough for some nor exotic enough for others (Egleson used to joke that his movie would have gotten more attention in America if he'd made it in Polish and subtitled it). It had a spotty release in theaters, but earned a New England Emmy after later airing on WGBH, prompting the station to help finance Egleson's follow-up, the Cambridge projects drama *The Dark End of the Street*.

The apparatus to get low-budget, American non-horror independent movies to audiences barely existed at the time. But Egleson's film reflected a growing rebellion against Hollywood hegemony. Like him, other moviemakers were taking to *their* streets, including Victor Nuñez (*Gal Young 'Un*) in Florida and the team of Rob Nilsson and John Hanson (*Northern Lights*) in Minnesota. Regional filmmaking was posing no threat to Hollywood, but it was bubbling under the surface. And *Billy in the Lowlands* had a ripple effect in Boston.

Among those who saw Egleson's movie were Robert Jones and the husband-and-wife duo of Randall Conrad and Christine Dall. All three had been making documentaries, but recognized that Egleson had shown how they could take their talents in a new direction. After seeing *Billy*, and as Egleson filmed *The Dark End of the Street*, these other moviemakers made their own fiction films—*The Dozens* (1981) by Conrad and Dall, *Mission Hill* (1982) by Jones.

"I think there was a craving to make films," Conrad recalls of the time. "Making films was a very '60s thing. People used to joke that, in Cambridge, if you tripped over an architect you fell over a filmmaker—they were so common. It was sacrosanct to make documentaries, for various reasons. (But) in some of our fantasies, we all wanted to make a feature film—a dramatic movie. I remember going over to see Jan and asking him a little bit of how he worked. Because I had zero experience making fiction films, a fact which was to be sorely tested during the shoot.

"Jan was very encouraging," Conrad adds. "He was very lonely out there by himself."

For Dall, making *The Dozens*—which she and Conrad shot in 1978 and 1979, shortly before they were married—wasn't chasing a dream, it was a practical solution. Although they'd originally imagined doing a movie about a just-released female convict as a documentary, she saw the logistical problems in that.

"One of the big problems we faced if we were going to do it as a documentary was being allowed into the real life of this person," Dall says. "Obviously, they're not going to want what they're doing and who they're associating with out there in the public."

So *The Dozens* became well-researched fiction, with a script the couple wrote with Marian Taylor, an ex-con who also acts in the movie. Debra Margolies brings fiery spunk to the role of Sally, a young woman with one foot in prison and the other in a drab, blue-collar world of limited opportunities, especially for a woman. Inspired by the

English movies of everyday drudgery made by Ken Loach and Roland Joffé, it's grim yet somehow lyrical.

Robert Jones, then teaching film at Boston University, felt the influence of *Billy in the Lowlands*, too. "Jan was definitely the primary influence—I really liked his films and his style," says the *Mission Hill* director. Like Egleson's films and *The Dozens*, *Mission Hill*, set in the neighborhood where Jones grew up (though filmed in other parts of Boston and its surroundings), is a blue-collar drama. But it spreads its focus over an entire family—a dissipated single mother (Barbara Orson) and the kids (Brian Burke, Alice Barrett and John Mahoney) who are still rattling their cages to escape their triple-decker flat.

Social realism isn't the only thing linking the movies. "The tech talent pool was very thin, so we all used the same camera people, editors, make-up people, etc., which augmented the feeling of community," recalls Jones.

Movies such as *Billy in the Lowlands*, *The Dozens*, *The Dark End of the Street* and *Mission Hill* received plenty of local attention and jump-started Boston independent moviemaking. There was even a 1983 Museum of Fine Arts panel discussion with all four directors which, putting a local twist on Scorsese's *Mean Streets*, branded their movies as "Beanstreets" movies. But the idea of self-sustaining regional cinema was not economically viable. In order for a movie to be attractive to the sort of independent film distributors that sprang up in the 1980s, it had to appeal to audiences nationwide, conforming to the accepted style and look of a "commercial movie" and, in the process, requiring an enhanced budget and losing some local flavor.

After *The Dark End of the Street*, Egleson was unable to secure financing for the follow-up he'd intended. Instead, he eventually found partial funding from PBS' new *American Playhouse* series for *The Little Sister*, a project that had a similar grass-roots genesis to his previous movies but, for better or worse, also had a much more professional rendering. His career since has been a mixture of PBS, Hollywood and Boston films, including the withering black comedy *A Shock to the System*, locally shot TV movies such as *Big Time* and *Original Sins* and a triumphant return to local moviemaking with 2001's *The Blue Diner*, the last in collaboration with the late Natatcha Estébanez. Since Egleson was not able to continue making movies only in Boston, *Billy in the Lowlands*, *The Dark End of the Street* and *The Little Sister* retroactively became known as his "Boston trilogy."

Egleson says he "always" has at least one Boston project he's trying to get made at any given time. "I live here and I love the city, I love the way it looks and everything else about it," he explains. "But I also like the idea that you do work that's rooted in where you are. It's just much less abstract. When you're making a film about your neighborhood or your city, it has a very different feel than when you go somewhere and make it all up. It's very different."

Despite winning a Grand Prize at the U.S. Film & Video Festival (later renamed the Sundance Film Festival), *The Dozens* did not open doors for Randall Conrad and Christine Dall. "There was no thought of sitting down with the studios," Conrad says, contrasting the situation with that awaiting today's Sundance award winners. And the pair wanted no part of the fund-raising struggle necessary to make another movie like their first.

"For me, it was the reality of (features) not really being about filmmaking and being able to make social justice movies," says Dall, explaining why there was no follow-up to *The Dozens*. "This was a business. It takes money, a lot of money, to do it. If you don't have access to it, it's a killer. You have no money, you can't support yourself. I wanted to have a family."

So it was back to documentaries for the couple. He made a short documentary about Shay's Rebellion (*A Little Rebellion Now and Then*), she made the 1989 music documentary *Wild Women Don't Have the Blues*. They taught, worked on other people's movies and stayed sane.

Similarly, Jones eventually returned to documentaries and teaching. He's been at the University of Central Florida for over a decade, with the makers of *The Blair Witch Project* counted among his students. More recently, he's been making low-budget comedies, his latest being *Fetus Fetish*.

■▫■▫■

So the idealistic "Beanstreets" movies came and went with barely a blip. Or did they? A more accurate description might be that they quietly planted a seed, and the crop is still being reaped today.

Put bluntly, the chances that Hollywood ever would have made Boston "neighborhood movies" like *Mystic River* or *The Departed* were it not for *Billy in the Lowlands*—a movie few people are even aware of today—are doubtful. But the dots are pretty easy to connect. *Billy* begat *Dark End of the Street*, in which a little tyke named Ben Affleck made his acting debut. Affleck's and Matt Damon's families were friendly with Egleson's before Matt and Ben were even born— Affleck's dad acted some with the Theater Company of Boston and the three families were all Cambridge neighbors. The influence of

Egleson's homegrown movies rubbed off on *Good Will Hunting*, and not just on Damon and Affleck's stubborn insistence that at least a good chunk of the movie be shot locally. As Affleck told me shortly before filming began on *Good Will Hunting*: "Part of what the movie's about on a subtext level is class and the way people deal with each other. In Cambridge, we were acutely aware of the stark contrast between university life and the lives of the people who live there." Working on Egleson's second movie surely wasn't the only way Affleck learned about class struggle, but it helped to shape the specific understanding of society that *Good Will Hunting* exudes.

Good Will Hunting isn't the only sprout that's the result of the "Beanstreets" movies. Robert Patton-Spruill, the Roxbury-based director and producer, is the son of another Theater Company of Boston alumnus, B.U. drama professor James Spruill. In the 1990s, when Patton-Spruill was working at Collinge-Pickman, the casting agency co-founded by Egleson's wife, Patty Collinge, Egleson took Patton-Spruill under his wing. The two collaborated on an unproduced script for *The Boy Without a Flag*, the Abraham Rodriguez, Jr. story Egleson had optioned. That project never came to fruition, but Patton-Spruill's first movie, 1997's *Squeeze*, grew out of his experiences with kids at the Dorchester Youth Collaborative, just as Egleson's early movies had been inspired by his Group School students. Like Egleson, Patton-Spruill cast untrained kids as his *Squeeze* leads.

Good Will Hunting and *Squeeze* are big parts of the impressive late-1990s cluster of Boston independent movies that also included Brad Anderson's *Next Stop Wonderland* and Ted Demme's Denis Leary-produced *Monument Ave*. These films, as much as *Blown Away, Housesitter* or *The Crucible*—Hollywood visits that pumped much more money into local coffers—kept Boston an *interesting* movie city and indirectly inspired Clint Eastwood and Martin Scorsese to fight their studios for a local shooting schedule—the entire movie for *Mystic River*, about half for *The Departed*. The momentum generated by such acclaimed movies also made it possible for Affleck to later direct his own Boston neighborhood movie, *Gone Baby Gone*—like *Mystic River*, an adaptation of a Dennis Lehane novel.

■□■□■

There was a feature on David Letterman's 1980s NBC show called *Limited Perspectives*, when a specialist reviewed a movie solely on the basis of his or her field of expertise—a dentist reviewing *One from the Heart*, a driver's ed teacher reviewing *The Road Warrior* and so on.

The last thing this book should be is the Boston movie equivalent of that *Late Night with David Letterman* segment. A scenic walk through the Common or a character living in a triple-decker does not automatically make a good movie. These are secondary concerns. I've tried to show which movies use Greater Boston locations with depth and cleverness, and which do not. But those that use locations well aren't always better movies than those that use them more generically, especially if the movie that uses locations well has a weak script.

People often ask what makes a movie a "Boston movie." For the feature films, I've used a "boots on the ground" rule. If, unlike *Legally Blonde*, *The Out of Towners* remake or *The Greatest Game Ever Played*, a movie takes the trouble to bring cast members to Boston to shoot action here, it is, to some extent, a "Boston movie" and deserves to be included here. Naturally, for the book's purposes, movies that take place partially in Boston usually aren't as significant as those set entirely in and around the city.

Documentaries are trickier. The area abounds with world-renowned non-fiction moviemakers such as Errol Morris, Frederick Wiseman and Ross McElwee. Although such directors do most of their production here, they don't often shoot here. But they're Boston filmmakers, nonetheless, and their influence has often crept into the features made here (remember, the "Beanstreets" cycle of movies never would have happened were it not for the pre-existing local documentary scene). I've attempted to give a taste of the work of the most prolific filmmakers in the area, as well as spotlight other non-fiction standouts that have sprung from the thriving Boston documentary community.

Regardless of any movie's genre, the aim here is to look at a group of movies through the same context and to put the small, homegrown movies on the same footing as extravagant Hollywood productions. The playing field leveled, hopefully the merits of the smaller movies will emerge and the relationship between the low-budget homegrown pictures and the costlier Hollywood productions will become clearer. I also hope the book's "pull quotes" give a taste of the intentions of both Hollywood and Boston moviemakers (unless otherwise noted, all quotes in the book are from interviews I've conducted over the years). A large number of homegrown movies—from *Ruby* and *Billy in the Lowlands* to *A Pound of Flesh* and *The North End*—have still not come out on any form of home video. Let's hope this book will be partially responsible for changing that situation.

PAUL SHERMAN
DECEMBER 2007

All the Rage

1997. Written and directed by Roland Tec. Based on his play *A Better Boy*. With John-Michael Lander, David Vincent, Paul Outlaw, Jay Corcoran, Peter Bubriski and Merle Perkins. Cinematography by Gretchen Widmer.

IT SOUNDS CLICHÉD, BUT leave it to a gay movie to produce one of the handsomest, best-groomed glimpses of Boston onscreen. As *Good Will Hunting* does for South Boston, *Monument Ave.* does for Charlestown and *The North End* does for Boston's Italian-American neighborhood, writer-director Roland Tec's movie brings another part of the city to the screen: the South End's gay community.

Looking much more luxurious than it ever really should, considering its under-a-million budget, *All the Rage* is one of the more resourceful movies shot around town in the mid-1990s. The producers sent out a letter to prospective "helpers" asking for donations or discounts on everything from paper plates and shooting locations to dry cleaning, and the appeal apparently worked. Tec shot much of the movie in private residences that owners let him use for free. And some of them, including Tec's own Columbus Avenue apartment, had roof decks with spectacular views.

Fashioning a blend of comedy and drama that's sometimes striking and sometimes awkward, *All the Rage*—based on Connecticut native Tec's 1994 one-man play *A Better Boy*—sets its critical sights on its protagonist, Christopher (John-Michael Lander). An A-list Boston lawyer with money, looks and libido, Christopher picks and chooses his boyfriends, and then loves 'em and leaves 'em. This slick slut claims to want more out of relationships than one-night stands. He gets his chance to prove it when he falls for Stewart (David Vincent), a nebbishy book editor who, unlike Christopher's usual conquests, doesn't want to rush things.

Some of the early comedy stems from Christopher's hedonistic friend Larry (Jay Corcoran) and his straight female friend Susan (Merle Perkins). She isn't brassy, a departure from the usual stock character, and is typical of how Tec's movie often breaks from conventions that sometimes littered 1990s gay moviemaking. *All the Rage* has no drag queens, campy gags or plucky underdog heroes.

Such boldness definitely buoys the movie. This is hardly a movie-by-numbers; it has all kinds of ambition. Still, only some of the humor works, and the story definitely sags during its mid-section. That's partially because new boyfriend Stewart is not quite as endearing as

Christopher tells others he is. Consequently, you don't feel the stupidity of Christopher later jeopardizing his new relationship as strongly as you might have.

But the relationship with Stewart allows *All the Rage* to start with a light tone and gradually darken as Christopher contends with the temptations that come along with monogamy—the biggest forbidden fruit he encounters being Stewart's famously endowed roommate (Alan Natale).

The movie's ability to avoid cliché keeps it interesting, and *All the Rage* is definitely decent for a low-budget first film. Although the storytelling sometimes strains to get its points across, the movie rebounds to a very strong ending in which Christopher encounters a sort of "ghost of one-night stands past" (Jeff Miller). The cutting climax doesn't totally erase the memory of the dull stretches, but it sends this bumpy ride out with class.

> I love having the Hancock Tower with the reflection of Trinity Church (on it). It's pitting the old against the new, which I think reflects part of what the main character is going through. He's 31, it's like, 'Is he an adult or an adolescent?'
> –Roland Tec

Although the Massachusetts Film Office often seemed to have little concern for homegrown movies like this, in the mid-1990s it began to pay more attention to them. Tec—who co-produced his movie with *A Pound of Flesh* director Catherine Burns—goes out of his way to thank the state agency during his audio commentary on the movie's DVD. *All the Rage* was a relatively low-maintenance film for the Film Office, no doubt, as it shot only in the city. In addition to the South End and the Back Bay, Tec also filmed part of *All the Rage* in Charlestown and at the longtime Fenway club, The Ramrod.

▶**Locations:** South End, Fenway, Back Bay, Charlestown, Boston.

▶**Accents:** "You're wicked cute," says one man to another in one of the movie's rare instances of local slang. But the upscale South End setting is light on accents.

▶**Local color:** There are some amazing views here: nearby skylines from South End townhouse rooftops, a walk down Stuart Street behind the John Hancock Tower, a look down on Copley Square and the Trinity Church from what appears to be a Prudential Center office (on the DVD commentary, writer-director Roland Tec reveals that he was allowed to use the office where the work scenes occur only on the "condition of anonymity" because it's a very conservative company). The people might not necessarily shout "local," but the city is definitely part of what defines them.

Between the Lines

1977. Directed by Joan Micklin Silver. Written by Fred Barron. With John Heard, Lindsay Crouse, Jeff Goldblum, Gwen Welles, Stephen Collins, Bruno Kirby, Jill Eikenberry, Lewis J. Stadlen and Michael J. Pollard. Cinematography by Kenneth Van Sickle.

JOHN SAYLES' NEW HAMPSHIRE-shot *The Return of the Secaucus Seven* (1980) and Hollywood's version of its 1960s-pals reunion premise, *The Big Chill*, weren't the first movies to look at the disillusionment striking baby boomers who'd lived through the idealistic counterculture. Joan Micklin Silver's movie came first, and though it would have been timelier a few years before 1977 (Fred Barron actually completed his script in 1975), *Between the Lines* captures the counterculture in mid-fizzle.

Barron had been a movie critic for *The Boston Phoenix*, and he based the movie's *Back Bay Mainline* on that and the area's other alternative weekly, *The Real Paper* (which later folded in 1981). The fictional publication is at all sorts of crossroads in *Between the Lines*: rumors abound that the once-vital, now-stagnant paper is about to be sold to an out-of-town company; the longtime staffers there are each

Between the Lines: Michael J. Pollard in Copley Square.

deciding whether to stick around or search for greener pastures; and, as one character says, everyone at a place like the *Mainline* is either "going up or going down."

There's a wonderful assortment of characters and, true to the movie's setting, they're played by an impressive cast, many of whom were indeed "going up." There's the star reporter who's now burnt out (John Heard), a photographer trying not to have a "career" (Lindsay Crouse), a rock critic who takes every advantage of his local fame (Jeff Goldblum), another reporter writing a book on the death of the counterculture (Stephen Collins) and a third reporter who realizes she's lost the passion for her work (Gwen Welles), among others.

When these people are together in bunches, their camaraderie sparks. In such instances, the journalists are always eager to ridicule Stanley (Lewis J. Stadlen), the advertising salesman who has no sense of humor. One of the movie's funniest scenes comes when a self-proclaimed "conceptual artist" (Raymond J. Barry) barges into the office and smashes a typewriter in hopes of getting noticed. The rock critic, eager to impress his co-workers, quickly outdoes the guy with "installations" of his own, punching a hole in a wall and ripping the buttons from—who else?—Stanley's shirt.

> We could only afford to shoot in Boston for two weeks. We couldn't afford to put up the cast for longer there. So we shot a lot in New York, where most of them lived.
> –Joan Micklin Silver

But you might say the party's over for most of these people. They either have to decide what to do with their lives, or such a decision will be made for them, especially after a business-minded new owner (Lane Smith) arrives.

Goldblum, whose charismatic critic is likely to cling to his low-paying position after the regime change, and Heard, who would mine male vulnerability further with Silver in her even better *Chilly Scenes of Winter*, come off strongest here. If Silver's direction is clunky at times, it only adds to the movie's scruffy personality. Made at a time when independent film was at low ebb, *Between the Lines* helped keep low-budget moviemaking for adults alive.

The movie didn't have to be set in Boston, but the city is one of only a handful where the radical sentiments of the late 1960s might have coalesced into a paper that lasted into the late 1970s. While Silver filmed many exteriors locally, just about all the interiors were done in New York. The opening sequence, with Michael J. Pollard as the *Mainline* hawker trying to entice drivers waiting at the Dartmouth Street traffic light between Copley Square and the Boston Public Library, is actually the most sustained use of Boston public locations.

The Charles Red Line platform is the setting for another scene, as is the Central Square fixture Cheapo Records. In fact, Cambridge is here more than Boston. Jeff Goldblum and Bruno Kirby walk through the "old" Harvard Square, seen via a nice rooftop shot, while the *Mainline* office is also across the river.

Had the plans of local filmmaker David Helpern (the documentaries *I'm a Stranger Here Myself* and *Hollywood on Trial*) come to fruition, *Between the Lines* might have been an all-Boston affair. A 1975 *Real Paper* article mentions his intention to direct Barron's screenplay, then called *Alternative Lives*. Presumably, bringing in Silver, who'd had an arthouse hit with *Hester Street*, made finding financing easier. There was a small spat when Silver tried to get a screenwriting credit on the movie after filming, but the Writers Guild of America deemed Barron the sole writer. Helpern and Barron eventually made 1979's romantic comedy *Something Short of Paradise* together, after relocating to New York City.

▶ **Locations:** Cambridge; Back Bay, Boston.

▶ **Accents:** Nothing here. In a more perfect world, the hawker might have been a local. But the bulk of the movie's characters are presumably transplants who came to Boston for college, and grew up elsewhere.

▶ **Local color:** There's more of a left-leaning-city-with-radicals-hanging-around flavor than a specifically Boston flavor. Better here than San Francisco or Philadelphia. Having a local band such as The Modern Lovers play the movie's party instead of Southside Johnny & the Asbury Jukes could have added something, but that wasn't to be.

Billy Galvin

1986. Written and directed by John Gray. With Karl Malden, Lenny Von Dohlen, Joyce Van Patten and Toni Kalem. Cinematography by Eugene Shlugleit.

THINK OF IT AS the anti-*Jazz Singer*. Instead of a father saying "I have no son" because his offspring won't continue the family business, this time Jack Galvin (Karl Malden) feels that way because his son (Lenny Von Dohlen) *wants* to do what his father does.

In this case, the family business is being a Boston ironworker, and the elder Galvin's stubborn insistence that his union not give 25-ish Billy a job is among several things that aren't quite convincing in writer-director John Gray's movie. Sure, it's natural for the old guy to want his son to have every opportunity in life and be an architect (though there's never any hint that Billy has any design flair). But even Malden—whose reflective scene with Alan North in a Blue Line station is a highlight—struggles with Jack's over-the-top childishness. Jack is essentially an emotionally blocked Archie Bunker, presumably minus the racism (though his union local is lily-white), especially in the scenes with Joyce Van Patten as his wife.

If Malden is well-cast but fighting a weak script, Von Dohlen, who had a few lead movie roles in the 1980s, seems badly miscast. The blue-eyed actor tries hard to be blue-collar, but (and this is no insult) his Billy comes off more like someone who *would* want to be an architect rather than an ironworker. His barmaid girlfriend Nora (Toni Kalem) can outdrink him and, once he pulls an end run around his dad to get on the union's latest big project, it turns out he's not so comfortable with heights.

Although it's obvious John Gray wants to show the heart in ironworking vets like Jack, the co-worker played by North and the building-site foreman (South Boston's Paul Guilfoyle), the writer-director—a Brooklyn native with an ironworking tradition in his family—has trouble developing characters beyond the generic. Just look at the posters on Billy's bedroom wall: The Beatles, John Lennon and Bruce Springsteen. I guess being a working-class hero means not having very distinctive musical taste (or the character development that might have come with it).

The contrived father-son conflict is only biding its time, though. Jack doesn't want Billy to become an ironworker, but Billy gets on the job anyway. The construction scenes were filmed 16 floors up as Marketplace Center was being built between Quincy Market and the old expressway. These scenes offer great views of other Boston high-rises from various eras, including the Custom House Tower, Harbor Towers and the John Hancock Tower.

> The flavor of the people at Marketplace Center was absorbed by all of us, but I particularly paid attention to the guys I met there and the people at Champions, the bar we shot at.
> –Lenny Von Dohlen

A mishap puts Billy's ironworking career in jeopardy, and it's up to Jack to help him get back on the job and avoid being laid off. But you know Jack's resistance will melt away, as surely as you know Billy's tiff with Nora will be smoothed over. There are few surprises to enliven *Billy Galvin*.

There aren't surprises, but there are a few unexpected choices in locations, for better or worse. While a movie made today would most likely put Billy's parents in a Southie triple-decker, they live in a South End townhouse in this 1980s drama. And it seems odd for an ironworker's retirement bash to be at the Hotel Lafayette (now a Hyatt) instead of at the union's own hall or a VFW post. The barroom action was done at Champions on Main Street in Everett ($10.50 for pizza and a pitcher!); chances are the place was *already* decked out in memorabilia reflecting the days in which the Celtics and Bruins always made the playoffs and few had expectations or passion for the perennially pathetic Patriots. The movie climaxes at Joseph's Aquarium Restaurant on the waterfront.

▶**Locations:** South End, Boston; Everett; Cambridge.

▶**Accents:** Like everything else in *Billy Galvin*, strain shows here. Malden, Von Dohlen and Keith Szarabajka, who plays Billy's pal Donny, all sport questionable, erratic accents. They would have been better off toning it down. The local native with the biggest role, Paul Guilfoyle, has a lighter accent than the others try to use.

▶**Local color:** No joke, this movie has great trash. Bags from Grossman's, Pizzeria Regina and D'Angelo's litter Billy's car and apartment, and they're a rare instance of the movie developing the right specifics about who this guy is. Too bad they mean nothing to anyone beyond 495, but someone on the production staff did his or her job well.

▶**Local celeb alert!:** That's comic Steve Sweeney as the diner owner at the greasy spoon where Billy briefly works.

Billy in the Lowlands

1979. Written and directed by Jan Egleson. With Henry Tomaszewski, Paul Benedict, Genevieve Reale and David Clennon. Cinematography by D'Arcy Marsh.

TO PARAPHRASE AN OLD line of dialogue, there's not a lot to *Billy in the Lowlands*, but what's there is choice. In many ways, Jan Egleson's homegrown movie began indie feature filmmaking in Greater Boston. The drama struggles to get going, but it ultimately kicks in and its offbeat coming-of-age tale definitely stays with you.

It takes a while to tune into *Billy in the Lowlands'* particular rhythms. Egleson was a theater actor who'd occasionally been in movies—he's the young soldier nervously selling guns in *The Friends of Eddie Coyle* and the guy whose bike is almost stolen here—and the style of his first movie is fairly primitive. Since there was no fiction filmmaking community in Boston at the time (the movie is actually a production of the famed Theater Company of Boston), Egleson's small crew was just as inexperienced as he was. He cast the movie with a combination of professionals (Paul Benedict, David Clennon) and non-professionals, including teens from Cambridge's The Group School for troubled youth, where Egleson volunteered as a drama instructor.

These kids' anecdotes provided the inspiration for Egleson's tale of Billy (Henry Tomaszewski), a trouble magnet who rests all his hopes on a reunion with his wayward father (Benedict). Billy's bad luck and poor judgment are evident right away when he punches out at his foundry job in Quincy, and a joy-riding friend pulls up and asks him if he wants a ride home—in a stolen car. Billy, who we soon learn is on probation, gets in, the cops catch them and Billy ends up in juvenile prison in Billerica.

When Billy gets a call about his grandfather's death and his father flying in for the funeral, he sneaks away from jail to find him, thinking his father will take him far away. Once he gets back to Cambridge and finds his friends from his housing project, who try to help him get to Lynn, where his father is supposed to be, the story takes on a real urgency and hits its stride. After the set-up, the last two-thirds of the movie take place over a 24-hour period.

Tomaszewski's nervous energy suits the urgency that grips the title character (of course, the fact that Billy has handcuffs he wants to shed adds to the kid's frenzy). The scenes with his friend Liz have a special spark, because Genevieve Reale, who plays her, has an unusually expressive face. Liz is sad-eyed, as if she knows more about what's ahead than Billy does. We know Billy is deceiving himself about his dad because, at various times, he tells others his father is an artichoke farmer, a trucker and an oil-well driller. Sure enough, once Billy finds his father, he's a drunk who doesn't live in Billy's land of dreams, California, but in Cleveland. There's a humorous, skin-crawling awkwardness to most of their scenes together, but the movie ends with hope, not despair, as the encounter awakens Billy to the fact that no one is going to shape him up but him.

> The Italians had done it with neo-realism and the English had done it with the kitchen-sink dramas. There was nothing like that in America. So we thought, 'Why don't we try?'
> –Jan Egleson

Of course, *Billy*'s lack of style *is* its style. It's a back-to-basics, grass-roots movie all the way. I assume Egleson had permits to shoot some scenes in Harvard Square, or else the Cambridge police would have quickly shooed him away, but some of the little moments—like Billy panhandling for change—feel as if the director just pushed

Billy in the Lowlands: Paul Benedict and Henry Tomaszewski in Hull.

Tomaszewski into a real crowd and filmed what happened. There's also a gritty beauty to shots like the one in which Billy, Liz and another friend ride towards the Paragon Park rollercoaster at dawn, while the sequence in Cardell's, the atmospheric Harvard Square greasy spoon that used to be across from the Brattle Theater, is pure Edward Hopper. The prison scenes are also in Cambridge (at the then-new Middlesex courthouse), while the Lynn scenes were done mostly in Hull (after plans to shoot in Revere were thwarted by the demolition of the rollercoaster there).

One of my favorite touches, which I'm sure no one thought twice about at the time, is that Billy has a Sears basketball near the end of the movie. Now that Sears no longer makes things like basketballs, it just seems so right. Billy and his friends are more likely to have things or frequent places that are old than they are to be enjoying the latest things. They don't live in a land of dreams.

▶ **Locations:** Cambridge; Quincy; Hull; Medford.

▶ **Accents:** All real, all the time. They ought to make Hollywood dialect coaches watch it.

▶ **Local color:** This one will definitely take you back, if you're old enough to remember, to a less slick time: Paragon Park! Zayre! Cardell's, Brigham's and the antiquated wooden-slats escalator in "old" Harvard Square! And there's a great view of the roster of stores at Fresh Pond Shopping Center, circa 1977.

Black Irish

2006. Written and directed by Brad Gann. With Michael Angarano, Brendan Gleeson, Melissa Leo, Tom Guiry and Emily VanCamp. Cinematography by Michael Fimognari.

WRITER-DIRECTOR BRAD GANN isn't Irish and he isn't Bostonian. But his *Black Irish*, a coming-of-age tale set in South Boston, is a modest success, partially because it has a light touch with its Irish "isms." The family at its center, the McKays, is the result of a marriage between an Irish-American (Brendan Gleeson) and an Irish immigrant (Melissa Leo). While some movies portray the Boston Irish as if they live in an Irish bubble far removed from everyday American life, Gann does not, and such an approach gives his movie a universal reach and a resistance to nagging clichés.

After all, its first images are of 15-year-old Cole (Michael Angarano) throwing a baseball into a painted strike zone on a schoolyard wall. There's no doubt he's American through and through, even if he is an altar boy contemplating studying for the priesthood. Part of the premise of *Black Irish* is that Cole is too nice for his rough-and-tumble family: an emotionally remote, hard-drinking dad who's always searching for work, a mother who's lost control of her husband, a big brother (Tom Guiry) who's a belligerent jerk and a big sister (Emily VanCamp) whose life has been derailed by an unplanned pregnancy.

It's typical of the movie that Kathleen's pregnancy doesn't result in stereotypical hysterics from her Catholic parents, even when she's thinking of having an abortion. Instead, the pregnancy is just another obstacle to be maneuvered around, like making ends meet and keeping

Terry, the big brother eager to pull Cole down to his level, in check. Such problems mesh when the price of "sending away" Kathleen to a home for unwed mothers (from which she soon bolts) means Cole has to leave his Catholic school for Terry's public school—jeopardizing his seminary plans and forcing him to have to make a different, better baseball team. He's more concerned about the latter.

Amidst all these little dilemmas is the main one, and that's whether "good kid" Cole can retain his essential goodness. Angarano, who has the dark features of Shia LaBeouf, and Gann convey Cole's goodhearted nature without making him too naïve (the running gag of Cole leaving a little trail of accidentally dead animals in his wake prevents him from being goody-goody). Aside from his outrage during one scene in which he sees his father humiliated, Cole is pretty levelheaded, and he's an engaging underdog.

Cole's levelheadedness epitomizes the entire movie's restraint. Gann has enough faith in his words to let his cast underplay the drama. Some of the characters have brief near-monologue moments, including Cole's mother and

> Originally it was set in Queens in the 1970s. But my producer suggested Boston, and we couldn't afford to keep the 1970s setting. Boston turned out to be a perfect match. I wanted to make the story as timeless as possible, and Boston gave it that kind of feel.
> –Brad Gann

his brother, but they're not delivered as "big moments." And when you have an actor as sturdy as Gleeson (1997's *The General*) you don't need to get fancy. As several crises come to a head and other opportunities arise for the characters, Gann's restraint becomes especially effective in the optimistic yet open-ended resolution.

Black Irish is not as hardcore a South Boston neighborhood movie as *Good Will Hunting* or *Southie*. It makes use of several local businesses, though, including Skip Scaro's Barber Shop, the Galley Diner and Casper Funeral Home, while some of its baseball action is at Foley Field (also seen in *Good Will Hunting*); the other baseball diamond, seen at the end of the movie, is at Tufts. But the movie mixes and matches a variety of neighborhoods: the family's house is in Dorchester, school scenes take place at East Boston High (as does the police station scene) and the church is St. John's Episcopal Church in Jamaica Plain (with the church office scene done in the mansion at Borderland State Park on the Sharon-Easton border). Waltham's Ristorante Marcellino is also central to the story, as is Roxbury's Jewish Memorial Hospital. Charlestown, Everett and Chelsea also appear, the last during the car crash scene.

▶**Locations:** Dorchester, South Boston, Charlestown, Roxbury,

Jamaica Plain, Boston; Waltham; Everett; Sharon/Easton; Somerville/ Medford.

▶**Accents:** None of the lead actors is local, but Brendan Gleeson, Michael Angarano, Tom Guiry and Emily VanCamp do a good job with their pretend accents, while Melissa Leo does a dandy *faux* Irish accent. It's ironic to have Irish Gleeson doing an American accent and American Leo doing an Irish brogue, yet the two do such a good job it's inconsequential.

▶**Local color:** Perhaps because of budget limitations, there isn't a lot of public action here (since that involves things like blocking off streets and hiring more extras). Most of the neighborhood scenes could have been filmed in any Northeastern blue-collar neighborhood. But the smattering of Southie businesses and parks on display bolsters the story's credibility.

The Blinking Madonna and Other Miracles

1995. Written and directed by Beth Harrington. With The People of the North End, Beth Harrington, Roberta Beyer, Trisha Zembruski, Lorenzo Perez, Melinda Lopez, Jeff Miller and Michael Harrington. Cinematography by Kyle Kibbe.

A 1991 VIDEOTAPE OF a North End feast shot by Beth Harrington inspired her wondrous hour-long movie. The Jamaica Plain native's tape became a Boston media sensation when it apparently showed a Madonna statue blinking. But in letting us share in Harrington's religious and personal reaction to the event and the subsequent hoopla, *The Blinking Madonna* covers much more ground than that mere "miracle."

Harrington establishes the context for her reaction to the incident through hilarious staged flashbacks that she narrates. In them, we see seven-year-old Beth (Roberta Beyer) in her early-1960s parochial school—complete with Bing Crosby-casual priest (Michael Harrington; no relation to Beth)—consuming herself in her religion during the heyday of Boston Catholicism (cue the clips of dashing JFK and gravel-voiced Cardinal Cushing). The kid's-eye-view interplay between wide-eyed Beth and the ominous yet very theatrical nun (Trisha Zembruski) who teaches her is a hoot to watch. (The Archdiocese of Boston changed its mind about letting Harrington shoot inside Braintree's St. Francis of Assisi School, causing her to film classroom interiors in Jamaica Plain's aptly named John F. Kennedy School.)

Staged flashbacks and newsreel footage of the changing world *beyond* Catholic school next combine to show how religion becomes less important in Harrington's life. Later, though, she moves to the North End to try to return to a more traditional life, culturally if not religiously. The move is also a way for Harrington to connect with her Italian-American mother's heritage. But, of course, even a half-Italian woman trying to fit in is still "an outsider" to North End natives, and *The Blinking Madonna* details her uneasy path to neighborhood acceptance with a characteristically light touch. Her social entrée was to start videotaping the cultural traditions around her in short films such as *Ave Maria*. (The cool, unmentioned fact that Harrington was also a backup singer for Natick's finest son, Jonathan Richman, during several of her 18 years in the North End should also be noted.)

The Blinking Madonna and Other Miracles: Beth Harrington in the North End.

The breakup of a long relationship, a move from one North End apartment to another and a lack of work lead to the vulnerable emotional state Harrington is in at the time of the blinking Madonna incident. Although she knows the "miracle" is a result of a glitch in her camcorder's auto-focus, the event turns out to be an emotional watershed for Harrington. It doesn't awaken any dormant religious faith, but instead makes her appreciate life's happy little accidents and blesses her with a new go-with-the-flow attitude.

The seed for this new attitude comes not only from the accident on the feast video, but also from the carefree new neighbors in her North Margin Street building that Harrington dubs the "airline angels" (flight personnel played by Lorenzo Perez, Melinda Lopez and Jeff Miller). As with the Catholic school sequences, the scripted scenes in which the neighbors loosen up Harrington are down to earth and funny, as are the recreations of the hubbub surrounding the video (featuring many non-professional North Enders, who do just fine before the camera).

Beneath the intentional surface comedy of *The Blinking Madonna*, there's a quiet wisdom that makes the ending very moving and the movie especially rich. Like so much of the best non-fiction moviemaking that's come out of Greater Boston, it's an affecting combination of soul-baring and storytelling.

The new go-with-the-flow attitude Harrington picked up in *The Blinking Madonna* stuck. Eventually, she left the North End for the Pacific Northwest to be with her future husband. She also showed that she could make an outstanding movie that looked beyond her own experiences when she traveled the lost highway of American music history to spotlight the fire-breathing, foot-stomping, fringe-shaking, rule-breaking, trailblazing women of country-tinged 1950s rock 'n' roll in 2002's *Welcome to the Club: The Women of Rockabilly*.

▶ **Locations:** North End, Jamaica Plain, Boston; Braintree.

▶ **Accents:** In spades. And they're real.

▶ **Local color:** If North End feasts, neighborhood tribalism, Cardinal Cushing clips and Catholic schools aren't Boston local color, nothing is. You can practically taste the fried dough during the feast footage.

Blown Away

1994. Directed by Stephen Hopkins. Written by Joe Batteer & John Rice. With Jeff Bridges, Tommy Lee Jones, Forest Whitaker, Suzy Amis, John Finn and Lloyd Bridges. Cinematography by Peter Levy.

IT WAS THE MOST expensive, complex and certainly *loudest* production to have ever come to Boston at the time. But *Blown Away*, the 1994 Boston bomb squad thriller, is a dud. Alas, sometimes even a raft of local locations can't improve a run-of-the-mill action-thriller.

Since the story unfurls as one of those "this time it's personal" action movies, the big failing is in the lead characters. *Blown Away* is neither Jeff Bridges' nor Tommy Lee Jones' shining moment. Bridges is always dependable for a certain level of performance—save for in *The Vanishing* remake—but he never totally connects with Jimmy Dove, the Irish revolutionary turned Boston bomb squad cowboy who must confront his past. Next to some of the other characters Bridges played during this very fruitful period for him, which includes *The Fisher King, Fearless* and *The Big Lebowski*, Dove is very forgettable. Less forgettable but more dismissible is embittered mad bomber Ryan Gaerity (Jones). Jones has a tendency to overdo his roles, but never has he chewed as much scenery as he does here. I don't care if the character *is* half-insane.

So you can appreciate the stunt work during the climactic fight scene between Dove and Gaerity on a decrepit boat docked at East Boston's Border Street Pier, but it's hard to really get into the action because you don't care about the characters. *Blown Away* was produced by the same people behind the Chicago-set firefighters film *Backdraft* and, like its predecessor, it's very conventional stuff that feels as if it were written by a computer that formulaically inserts emotional baggage, dangerous situations, relationship trouble and occasional good times into the script. If it's not the strained "old country" backstory that links the two lead characters, it's the "retired" guy pulled back into danger. If it's not the periodic tragedies—how many times does poor Jimmy have to run towards someone's imminent death and not be able to get there in time to help?—it's the repeated use of Dove's musician wife (Suzy Amis) and stepdaughter (Stephi Lineburg) as objects in jeopardy. If it's not the ominous music that cartoonishly accompanies Gaerity's every move, it's the fact that, despite the expected "inside" view of the bomb squad, many of the suspense scenes culminate in that old cliché, the snipping of the wire. I mean, c'mon, the heavy kills the hero's *dog* in *Blown Away* (the writers couldn't do any better than that?).

Some of the action works well. There's genuine suspense in the rather playful sequence in which the wife and stepdaughter unwittingly

> I developed a respect for these guys on the bomb squad who risk their lives. They're just very unusual guys that get hooked to a certain extent on the adrenalin.
> –Jeff Bridges

turn on appliances that may or may not be rigged with explosives, and in the scene in which Dove tries to defuse the rigged headphones of bomb squad colleague Anthony (Forest Whitaker). In fact, most any time Whitaker is onscreen things are interesting. Although making this "new guy" character a real Boston townie might have upped the amount of local color here (since there's no such character in the movie), Whitaker supplies a needed energy, and Anthony's quest to discover what's behind the bombings gives the plot a little nudge.

Blown Away: Copley Square.

Cocky Anthony and wizened Dove are initially suspicious of each other, but a mutual respect develops between the two and theirs turns out to be the only genuine relationship in the movie. The lack of connection among its characters is a reason why, arriving a scant month after *Speed*, *Blown Away* was a real also-ran as a "mad bomber" thriller, lacking the cleverness or chemistry of its competition.

For all the Boston locations on display, this is not a movie in which the city becomes a character in the story. It's not *that* specific.

But there's an impressive cross-section of the city here, from movie-familiar Longfellow Bridge and Fenway Park to the Charles River Dam Bridge and Charlestown (including the St. Francis de Sales School). In Cambridge, there's the Harvard-Epworth Church and M.I.T. The movie also ventures to Gloucester's Wingaersheek Beach (for one of the sillier Jones sequences). Because so much of the action takes place outside, only some of it—including the Dove-Gaerity fight climax and the backyard scenes—was filmed in a studio back in Los Angeles. The best area locations mix the different looks of Boston, especially the Copley Square exploding-van sequence, with the action framed by such structures as Trinity Church, the John Hancock Tower and the ornately decked-out top floors of Boylston Street office buildings.

▶**Locations:** Back Bay, Charlestown, Beacon Hill, East Boston, Boston; Cambridge; Gloucester.

▶**Accents:** Problematic stuff. John Finn, as the bomb squad captain, is the cream of a poor crop. Bridges struggles with his dialogue, sometimes flattening out his a's in a quasi-Boston accent, other times talking in a more generic dem-and-dose workingman's voice and occasionally in a faded Irish accent; it's as if no one quite decided what this Irish native who moved to Boston and has tried to lose his accent should sound like. No one else in the bomb squad tries to sound local: sometimes they've even been given character names designed to excuse them from an accent, like Cortez (Chris de Oni) or Bama (longtime Bridges comrade Loyd Catlett), while Forest Whitaker, who was the last person cast in the movie, said in interviews that his character, who was written as Italian-American in the original script, was (like the actor) from New York. On the non-Boston front, Jones' Irish brogue is totally over the top but, for better or worse, the actor plays everything about him that way. Jeff Bridges' dad Lloyd, playing his uncle here, does a more convincing brogue.

> There was this place, Serendipity, and I said, 'I'm never going there again.' Every time I'd go there, (in the next day's paper) it was like, 'He's eating onion rings again.'
> –Forest Whitaker

▶**Local color:** It's a change from the norm, with so many pre-*Good Will Hunting* movies interested in only one sort of Boston: academic/medical, ethnic neighborhoods, etc. But the variety within Boston spices *Blown Away*. Another nice juxtaposition place a runaway-car action sequence on staid Beacon Hill's Joy Street.

▶**Off the set:** *Blown Away* had a very *reverberating* effect on some of the neighborhoods where it filmed, especially East Boston. When the moviemakers took an old tuna boat named Sarah, refitted it, renamed it The Dolphin, used it as the villain's lair and blew it up on the East

Boston side of Boston Harbor, the 24 pounds of gunpowder, 1,700 feet of depth cord and 540 gallons of gasoline turned out to be even more explosive than imagined.

Despite the predictions of reverberation consultants, evacuation of the two blocks closest to the blast, mass boarding-up of windows and the distribution of 4,000 pairs of earplugs, the production received over $100,000 in insurance claims from East Boston residents, along with countless complaints. The evacuees put up at the Ramada complained about the pizza dinner served to them, Al's Shoe Store put up a sign in its broken window saying *"Blown Away* Blew Us Away" and the East Boston Chamber of Commerce lamented that no local window-replacement companies were hired for the cleanup.

The explosion really was something. I was standing on the opposite, Charlestown side of the Harbor and could feel the heat when the crew set it off. Bridges, Jones and Whitaker were, of course, nowhere near the scene at the time.

▶ **Don't blink!:** Look for future Oscar-winner Cuba Gooding, Jr. in the classroom training scene.

The Blue Diner

2001. Directed by Jan Egleson. Written by Natatcha Estébanez and Jan Egleson. With Miriam Colón, Lisa Vidal, Jose Yenque, William Marquez, Jaime Tirelli and Jack Mulcahy. Cinematography by Teresa Medina.

AT ROUGHLY THE SAME time Hollywood released *What's the Worst That Could Happen?*—an unsatisfying multi-cultural Boston movie—a little independent film was arriving, too. But its multi-cultural Boston is a lot more entertaining and clever than its Hollywood counterpart's. *The Blue Diner* is the result of a collaboration between WGBH documentary producer Natatcha Estébanez and pioneering Cambridge independent director Jan Egleson (*Billy in the Lowlands*). Chance meetings in the hallway at WGBH, where each was working, led to the pair partnering on a bilingual script focusing on a Puerto Rican mother and daughter living in Boston's Hispanic community.

Elena (Lisa Vidal) is the daughter and Meche (Miriam Colón) the mother who's all too eager to remind her grown child how much she sacrificed to come to the mainland to give Elena more opportunities in life. But straddling mainstream American culture and the Hispanic subculture of her neighborhood (with street scenes filmed in Dorchester's colorful Uphams Corner) is all too much for Elena. Ironically, she feels bad because Meche is pushing her *away* from her roots, not because her mother won't let go.

Bilingual Elena works in sales at a casket company where she's romantically drawn to two co-workers: Brian (Jack Mulcahy), one of the Anglo bosses, and Tito (Jose Yenque), a South American artist toiling as a casket builder until he can get a visa that will allow him to stay in the country. Magical realism enters the story when the stress of deciding between safe Brian and romantic Tito (whom Meche takes every opportunity to badmouth) causes Elena to have a panic attack. After the attack, she can no longer understand or speak Spanish.

This cultural amnesia might have been a heavy metaphor for *The Blue Diner* to bear, but there's such a breezy, colorful air to the story that it works. Elena's condition not only forces her to assess her relationship to her heritage. It also forces everyone around her to ponder that relationship, including Meche, who's been withholding info about Elena's father from her, and Papo (William Marquez), the Cuban-American cook at the eponymous diner that's trying to get a loan from a white banker (Ken Cheeseman). Naturally, the truth must manifest itself before Elena's Spanish reappears, but you never get the feeling *The Blue Diner* is following a formula.

The Blue Diner: Lisa Vidal in Dorchester.

That's because its style is just unconventional enough to feel spontaneous. In the years after *The Little Sister*, the last of his homegrown "Boston trilogy," Egleson flitted between PBS productions, network TV movies (including the locally shot *Original Sins*) and non-Boston features (including 1990's very funny dark comedy *A Shock to the System*). Obviously he's a much more professional filmmaker in *The Blue Diner* than he was in 1980 (Teresa Medina's cinematography and photogenic Vidal make this an unusually attractive movie). But returning to his Boston neighborhood movie roots, Egleson finds another way to inject documentary style into the movie, and that's by having characters periodically talk to the audience. These inserts aren't deep monologues or distracting asides within other scenes; they're totally conversational, and add to the friendly tone of the movie. Estébanez, who died in 2007, created that tone as much as Egleson, and he shares the director's customary "A Film By" credit with her.

> Natatcha and I are called producer and director. But that's a mistake. We really did everything side by side. We quickly discovered that people would attribute authorship of the film to me, and that was really wrong.
> –Jan Egleson

Part of the handsomeness of *The Blue Diner*, which played in film festivals but could not secure theatrical distribution before airing on PBS, is in its locations. Circumstances necessitated creativity: when the Museum of Fine Arts (where Meche works as a cleaner) thought twice about letting the movie shoot there, Egleson, Estébanez and their crew let interiors in the Boston Public Library and the Mass. Historical Society stand in for the MFA. Similarly, the real-life Blue Diner (on Kneeland and South Streets) had moved, its space taken over by a new restaurant; what we see here is the outside of that diner (now called South Street Diner) and the interior of Wilson's Diner in Waltham. The movie also shot at East Boston's New England Casket Company and in the back room of an Irish bar on Boylston Street in the Fenway, while the scenes in Elena and Meche's apartment were filmed in Brookline.

▶ **Locations:** Waltham; Dorchester, East Boston, Back Bay, Fenway, Jamaica Plain, Boston; Brookline.

▶ **Accents:** Sí. But not Boston accents.

▶ **Local color:** The bright colors provide a welcome contrast from the stately brick that dominates most Boston movies. *The Blue Diner* is sunny and summery, unusual qualities for the city and its movies. Avoiding oft-seen locations adds to the refreshing quality of the genuinely feel-good bilingual tale.

The Boondock Saints

1999. Written and directed by Troy Duffy. With Willem Dafoe, Sean Patrick Flanery, Norman Reedus, Billy Connolly and David Della Rocco. Cinematography by Adam Kane.

NEW HAMPSHIRE NATIVE TROY Duffy's bloody comedy-drama might have been the best of the otherwise blah 1990s Quentin Tarantino wannabes—if it had actually come out in the 1990s. But its long road to the screen was such a bizarre crash and burn that it spawned a whole other movie, the 2003 documentary *Overnight*, made by two colleagues who'd had a falling out with Duffy.

Miramax Films had bought then-bartender Duffy's script in 1997 for him to direct and his band to score, even offering to buy him part-ownership of the Los Angeles bar he tended. Much publicity was made of this yob-makes-good tale, but following casting disputes, Miramax dropped the project. Less generous, independent funding was scraped together and Duffy filmed his movie in 1998, but—perhaps as a consequence of the shocking, real-life gun violence of 1999's Columbine shootings—*The Boondock Saints* had only a low-key release. It played in only five theaters nationally, two of them in the Boston area, and that was only on the eve of its DVD release.

The interesting irony here is that not only is the behind-the-scenes success-story-gone-awry compelling, but so is *The Boondock Saints*. Its mix of gun-toting dark comedy isn't exactly original after Tarantino's *Reservoir Dogs* and *Pulp Fiction* had spawned imitations like *Things to Do in Denver When You're Dead*. But Duffy's movie has an unmistakable spark.

In Tarantino's movies, people get medieval; in Duffy's film, the fraternal-twin McManus brothers (Sean Patrick Flanery, Norman Reedus of *Floating*) get biblical. These hard-living Irish-immigrant Southie brothers hear a calling from above and feel they've been chosen to be avenging angels that violently rid the world of evildoers.

Duffy regularly puts absurd twists on the brothers' subsequent Guinness-soaked encounters with Russian mobsters and the local Italian Mafia. The brothers bicker between bullets; the FBI agent (Willem Dafoe) trying to solve the murders, who loves to give Boston detectives grief, is flamboyantly gay; the brothers' Mafia bag-man friend (David Della Rocco) is a hilarious knucklehead; and wild-eyed Scottish comic Billy Connolly, as the Manson-like hit man the Mafia send after the brothers, is an amusing coil of malevolent energy. Duffy also offers creative storytelling—he regularly takes us to the moment the brothers strike, flashes forward to the FBI man trying to make sense of the carnage and then flashes back to the actual incident. In the movie's most graceful sequence, Duffy merges the incident and the aftermath, having the agent in the same room as the shooters, acting out the killings as they commit them, side by side.

Like many movies trying to be both brutal and funny, *The Boondock Saints* sometimes tries too hard to succeed. But it has energy to burn, and though it felt like a real Johnny-come-lately upon its release, it's certainly not the last movie to ape Tarantino. One victim of the movie's troubled production and its lowered budget was local shooting. Duffy shot almost all of his movie in Toronto, with only a few locations and a helicopter flyover in Boston. Among the genuine landmarks mixed in are Newbury Street's Church of the Covenant, the old Charles Street Jail and both the Longfellow and Northern Avenue Bridges.

To a certain extent, Duffy had the last laugh. Despite making *The Boondock Saints* on a reduced budget, seeing it essentially bypass theaters and being portrayed unflatteringly in *Overnight*, the movie has been popular on DVD, enjoying a two-disc special edition re-release. There's even been talk of a sequel. Regardless of what happens, Duffy made a movie that, despite the odds, found its audience.

▶ **Locations:** Back Bay, Beacon Hill, Boston.

▶ **Accents:** The title characters are Irish, not Bostonian (with Sean Patrick Flanery's brogue definitely more consistent than Reedus'). Duffy mixes in Bostonians here and there, most notably comedian Bob Marley as the Boston cop whom Willem Dafoe's character most likes to befuddle.

▶ **Local color:** Lacking in many Boston locations, *The Boondock Saints* squeezes a little local color from the Irish Catholicism that spurs its title characters' killing spree. An eye for an eye, a bloodbath for a bloodbath.

▶ **Local celeb alert!:** Comic Jimmy Tingle plays the priest taking confession with a gun pointed to his head.

The Boston Strangler

1968. Directed by Richard Fleischer. Written by Edward Anhalt. Based on Gerold Frank's book. With Tony Curtis, Henry Fonda and George Kennedy. Cinematography by Richard H. Kline.

OF ALL THE BOSTON "true story" movies—from *Six Bridges to Cross* to *The Perfect Storm*—this might be the most purely interesting. With the infamous 1962-64 murders of 13 women as its focus, star Tony Curtis turning his back on his pretty boy image and director Richard Fleischer employing the split-screen technique of the influential Expo '67 films, *The Boston Strangler* is a very ambitious blend of realism and abstraction.

The movie, partially shot locally, is remarkable for another reason. Its title character—Albert DeSalvo (Curtis), the Malden resident who confessed to the crimes but was never charged with them (no one was)—doesn't appear until an hour into the film. Gerold Frank's book, which Fleischer and screenwriter Edward Anhalt adapt, not only named DeSalvo as the killer but also detailed the panic the killings drove the city into. Here's where the split screens are so effective. With five or even more panels in the widescreen image, the movie really can be in more than one place at a time. Sequences in which law enforcement (represented by Henry Fonda's and George Kennedy's characters, among others) rounds up sex offenders for questioning, or in which women take precautions to protect themselves, economically suggest the way the crime spree preoccupied people throughout the area. The latter sequence becomes even more of a sensory overload with the overlay of newsreel audio from actual woman-on-the-street interviews at the time of the killings.

It's this kaleidoscope of sights and sounds that pulls you into *The Boston Strangler*. It also creates the sense of danger once we finally do see DeSalvo, a role for which a plumped-up Curtis uses a prosthetic nose and wears brown contact lenses. When we see a woman (Sally Kellerman) ironing on the right of the screen as DeSalvo, on the left, peruses apartment mailboxes and doorbells, jimmies a lock and looks for an apartment to try to get into, the suspense builds and builds. The subsequent attack is harrowing (inserts of DeSalvo's hands are actually not Curtis, but longtime Colonnade Hotel employee Ray Latino).

The Boston Strangler has an unusual sexual frankness for a mainstream 1968 movie with old school stars like Curtis and Fonda. Its underlying premise is that sexual peculiarities abound everywhere (as one cop says, "It's a horny world"). Sometimes this is sad, as in the case of the suspect (William Hickey) who punishes himself for his impure deeds; sometimes it's amusing, especially the pickle salesman (George Furth) who's been scoring all over town impersonating a colonel. And it's disturbing in the case of DeSalvo, whose sheer brutality is shocking. The last section of the movie, with Fonda's investigator interviewing DeSalvo, indulges in pop psychology, with "family man Albert" cracking up once he realizes the existence of "strangler Albert." In fact, DeSalvo had a long criminal record, so the multiple personality disorder of the movie strays from the facts of the case. Still, Curtis is genuinely eerie portraying DeSalvo's breakdown.

Filming in Boston in early 1968 before heading to Los Angeles for most of the interiors, *The Boston Strangler* rarely uses exteriors for important action. The Public Garden appears briefly, as do the Animal Rescue League on Chandler Street, Louisburg Square (home of the lesbians questioned by police), Memorial Drive (where the beatnik attacks his wife), St. Stephen Street and Malden's Forestdale Cemetery, where the lone black victim's funeral occurs. The State House exterior is seen and a tight shot of the Museum of Fine Arts entrance is used as the Boston City Hospital entrance. Most of the apartment buildings where DeSalvo strikes are tucked away on Beacon Hill and Back Bay side streets. The production filmed exteriors at the house where DeSalvo lived in Malden, but they apparently are not in the movie. I don't know if an arrest scene was filmed in Boston and deemed unsatisfactory, but the foot chase beginning in Boston actually concludes with police arresting DeSalvo on a street in San Francisco, with a Boston police car imported to create the illusion we're really still in Massachusetts.

Of course, many have investigated the guilt of DeSalvo, who was killed in prison in 1973, since *The Boston Strangler* came out. Using newer forensic technology, most have discounted the possibility DeSalvo was the strangler, or that the crimes were even committed by just one person.

▶**Locations:** Beacon Hill, South End, Back Bay, Boston; Cambridge; Malden.

▶**Accents:** Unlike in *Six Bridges to Cross*, in which he played a fictional character, Curtis goes with an accent for DeSalvo. He does a decent job, too, and the accent is one of the many reasons we see DeSalvo and not Curtis in his sturdy performance (his Bronx accent sometimes sneaks through). George Kennedy's isn't nearly so convincing or consistent.

▶**Local color:** This isn't the "old, old Boston" of *Walk East on Beacon!* and *Six Bridges to Cross*, but it's still an "old Boston" where characters mention Jordan Marsh and the Statler Hilton Hotel, newspapers are how people get their information and Bostonians are mostly apartment dwellers. The "it's a horny world" premise also gains strength by being offset against repressed, Catholic Boston. It wasn't for nothing that the Standells sang of "frustrated women" in "Dirty Water."

▶**Off the set:** Medford native Alex Rocco, not yet a prolific character actor—that would come after he played Moe Greene in *The Godfather*— was brought back from Hollywood to be Curtis' dialect coach. According to an issue of the *Malden Evening News and Medford Daily Mercury* from early 1968, "An M.I.T. professor was hired first for Curtis, but the actor felt his manner of speech a bit too refined for the part." Rocco also has a small part in the movie as the Cambridge detective talking about the 10th victim's thesis. Rocco would return home again for *The Friends of Eddie Coyle.*

▶ **Local celeb alert!:** Longtime Boston TV fixture Jack Hynes plays a newsman filing a remote report from Cambridge. Boston movie theater mogul Ben Sack is another reporter.

The Bostonians

1984. Directed by James Ivory. Written by Ruth Prawer Jhabvala. Based on Henry James' novel. With Vanessa Redgrave, Christopher Reeve, Madeleine Potter, Jessica Tandy, Wesley Addy and Nancy Marchand. Cinematography by Walter Lassally.

THE DIRECTING-PRODUCING TEAM of James Ivory and Ismail Merchant made several good movies, but they made many more that choked to death on their cold, well-crafted tastefulness. Though it could use a trim in its second half, the Merchant Ivory version of Henry James' *The Bostonians* lands in the first category. Not only was it the financial breakthrough that helped to turn Merchant Ivory into a well-known brand name of sorts—locally, it set a house record at then-new Copley Place Cinema—it also makes great use of real locations. In fact, despite being set in the mid-1870s, it was shot entirely in existing buildings, including Beacon Street's Gibson House and Harvard University's Memorial Hall.

There's simply more going on in *The Bostonians* than there is in the lesser Merchant Ivory movies. Its tangle of affections begins when rich-spinster suffragist Olive Chancellor (Vanessa Redgrave) first lays her eyes on young Verena Tarrant (Madeleine Potter), who espouses the female-rights views Olive holds with more grace and eloquence than the spinster could ever muster on her own. She's smitten. She takes Verena under her wing and starts to school her in literature and politics, grooming her to be the next star of the suffragette movement.

But she's not the only one who's smitten. Olive's own distant cousin, Basil (Christopher Reeve), a dashing Southern lawyer who's trying to start a practice in New York, sees Verena speak, too, while visiting Boston—and soon arranges to see her behind his cousin's back. Henry (John Van Ness Philip), a Harvard student with a well-to-do mother (Nancy Marchand) who wants to show off Verena in New

York, hopes to marry her. And Pardon (Wallace Shawn), a newspaper reporter, wants to help promote Verena's speeches and share in her glory. To complicate matters further, Olive's sister Adeline (Nancy New), is trying to land Basil.

But Basil, despite thinking everything Verena says in her speeches is foolish, cares only for the fresh-faced suffragist. With Olive and Verena in one of those intimate, semi-physical relationships between 19th-century feminists that actually came to be known as a "Boston marriage," *The Bostonians* emerges as a battle not just between protective liberal Olive and seductive conservative Basil, but between Verena's head and her heart.

That Verena would fall for Basil, who thinks a woman's place is only in the home, is a stretch, but Reeve is actually less stiff than usual here, and his strapping Mississippi native has an exotic flavor next to the crusty, bookish New Englanders (just look at him tower, Gulliver-like, over Jessica Tandy and Linda Hunt). And you can't blame Verena for seeking an alternative to Olive. Olive's affection for Verena practically oozes out of her pores, but she's emotionally smothering her protégée. Thanks to the cast, neither Olive nor Basil comes off as a villain, and in Redgrave's hands Olive is a convincingly fragile idealist.

The actress was always Merchant and Ivory's choice for the role. But she originally turned it down, and Julie Christie (with whom they'd worked on *Heat and Dust*) was to play Olive. But Christie dropped out and Glenn Close was cast. Close had also landed a role in *The Natural*, and when scheduling conflicts arose in pre-production, the partners went back to Redgrave and she was soon in Boston lacing up a corset.

Also shot in Newport, New York City and Troy, New York, *The Bostonians* is a filmmaking lesson in conjuring up the Victorian era by its wise use of the Back Bay (Olive's home is the Gibson House Museum at 137 Beacon), the South End (Adeline's New York home and the N.Y. boarding house where Olive and Verena stay) and Cambridge (the Longfellow House on Brattle Street is Henry Burrage's home; Verena's parents' house is on Pemberton Street). Other locations include the Boston Athenaeum, Charlestown's Monument Square and the Dedham bank of the Charles River. Like all good low-budget independent movies, this is a resourceful one.

▶**Locations:** Back Bay, South End, Beacon Hill, Charlestown, Boston; Cambridge; Dedham; Martha's Vineyard.

▶**Accents:** How did well-heeled Boston liberals speak in the 1870s? Damned if I know. We get a blend of Brits (Redgrave), Americans who talk in pseudo-English theatrical voices (Jessica Tandy, Linda Hunt, Nancy Marchand) and just plain American voices (Potter,

Wesley Addy). It's a common mix for a period piece, and who knows how authentic it is, but it works just fine. Reeve does a decent, albeit generic Southern accent.

▶**Local color:** Again, the period setting of James' story calls for a leap of faith from the viewer. But the city is just right for characters such as Olive, a former abolitionist who's channeled her political energies into the early suffrage movement, and the more comic, opportunistic characters (Verena's quack faith-healer dad, the newspaper reporter) fit in, too. After all, it wouldn't be right for a movie featuring a "Boston marriage" to be set anywhere else. The use of authentic, old-fashioned nooks and crannies within the modern city makes the leap of faith a small one.

The Brink's Job

1978. Directed by William Friedkin. Written by Walon Green. Based on Noel Behn's *Big Stick-Up at Brink's*. With Peter Falk, Peter Boyle, Allen Goorwitz, Warren Oates, Gena Rowlands and Paul Sorvino. Cinematography by Norman Leigh.

THE "CRIME OF THE century" becomes a caper comedy, with bumbling, two-bit thieves lucking into a big haul in director William Friedkin's rendering of the legendary January 17, 1950 Brink's robbery. Based on Noel Behn's fact-based *Big Stick-Up at Brink's* and scripted by *Wild Bunch* writer Walon Green, *The Brink's Job* uses the ultimate heist comedy, Italy's *Big Deal on Madonna Street*, as its model.

Not surprisingly, the 1978 comedy never reaches its predecessor's level of lunacy in character and deed. But it unearths a few hidden corners of the city (like the "ghost sign" on the back of the Gaiety Theater in its opening sequence), lets production designer Dean Tavoularis (*The Godfather*) loose in recreating bygone Boston and emerges as an agreeable enough diversion from the director of *The French Connection* and *The Exorcist*.

There are no bad guys in *The Brink's Job*, a perspective accentuated by the casting of charismatic Peter Falk as its hero. His Tony Pino is a crook destined never to taste the big time as the movie starts. He gets pinched in a botched slaughterhouse robbery and, when he gets out and gets back to work, his break-in of a candy factory, complete with pratfalls in piles of gumballs, is almost as comical as it is unproductive. Tony might be unlucky, but brother-in-law Vinnie (the always amusing Allen Goorwitz) is just plain stupid. The way they stumble upon a

The Brink's Job: Gerard Murphy and Peter Falk in the North End.

Brink's depot, in which stacks of money are being casually toted from armored cars, is dumb luck—but Tony's determination to penetrate the company's counting rooms and vault, which "smarter" guys might have assumed are well-secured, is actually admirable.

This is a motley-crew movie, and in addition to Tony and Vinnie, there are also bookie Jazz (Paul Sorvino), demolitions expert Specs (Warren Oates), fence McGinnis (Peter Boyle) and lifetime crooks Sandy (Gerard Murphy) and Gus (Kevin O'Connor) in on the job. There's a definite Runyonesque flavor to their antics, and the comedy hits a groove when the bunch plans the heist (it's a riot how Specs originally wants to fire a bazooka into the vault from across the street, and can't imagine how that might be a *little* conspicuous). When the guys actually carry out the heist, it's staged as a relatively straight suspense sequence. Mirroring the lunacy of the crew is that of obsessive J. Edgar Hoover (Sheldon Leonard), who theorizes the robbery is the "missing link" between Communism and organized crime (in reality, Hoover's FBI spent $29 million and only ever recovered $52,000 of the $1.2 million in cash and $1.5 million in checks and securities).

The Brink's Job stumbles in its late action, giving a poor sense of elapsed time and omitting much bizarre, real-life intrigue (is this perhaps a consequence of the movie somehow going from 118 minutes in its original release to 104 on video?). The clumsy resolution mutes the movie's charms. While the locations don't always scream Boston, they are very effective: the North Terminal Garage Building at Prince and Commercial streets (the same structure where the real robbery happened), the old Dudley elevated Orange Line stop, the Custom House Tower steps for the last big crowd scene, Tony taking his wife (Gena Rowlands) to Rino's restaurant in East Boston and Stoneham doubling for a Pennsylvania town's Main Street.

Not yet released on DVD as of this writing and out of print on VHS, *The Brink's Job* has been all but forgotten by most. But its effect on the relationship between Boston and Hollywood lingered for decades (see below). Of course, that had nothing to do with its content.

▶**Locations:** North End, Financial District, East Boston, Charlestown, Roxbury, Boston; Stoneham.

▶**Accents:** This is a movie you trot out whenever people talk about mangled Boston accents. With Peter Falk, Peter Boyle, Warren Oates, Paul Sorvino and Allen Goorwitz (a/k/a Allen Garfield), among others, *The Brink's Job* has as colorful a 1970s ensemble cast as you could hope for. Boyle's character is an Irishman, so he's exempt, but Falk's and Goorwitz's New York accents dominate, as does Oates' Appalachian drawl. Falk's Tony Pino is even given a good favorite Boston exclamation ("Mothah ah Gawd"), but the actor's attempts to do the accent are middling at best, as are Oates'. Sorvino, who'd played a Boston cabbie in 1972's *Dealing*, does better, but is still not that convincing. The amazing thing is that the strongest Boston accent comes from the judge who sends up Specs and Gus, and he's supposed to be in Pennsylvania.

▶**Local color:** It's great to see some of the locations here in a movie, like the North Washington Street Bridge. But, in a way, most of the locations are so tucked away that they could be anywhere (since the movie takes place in 1938, 1944 and the 1950s, they *had* to use tucked-away places that hadn't been modernized). So local color is lower than expected. There are old Hood and Moxie signs on display and a mention of Narragansett (the race track, not the beer), but not very much "public" action.

▶**Off the set:** The shenanigans surrounding *The Brink's Job* forever overshadow the actual movie. First off, the North End's narrow streets are not friendly to the convoys of trucks and trailers that accompany a major motion picture production. Just try turning an 18-wheeler down Sheaf Street. And stories—some no doubt true, some legend—abound of neighborhood residents finding creative ways of getting courtesy payments to take down TV aerials, air conditioners and other visual impediments to the movie's authenticity.

But these are not the most extreme shenanigans. Two episodes stand out. One is when gunmen barged into the movie's Stuart Street production office and stole several cans of film from the editing room. In a case of life imitating art, the misinformed robbers then tried to ransom the film, which was practically worthless, since the negative was still in the production's possession.

The worst was yet to come. As detailed in Nat Segaloff's book *Hurricane Billy: The Stormy Life and Films of William Friedkin*, an investigation into the extortion of five film productions, including *The Brink's Job*, by The Federal Organized Crime Task Force led to charges being filed against five Boston area Teamsters. Although Friedkin denied knowledge of any such payments during a 1978 press conference, having been working solely on the creative end of the production, executive producer Dino De Laurentiis told NBC the movie spent over a million dollars hiring more Teamsters than necessary. From this point on, "Brink's job" must have become a two-word Hollywood code for "Why would you ever want to shoot a movie in Boston and put up with that, you schmuck?"

Celtic Pride

1996. Directed by Tom DeCerchio. Written by Judd Apatow. With Daniel Stern, Dan Aykroyd, Damon Wayans, Gail O'Grady, Christopher McDonald and Paul Guilfoyle. Cinematography by Oliver Wood.

THE BOSTON GARDEN DESERVED a better send-off than this. The old arena was closed for business by October 1995, months after the Celtics and Bruins had finished their 1994-95 seasons and moved into the (then-)Fleet Center. But the shuttered home of so many Boston hoop memories played host to this barren comedy that, instead of a tribute, felt more like a slap in the face when it was released the following spring.

Even in 1996, a story putting the Celtics in the NBA finals felt like a cruel joke, because the franchise of Cousy, Russell, Havlicek and Bird had already plummeted in performance and prestige (though mid-1990s mediocrity would be preferable to the decade that followed). But to have that premise arrive in such a witless comedy was even worse. *Celtic Pride* acts as if it has all sorts of intimate knowledge of Bostonians, when in fact it doesn't. Just look at how its knucklehead heroes—gym teacher Mike (Daniel Stern) and plumber Jimmy (Dan

Aykroyd)—enter the Garden for their beloved Celtics' playoff game against the Utah Jazz: they stop on the ramp, kneel in devotion, kiss a finger and touch the finger to the loge sidewall.

Huh? This isn't Fenway Park, with its breathtaking green vista, this is the Garden. If I or anyone who ever went there did that, a tetanus shot might be needed. The Garden itself was a filthy sty, and everyone knew it. If the buddies had walked down to the beloved parquet floor and kissed *that*, the scene would have worked. But writers Judd Apatow and Colin Quinn (the latter got a story credit)—comedy vets who usually do better than this—bring little insight to the story. They're New Yorkers, and probably only chose the Celtics because, at least back in the mid-1990s, it was one of the few sports franchises whose legacy meant something even to non-sports fans.

In *Celtic Pride*, the two die-hard Celts fans grieve over the team's game six loss to the Jazz and star Lewis Scott (Damon Wayans) and, before the championship-deciding seventh game, kidnap him. Much of the proverbial wacky mayhem is supposed to ensue after the locals get Lewis drunk at the Roxy and tote him back to Jimmy's memorabilia-filled Charlestown apartment. But the comedy here is D.O.A. The sequence in the apartment drags, and there really needs to be more action to cut away to that might divert our attention. Eventually, after an escape attempt and a ride in Jimmy's plumbing van, a few emotional developments happen, as Mike goads selfish superstar Lewis for not appreciating all that he has and the jock in turns tells the Celts fans they need to find more in life than just sports.

> I checked out from the Celtics after the Larry Bird bone-spur injury like everyone else did. But we're hoping the movie will put some positive focus on the Celtics.
> –Dan Aykroyd

But it's not as if the movie ever actually turns *good*. When Jimmy pulls his plumbing van over in East Boston's LoPresti Park, so Lewis and Mike can have a one-on-one grudge match on the basketball court there, the plumber impersonates Bob Cousy doing play-by-play. Cousy's French accent is one of the most distinctive of all ex-jocks, yet the impersonation here is a semi-*Boston* accent. That's indicative of how *Celtic Pride* never really did the work that might have made it a good Boston movie or, more importantly, an enjoyable comedy. In addition to the Garden, Charlestown, Eastie, The Roxy and a few scattered shots of the Back Bay and the South End (mainly following the cop car of Bostonian Paul Guilfoyle's character), *Celtic Pride* also visits two familiar movie spots, the Charlestown steps and Doyle's in Jamaica Plain. The cast also shot on sets built in Waltham.

The destruction of the Garden after the end credits is not the real thing, by the way; it's an explosion of a miniature done by special effects technicians in California. The real Garden wasn't demolished until 1998.

▶**Locations:** North End, Charlestown, East Boston, Jamaica Plain, Boston; Waltham (sets).

▶**Accents:** Fortunately, Daniel Stern and Dan Aykroyd didn't try local accents. Theater Company of Boston alumnus Paul Guilfoyle, who long ago moved away, sometimes slips back into one, especially for a nifty "This is biz-*ahhh*."

▶**Local color:** The local sports memorabilia in Jimmy's apartment, a Dukakis reference, the cameos and the last use of the Garden are great. But the gaffes and generally poor quality of everything here taints the local color. For instance, the game scenes are lit very differently than the Garden was during games. Consequently, the arena looks unlike it really did during such contests. No one was deluding themselves with the thought that they were making great art here but, still, the movie mucks up so much.

▶**Local celeb alert!:** Three former Celtics appear—Larry Bird, Bob Cousy (who's a big improvement on Aykroyd's bad imitation of him) and Bill Walton, who does the fake play-by-play on the playoff games with Marv Albert. Red Auerbach, John Havlicek and longtime Garden janitor "Spider" Edwards get thanks in the credits, so maybe there were other cameos cut in the editing.

Charly

1968. Directed by Ralph Nelson. Written by Stirling Silliphant. Based on Daniel Keyes' *Flowers for Algernon*. With Cliff Robertson, Claire Bloom, Lilia Skala and Leon Janney. Cinematography by Arthur J. Ornitz.

CLIFF ROBERTSON WON AN Oscar for playing the mentally retarded title character who undergoes a brain operation that makes him smarter, but the effects of which turn out to be unexpectedly temporary (a premise similar to subsequent movies such as *Awakenings* and *Phenomenon*). Although *Charly* threatens to go off the deep end several times, somehow it remains respectable, if not always as dramatic as intended.

Robertson, most recognizable to younger moviegoers as Uncle Ben in the *Spider-Man* series, had seen other live-TV dramas in which he'd starred, including *The Hustler* and *The Days of Wine and Roses*, go to the big screen without him. So he optioned the rights to Daniel Keyes' *Flowers for Algernon* after he starred in its 1961 TV version and shepherded the film himself (the movie's Boston setting is a change from previous incarnations). Robertson's Oscar win was partially a nod of respect for his smarts and perseverance, but his portrayal of Charly's affliction is also nicely underplayed.

Charly first appears as a limited man who's not afraid to push himself to learn, whether it's in the ESL class taught by Alice (Claire Bloom) or at the clinic at The Gamble Mansion (5 Commonwealth Avenue) where she brings him for therapy. There, scientists measure his smarts against those of a mouse named Algernon, who's had the same brain operation Charly eventually does. One sequence in the story finds Charly not only gaining normal intelligence after the operation, but improbably becoming a genius.

Another reach is his deepening relationship with Alice. *Charly* dimly links sexual urge with brain power, figuring that the boyish Charly of the opening has no urges, but post-op Charly is suddenly a torrent of hormones. What's worse, emotionally immature Charly jumps Alice's bones and she fights him off, only to soon dump her fiancé for the guy who attacked her. In between, there's the movie's jaw-dropping "freak-out" montage in which Charly apparently becomes a biker; I thought this sequence had to be some sort of rage-fueled fantasy in

Charly: Cliff Robertson and Claire Bloom at Faneuil Hall.

Charly's head, but in the next scene, in which Alice returns to him, she does indeed make passing reference to his motorcycle, which he has decided to sell (so why include the biker "freak-out" at all?).

Charly has pretty much run off the tracks at that point. What keeps the drama somewhat tethered is the earthiness director Ralph Nelson, another live-TV vet, gives the story. *Charly* is not nearly so slick as it might be today (there was a 2000 cable remake and a 2006 French-TV remake, neither of which was shot in Boston and neither of which I have seen). The shots of Charly's Southie neighborhood, and the way his eyes open to the world around him, unexpectedly recall the emotional journey of Marlon Brando's Terry Malloy in *On the Waterfront*. Similarly, giving Charly a job at Kasanof's Bakery in Roxbury is an evocative, unglamourous touch.

But while the atmosphere holds up, the message in *Charly* doesn't date so well. Charly discovers the effects of the operation might be temporary just before the clinic's scientists trot him out as their prized patient at a John Hancock Hall conference. He then unloads on the attending scientists for wanting to mess with him or anyone else. *Charly* is a 1960s cry for respecting nature's ways, but the message gets awfully muddled by the fact that, after his big speech, genius Charly spends the next scenes trying to come up with scientific ways to head off the regression. Today, it feels as if Charly is madder at the scientists for botching the job than for using him as a guinea pig.

In addition to the Back Bay and Southie locations—Charly lives on G Street—there's also action at Tufts University and Hanover's St. Coletta School for Exceptional Children (since renamed Cardinal Cushing School and Training Center), and a cross-section of tourist-friendly sites on Charly's Sunday bus ride. The beach sequence was reportedly done in Nahant.

As late as 1996, while doing interviews for *Escape from L.A.*, Robertson was touting the script he wrote for a *Charly* sequel to be shot in Boston. "It will be the first sequel that, 20 years later, the core of the cast will be back," he told me. "All my guys in the bakery (where Charly works), they all want to do it." Robertson had long tried to raise the budget for the movie. Back in the fall of 1980 locations were selected and local actors were even cast in supporting roles for the film, which was all ready to go. But the movie, which was to have been independently financed, didn't go before cameras—in 1980 or 1996.

▶**Locations:** Back Bay, South Boston, Roxbury, Charlestown, North End, Boston; Hanover; Medford/Somerville; Nahant.

▶**Accents:** Charly Gordon *should* have a Boston accent. After all, he's probably never left the city. But he's played by a star, so you get the star's normal voice. Aside from the tour bus guide, the closest thing to local accents comes from Charly's co-workers at Kasanof's, though some, like New Yorker Barney Martin (future TV dad to Jerry Seinfeld), just have their New York working-class voices. But *Charly* earns points for giving Quincy native Edward "Skipper" McNally— who plays Gimp, the practical-joke instigator at Kasanof's—his biggest screen role. McNally, who died in 1987, had long ago left the area. He was a sometime character actor who made a bigger name for himself in sports circles as a ticket hustler and Super Bowl gate-crasher. His most famous exploit came at Super Bowl IV, when he snuck onto the sidelines and was among those who hoisted Kansas City Chiefs coach Hank Stram in the air following victory.

▶**Local color:** Boston's status as an educational and medical outpost was no doubt the reason to set this story of the mind here, and the mix of neighborhood and medical/academia works, even though locals will chuckle at the thought of excited Charly running from his G Street South Boston apartment to the brain clinic at 5 Comm. Ave. That's not as big a laugh as we get during Charly's tour-bus ride, when the guide's audio has little semblance to reality (for instance, when the bus is on Comm. Ave. near B.U., heading away from the Back Bay, he tells riders to turn to their right to see the Boston Public Library). *Charly* would have the worst kind of *Mrs. Winterbourne* postcard view of Boston if these sorts of exteriors were the only local footage used. But the movie sprinkles exterior locations into the drama, which unfurls mainly indoors. It actually has an interesting, albeit brief, view of the pre-renovated Faneuil Hall area and the backside of under-construction City Hall (with the office tower at 28 State Street, also still being built, visible in the establishing shot). And did they really have jitneys like the one here going through the Public Garden?

A Civil Action

1998. Written and directed by Steve Zaillian. Based on Jonathan Harr's book. With John Travolta, Robert Duvall, William H. Macy, Tony Shalhoub, Kathleen Quinlan, Bruce Norris, John Lithgow, Zeljko Ivanek, James Gandolfini, Dan Hedaya, David Thornton, Stephen Fry and Sydney Pollack. Cinematography by Conrad L. Hall.

ONE OF GREATER BOSTON'S biggest environmental tragedies and legal tussles of the 1980s comes to the screen in a film featuring a bevy of area locations. The 1995 non-fiction book *A Civil Action* adapts, by

Northampton-based author Jonathan Harr, details the lawsuit brought against W.R. Grace & Co. and Beatrice Foods for polluting local water supplies, filed by several Woburn parents of children who'd died of leukemia. In the book, the truth *is* the story. It's an intricate chronicle of how the judicial system sometimes fails to serve the truth.

As with any 115-minute movie tackling a 500-page book, writer-director Steve Zaillian streamlines and simplifies the David and Goliath story. Sometimes the compression works, sometimes it doesn't. Unfortunately, Zaillian introduces a movie cliché right away when he presents protagonist Jan Schlictmann (John Travolta), a personal injury lawyer, as an "ambulance chaser" whose opportunism gradually turns to caring as he starts working on the Woburn case.

Despite the way he's presented, Schlictmann, who staked his personal and professional life on the case—and, for the most part, lost—generally comes off as the same driven individual he is in the book. Here, too, he becomes consumed by the struggle his small firm launches against multi-national defendants represented by venerable Boston law firms, in the form of crafty Beatrice defender Jerome Facher (Robert Duvall at his best) and straightlaced Grace counsel William Cheeseman (Bruce Norris).

Once it gets into the legal machinations, the movie turns more involving. The condensation gives short shrift to Schlictmann's Charles Street partners (Tony Shalhoub, Zeljko Ivanek), though William H. Macy gets more to do as the firm's watchful business manager. Similarly, only two of the victims' parents become genuine characters. But the performances of Kathleen Quinlan and David Thornton (he gives a devastating deposition that includes flashbacks shot on the Southeast Expressway) both have a big impact. As Schlictmann starts deposing Woburn residents and employees of the chemical-heavy tannery nearby, and Facher starts maneuvering like a chess master, the movie often captures the spirit of the book. A pre-*Sopranos* James Gandolfini and Dan Hedaya, as characters from the tannery, make the most impact among those playing employees.

> I knew how to solve this guy, as far as his coldness, his egocentric qualities. And that was to make him unaware that he was behaving this way. (To him,) everyone is celebrating Jan Schlictmann.
> –John Travolta

Like the large cast, the locations feel very realistic. The Woburn neighborhood scenes were actually shot on Riverside Drive in Dedham, the road to get there is in Palmer and the tannery scenes are outside Waltham's Metropolitan State Hospital. The Boston Athenaeum doubles as both a law firm and New York's Harvard Club, while Liberty

A Civil Action: John Travolta in Palmer.

Square and Jamaica Plain's Centre Street are also seen, as are parts of Northbridge and Brimfield.

Schlictmann's voice-overs relate the defendant-friendly obstacles the personal-injury lawyer has to overcome, most importantly having to finance the case and gamble that he'll win. *A Civil Action* is best at capturing Schlictmann's fatal flaw: his belief that he could be some sort of avenging angel who could make the corporations pay through the nose to right the wrongs inflicted on the Woburn families.

But it's not as adept at capturing the book's exposé of the sometimes cozy relationship between big money and the judicial system. The character of Judge Skinner (John Lithgow), whose repeated courtroom rebuffs against the plaintiffs comprise some of the most disturbing action in the book, has been reduced to a curmudgeon who merely dislikes upstart Schlictmann.

As one might expect, the movie struggles with the case's very ambiguous ending. The big-money lawyers outscheme Schlictmann, while the Environmental Protection Agency ultimately validates the charges against Grace and Beatrice after the case has been settled

The Unseen 'A Civil Action'

Half of *A Civil Action* was shot in Boston, half in Los Angeles. Because the nearly-three-hour *Meet Joe Black* and *Beloved* were big flops in the months before *A Civil Action*'s theatrical release, writer-director Zaillian cut several sequences to get his movie under *two* hours. So a good portion of local filming turned out to be for scenes that ended up getting cut from the movie and as yet have not resurfaced as DVD bonuses.

One is a scene shot over four days in the fall of 1997 at Fenway Park, in which a desperate Schlictmann goes to see Red Sox-mad Facher at a game, asking for, but not getting, mercy (with college players standing in for pros on the field; according to an old Peter Gammons *Globe* baseball notes column, among the collegians was Haverhill's and Northeastern's Carlos Peña, later on the Sox for part of the 2006 season, before having a prodigous 2007 season with Tampa Bay). The production even returned to Fenway in April 1998 to get real Sox footage to mix into the scene. "The scene was basically Jan's going there to tell Facher he's in trouble," said Zaillian. "I realized that the Jerry Facher character, the Duvall character, is not a bad guy. And to have a scene where it was like (him saying), 'Ha, ha, I got you,' at the end of the movie stuck in my craw." Presumably, the helicopter shot of Kenmore Square towards the end of the movie was originally intended to set up the scene inside the scenic ballpark.

There are also two other Charles Street scenes that highlight the financial bind in which "the Woburn case" puts Schlictmann and his partners. In one, the flashy lawyer's beloved Porsche gets repossessed. In another, shot at Charles Street Cleaners, Schlictmann pleads to get a suit back even though he can't pay for the cleaning.

"It was so good!" John Travolta said of this scene. "It's so wonderful, because you see this man is having a nervous breakdown, but it looks like he's on top of the world. It's funny, it's sad, it's powerful." •

for a fraction of what Schlictmann once believed he could get. The Hollywood gloss and the ambiguous resolution uneasily mix, but years removed from the actual events and Harr's book, Zaillian's legal thriller holds up very well.

▶**Locations:** Beacon Hill, Jamaica Plain, Charlestown, Boston; Waltham; Dedham; Palmer; Northbridge; Brimfield.

▶**Accents:** There's just enough here to remind that we're in Massachusetts. A couple of the deposed tannery workers sport Boston accents, while the big standout is David Thornton's Richard Aufiero, whose deposition is a big turning point in the story. Thornton nails the accent. It would've also been a nice touch to have a bailiff dropping his r's during the courtroom scenes, which were filmed in Los Angeles, but that's not the case.

▶**Local color:** The action in *A Civil Action* offers a pleasing cross-section of elements: city and suburbs, white collar and blue collar, scenic and not-so-scenic. It's not the concentrated dose of Boston you find in some movies, but it's very realistic in that regard and thankfully it's never gimmicky.

▶**Local celeb alert!:** Howie Carr interviews Schlictmann on his radio show during an early scene.

▶**Off the set:** Tango aficionado Robert Duvall shimmied up a storm at Friend Street's Jeanette Neill Dance Studio while in town.

Could Be Worse!

2000. Directed by Zack Stratis. Written by Zack Stratis and Vilma Gregoropoulos. With the Stratis family. Cinematography by Vilma Gregoropoulos.

THERE'S NOTHING *USUAL* ABOUT Zack Stratis' one-of-a-kind movie. Not the content—a genre-bending stew of family history, musical comedy, cooking show and gay-pride statement. Not the venue at which it had a local run—a "legitimate" theater that *had* been a movie theater in earlier days. And not the movie's snaky path to audiences—from the high of the Sundance Film Festival to the struggles of self-distribution.

Stratis had previously made the amusing featurette *Midburb*, his cockeyed tribute to his hometown of Everett, also home to Richie's Slush, big-haired girls and Mike's Donuts (R.I.P.). You might call *Could Be Worse!* his cockeyed tribute to his closely knit Greek-American family. Stratis had come out to his family years before, he explains in the movie, but since then his homosexuality had hardly been spoken of. But Stratis wanted more than a "don't ask, don't tell" relationship with his traditional parents. With their 50th anniversary approaching and older brother Stathi returning from Greece for the festivities, Stratis seized the opportunity to get his parents and siblings to talk about the family and themselves individually.

That's "talk" in the loosest sense of the word, as the most unusual thing about *Could Be Worse!* is its fondness for fantasy musical numbers—despite the fact that Zack and his family aren't trained performers (though Stathi teaches dancing in Greece). Zack expresses his desires for his cinematic experiment in the first song, which also conveys the movie's embrace of the tacky, whether it's his singing voice or the close-ups of him riding his bike in front of a green-screen outdoor scene. His family's skittishness about the project follows

> Even though the singing is dreadful and the acting is terrible, it somehow works.
> –Zack Stratis

in such songs as father Gus' "I'm Your Father, Listen to Me," newlywed sister Tedi's "Leave Me Alone" and old-country-loving Stathi's "Tears and Pain."

Could Be Worse! slumps in its mid-section, once the novelty of the "bad" music has faded, the reluctance of Zack's parents to discuss his homosexuality has long been established and the issue of whether he can pull his project together has been beaten into the ground. But the movie suddenly gets better, once Zack wears down everyone's resistance enough to get them to sit for separate interviews. "It's a chance for us to come out, all of us," Zack tells his dad, and there's a real poignancy to many of the subsequent interviews, especially his mother Olympia talking about being "molded" to fit the role expected of young women in the 1940s (she also has a song, "Try Growing Up a Woman," on the topic). In a similar vein, sister Evmorphia talks about her medical problems and Tedi speaks of her battles with her weight.

The anniversary bash approaches, which means lots of on-camera food preparation (spanikopita, baklava and more) and Zack's wished-for grand finale at the party, including the title song, which takes its inspiration from the translation of a Greek word. By this point, it's hard not to be won over by Stratis' movie, his family and the amusing case for tolerance *Could Be Worse!* makes. The organizers of the Sundance Film Festival were certainly won over, and the movie was the only Boston work in 2000's edition of the fest. Despite being well-received at Sundance and having further exposure at other festivals during 2000, no national distributor snapped up *Could Be Worse!* (alas, this was before *My Big Fat Greek Wedding* became the surprise hit of the

Could Be Worse!: Zack Stratis (lower right) and family in Everett.

decade). In keeping with Stratis' "let's put on a show" sensibility, his movie ended up opening locally at the Stuart Street Playhouse (in the former site of the Sack Cinema 57) in early 2001, where it played for 10 consecutive Mondays, complete with accompanying stage shows.

▶**Locations:** Everett; Cambridge; Boston; Revere; Manchester-by-the-Sea; Marblehead.

▶**Accents:** It's not a huge part of the story, but Greek-Americans in Cleveland don't talk like this.

▶**Local color:** In keeping with the intimate theme and the low budget, the movie doesn't stray from the Everett family home very often, just for the brief scenes at Zack's Cambridge apartment, his walk through the Esplanade during his big song and shots of the ocean at Revere, Marblehead and Manchester-by-the-Sea.

The Crucible

1996. Directed by Nicholas Hytner. Written by Arthur Miller. Based on his play. With Daniel Day-Lewis, Winona Ryder, Paul Scofield, Joan Allen, Bruce Davison and Rob Campbell. Cinematography by Andrew Dunn.

PLENTY OF FILMS REFUSE to shoot in Greater Boston because it's just too *complicated*. But *The Crucible* is an entirely different story. The logistics of its 1995 shoot are unprecedented in local filmmaking.

For his adaptation of Arthur Miller's 1950s play, director Nicholas Hytner and his cast and crew took over Hog Island, a secluded bump of land off of Essex that's part of the Crane Wildlife Refuge, and there they built Salem Village, circa 1692.

But it wasn't as easy as that might sound. See, there isn't a road to Hog Island, let alone *on* Hog Island. So the production enlisted the help of the Massachusetts National Guard and its 108-foot floating bridge. Most every bit of wood, hardware and manpower needed to build the movie's village was trucked over the floating bridge, as well as food and water for the cast and crew.

The setting—this vulnerable edge of coastal New World land where Puritans have settled and are still finding their way—is the real star of the movie. That and the legacy of Miller's play, which famously drew parallels between the Salem witch trials of the 1690s and the drive to root out American Communists (whether they existed in significant numbers or not) during the 1950s. Unfortunately, these things overshadow the actual movie, which, despite rallying late into its two hours, lacks the expected intensity.

What's the problem? Surprisingly enough in this movie reuniting the stars of 1993's *The Age of Innocence*, it's the lead characters: farmer John Proctor (Daniel Day-Lewis) and teen Abigail Williams (Winona Ryder). Abby is the instigator here. After being caught dancing and casting romantic spells with other local girls, she soon realizes that she's free from punishment if, instead of merely owning up to what she did, she accuses others of doing worse. To get off the hook, she tells the village elders that any witchcraft was perpetrated not by her, but by others. She tells them what they want to hear. She names names.

John, the married farmer with whom she had a fling and whom she still fancies, is the only person she tells about what really happened. This is shortly before Abby turns into nothing but a cold, calculated villain and the charges of witchcraft spread beyond her direct doing. Soon, everyone involved in a feud is charging his or her rival with witchcraft. In the Catch-22 of colonial justice, the accused is in a no-win situation. Telling the truth and denying the charge results in hanging, while confessing to imaginary crimes and soiling your good name will save you from the gallows.

> I had a horse who met me every morning when I got off the boat. This other world had been recreated so beautifully. I couldn't bring myself to climb into a golf buggy to go to the set. So I had a horse. A horse and a beeper.
> –Daniel Day-Lewis

While Abby fails to emerge beyond her villainy into a fully rounded character, John is an almost laughably dashing hero. One of the only men to see through the morally shaky witch hunt, he is an open-shirted, hale and hardy hunk dressed in leather amid a sea of grey or pasty fellow villagers dressed in buttoned-up "authoritative" clothes or sackcloth like that worn by the town parson and the trial judges (both the church and courtroom scenes were filmed inside Beverly's old United Shoe Building).

So too much of the movie's action is pat. We know who's wrong and who's right, and there's little middle ground. Things get much more dramatic in the second half, when John is moved to speak out against events and when the authority figures who then want to punish him balance their doubt over the proceedings with their desire to cover up any of their own improprieties. But the movie needed to get to this point much sooner.

The tale's diminished punch is frustrating, because it's easy to think of how *The Crucible* is still relevant. In interviews, Hytner and his cast cited such post-1950s events as China's Cultural Revolution, the McMartin child abuse case and the then-recent public grilling of Richard Jewell, a suspect in the Atlanta Olympics bombing. So there are plenty of reasons why *The Crucible* should have worked in the 1990s (in the years after the movie, you could add the passing of The PATRIOT Act to the list). The authenticity is there—many of the extras we see are actually descendants of real Salem villagers—but the drama is often absent.

▶ **Locations:** Hog Island, Essex; Beverly.

▶ **Accents:** You get the age-old, starchy accents movies have been supplying for colonial tales. Par for the course.

▶ **Local color:** It's not contemporary and it's not pleasant, but the Salem witch hunt is a big part of our local history (and tourism). So *The Crucible* rates very highly here.

▶ **Off the set:** During production, a group of *Crucible* cast and crew members took a field trip to see the much-derided, then-new version of another colonial morality play, *The Scarlet Letter*, starring Demi Moore and Gary Oldman. "It was just basically to show us all what not to do," Ryder admitted, wincing. "It's so mean."

The Dark End of the Street

1981. Written and directed by Jan Egleson. With Laura Harrington, Henry Tomaszewski, Michele Greene, Lance Henriksen, Pamela Payton-Wright, Albert Eaton and Terence Grey. Cinematography by D'Arcy Marsh.

The Dark End of the Street: Laura Harrington, Ben Affleck and Janice Brown in Cambridge.

TWO YEARS AFTER BRINGING grass-roots fiction filmmaking to Greater Boston with *Billy in the Lowlands*, Theater Company of Boston vet Jan Egleson returned to the streets of Cambridge for another life-sized drama. Billy Shaughnessy (Henry Tomaszewski), whom we left trying to right his life after legal troubles in *Billy*, is back in *The Dark End of the Street* (like its predecessor, named for a song). In the follow-up, vulnerable Billy's need to steer clear of the law is again a big factor, but he's not the main focus. Girlfriend Donna (Laura Harrington) is.

The intrigue begins after some post-softball partying on a roof in the Cambridge projects where they live. Billy and Donna hang around so they can be alone, but they're joined by Ethan (Terence Grey), a drunk friend who teases them, horses around a bit and then falls from the roof. The couple doesn't tell the police for two reasons. One is Billy's probation; he's sure any hint of wrongdoing will land him back in juvenile prison (it's an inside joke when he says, "I'll be in Billerica until I'm 90," a line he first utters in *Billy in the Lowlands*). The other is the fact that Ethan is black, and Donna and Billy are not. The chance of a race-related crime will surely make the police aggressively investigate the incident.

Not being able to tell anyone what happened hits Donna hard—in totally convincing, everyday ways. Her best friend is African-American

Marlene (Michele Greene), whose brother Brian (Albert Eaton) becomes the subject of the police investigation, since he and Ethan had quarreled earlier. When she hears that Donna might have seen what happened, the two fight in a disco and end up in jail overnight. Donna's attempts to get Billy to go to the cops with her also threaten that relationship. She's soon missing shifts at the greasy spoon where she works, and taxing her already overburdened mother (Pamela Payton-Wright) who, like Billy's mom in the earlier movie, is raising her kids alone. Ethan's death after several days in the hospital eliminates the one other person who could explain the incident. (That's Boston power couple Flash and Bennie Wiley playing Ethan's parents.)

As with *Billy in the Lowlands*, the filmmaking in *The Dark End of the Street* is basic, and the dialogue sometimes flat, particularly in the big speeches by the detective (Gustave Johnson) investigating Ethan's death. But the pleasure of the movie is in the intimate world it etches out, not just the plot. In a less intimate movie, the race question would swell into big crowd scenes with angry project residents and police barricades, and Donna and Marlene's friendship might get lost in the shuffle. Similarly, the scenes with Donna's weary mom, who's so well-played by Payton-Wright, wouldn't make the cut, since they don't often advance the central plot. Straddling the plot and the more observational scenes is Jimmy,

> In *Dark End of the Street*, we were creating a world a little more. In *Billy in the Lowlands*, we would just go into the real world and shoot.
> –Jan Egleson

the exotic truck driver and the mom's boyfriend, played with flippant charisma by Lance Henriksen, who'd worked in Boston theater and later scored in such cool movies as *Near Dark* and *Stone Cold*.

The Dark End of the Street doesn't deliver a knockout the way bigger movies sometimes can, but it portrays the delicate balance of everyday life in ways most movies overlook. The world doesn't change much over the course of its action. Life is just as much of a struggle for its characters as it was before, and the earthy characters (many played by non-professionals) remain in the same station in life. Since Hollywood was turning away from its uncharacteristic 1970s adventurousness, this and Egleson's other Boston movies were a welcome departure from the crush of sequels, remakes and save-the-world escapism.

Unlike the on-the-run plot of much of *Billy in the Lowlands*, *The Dark End of the Street* sticks closer to home: the most prominent Cambridge locations are where the characters live and work, including the Roosevelt Tower projects and Sexton Can (formerly in East

Cambridge). The donut shop where Donna works is Linda's, over the line in Belmont. We also see Flapper's, a one-time club where Alewife Station now stands, as well as the old Howard Johnson's off the expressway in South Bay and the Quincy quarries.

▶**Locations:** Cambridge; Belmont; Dorchester, Boston; Quincy.

▶**Accents:** Unlike most of the young cast, Laura Harrington is not from the projects. But the former B.U. student does a great job of blending in with her fellow actors. As with *Billy in the Lowlands*, the genuine accents are part of the deep credibility of the movie.

▶**Local color:** With its plot in which characters try to get through their daily lives, the color is more class-based than geographical. Just about everything we see is related to work, home or play—where Billy and Donna work, where she lives, where they hang out. This is working-class life shown with no desire to glorify it or gloss up its bleakness. And considering that much of it is in East Cambridge before it changed from an industrial area to a high-tech area, this is working-class life from a specific time.

▶**Don't blink!:** Yup, that's little Ben Affleck making his movie debut in the silent role of Donna's brother Tommy.

The Departed

2006. Directed by Martin Scorsese. Written by William Monahan. Based on *Infernal Affairs* by Alan Mak and Felix Chong. With Matt Damon, Leonardo DiCaprio, Jack Nicholson, Mark Wahlberg, Martin Sheen, Ray Winstone, Vera Farmiga and Alec Baldwin. Cinematography by Michael Ballhaus.

MARTIN SCORSESE'S AWARD-WINNING crime drama is one of the best Boston movies. But, like many others, it's a mix of real Boston and fake Boston. After all, *Mean Streets*, *Raging Bull* and *GoodFellas* director Scorsese is the foremost New York director of his time. And more of *The Departed* was shot in his hometown than in the city where it takes place.

But Bostonian William Monahan wrote it, putting a Boston overlay on *Infernal Affairs*, the cleverly plotted 2002 Hong Kong movie about a crook pretending to be a cop and a cop pretending to be a crook. And homegrown Matt Damon and Mark Wahlberg are in its cast. Take *The Departed* out of Boston and you wouldn't just lose the repressed atmosphere in which everyone, especially the two moles, is stingy about personal details. You'd have to lose one of its essential

The Departed: Leonardo DiCaprio and Martin Sheen in South Boston.

scenes, and its best Boston moment. That's when State Police sergeant Dignam (Wahlberg) tries to goad just-graduated State Police cadet Billy Costigan (Leonardo DiCaprio) into going undercover in the South Boston mob by targeting Costigan's embarrassment over coming from a family of underachievers, and his identity crisis from having split his youth between his "lace curtain" remarried mom on the North Shore and his downscale father in Southie. "You had different accents," Dignam prods. "You did, didn't you, you little fuckin' snake?" Dignam has found a weak spot to squeeze and he won't let go.

The scene doesn't just mark Costigan as a character who could only be from within the confining loop of Route 128. It also taps into Bostonians' tendencies to skip the pleasantries and rub each other raw. This isn't the playful "You talking to me?" or "Whadya mean, I'm funny?" Scorsese cursing by Robert De Niro or Joe Pesci. It's a hailstorm of dropped-R, in-your-face, smart-ass expletives worthy of the verbal sparring in George V. Higgins' *The Friends of Eddie Coyle*. *Yes*, I'm talking to *you*. These Staties are like hockey dads, with guns. They're just looking for an excuse to go after somebody.

The writing in the scene and the specific Boston qualities of Costigan are among the best instances of *The Departed* embellishing *Infernal Affairs*. Almost all of the plot comes from the Hong Kong film, from such big elements as a mob boss having a young protégé become a cop so he'll have a friend inside the department (this time, the characters are Jack Nicholson's Frank Costello and Damon's Colin Sullivan), to little things such as Costello smashing Costigan's arm cast (lest it contain a recording device) and two henchmen joking about how you can tell who's an undercover cop.

In its bulk-up from Hong Kong action drama to big-budget Hollywood blockbuster, *The Departed* certainly has problems here and there, though. It distressed this longtime Scorsese fan to see his *Mean Streets* innovation of using a rock-song score devolve into nothingness—wall-to-wall use of songs in which few of them actually have dramatic meaning—while the expanded character of a female psychologist (Vera Farmiga) comes off like a Hollywood convenience who's around just to have affairs with the two conflicting male leads.

One of the local aspects of *The Departed* that's been overly doted upon is that Costello is based on one-time South Boston mob boss and longtime fugitive James "Whitey" Bulger. Monahan's script adds a Whitey-like touch to Costello now and then, including the strong suggestion that he's an FBI informant. But 95% of the character is from *Infernal Affairs* and Nicholson, whose trademark leering sometimes detracts from the drama.

Like the Whitey connection, the locations used in *The Departed* supply an extra dimension for those aware of them. Scorsese and crew shot here for six weeks, using Staniford Street's butt-ugly Hurley Building for State Police headquarters, Charlestown's Flagship Wharf condos for Costello's luxurious digs and the Quincy Shipyard for the microchip-sale stakeout and the climactic showdown between Costello's crew and the police. You can also spot Boston Common in the opening rugby scene, Quincy Bay as the remote spot where Costigan has a rendezvous with his police contacts, the exterior of the Moakley Courthouse (from where Costigan makes a phone call), the Lewis Wharf area (where Dignam and his boss confront Costello) and the Park Street and South Station Red Line stations. The rooftop scenes take place in the Fort Point Channel area, off of Farnsworth Street, Costigan pursues Sullivan down Tyler Street and into the Chinatown parking lots bordered by Edinboro, Ping On and Oxford Streets, and such other spots as Charles Street (where the exterior of Charles Street Cleaners was made over as a bistro) and the ever-familiar Zakim Bridge are also visible. Sullivan's condo with a sweet view of the State

House is a fake, though. Those scenes weren't done locally, and were presumably done on a New York soundstage with a photomural for its powerful "view."

With a sequel for *The Departed* now in the works (featuring Wahlberg's Dignam) and tax breaks now in place that make it more desirable for Hollywood productions to shoot in Massachusetts, chances are any *Departed* follow-ups will shoot in Boston more than the original did.

▶**Locations:** South Boston, Charlestown, Chinatown, Seaport District, Beacon Hill, Dorchester, East Boston, Boston; Quincy; Cambridge.

▶**Accents:** Matt Damon and Mark Wahlberg amp up their lingering accents and give *The Departed* a sense of authenticity. Others in the cast are hit and miss. Costigan's accent is supposed to be weak, thanks to his childhood split between his upwardly mobile mother and his Southie dad, and DiCaprio does fine with the light accent. Nicholson and Alec Baldwin are inconsistent, Vera Farmiga is passable, Martin Sheen just cranks up the Kennedy accent he used playing both John and Bobby in different TV movies and Ray Winstone's accent is an unpredictable mix of Boston, generic American and his own English accent (big deal—he's always been a ferocious actor, and he's a force here). All in all, above average, as nobody is awkward enough to spoil his or her performance.

▶**Local color:** As in *Mystic River*, there's much use of the Staties nickname for the State Police. But William Monahan's script gets even littler details right. It's just perfect that the Staties' secretary we see is named Darlene. Who *didn't* go to high school in Greater Boston during the 1970s or 1980s with a Darlene, a Darlene that might go on to have a job just like that? Throw in The Dropkick Murphys' anthemic "I'm Shipping Up to Boston," a clip from the old Channel 56 news and a Brigham's reference, and the local flavor gets stronger. And you just have to grin at any line of dialogue describing someone once holding down the job of "carpet layer for Jordan Marsh."

Diaries (1971-1976)

1981. Directed by Ed Pincus. Cinematography by Ed Pincus.

BEFORE "REALITY TV" REARED its ugly head, before even PBS' landmark *An American Family*, Brooklyn-born M.I.T. film/video professor Ed Pincus put camera on shoulder and started filming his *own* life. And although the 200-minute length of his subsequent *Diaries (1971-1976)* can be trying, Pincus' life turns out to be *full* of remarkable drama.

Though too old to be flower children, he and wife Jane live in the shadow of the 1960s over the course of the movie, trying to balance a post-sexual-revolution open relationship with the rearing of their two young children and each's own artistic aspirations (Jane is a batik artist and a member of the Boston Women's Health Collective, the group behind the influential book *Our Bodies, Ourselves*).

Although we hear only occasionally of Jane's extramarital relationship with lover Bob (who may or may not be the reason she visits Paris at one point), Ed's time with such women as Anna and Christine often fills the screen. Much of the drama stems from the fact that Ed appears to be more into seeing other people than Jane is, and you can see him flash the impish smile that no doubt charmed many lovers (in the footage, which Pincus purposely let sit for five years before editing, the filmmaker looks like David Lee Roth's mischievous little brother). Through Ed and Jane, the movie becomes a moving look at the battle between monogamy and freedom, the tension ultimately giving way to a moment of calmness that suggests a truce in this battle (the couple remains together today).

The movie also veers into a fruitful direction in the road trip Pincus takes with friend and sometime collaborator David Neuman. Not only are the sights in Las Vegas and the Grand Canyon scenic, but there's a sense of existential drifting here that helps to make the serene, rooted ending, at the Vermont farm where the Pincuses have moved, connect that much more.

Diaries (1971-1976) definitely takes place within the private world of Ed and Jane Pincus. We only see the outer world *through* this private world, sometimes literally, as in the park viewed through the bay windows of the Pincuses' Cambridgeport home on Cpl. McTernan Street or the city streets seen through car windows. Although there are a few sequences taking place in restaurants and coffee shops such as La Patisserie and Joyce Chen, there are no exteriors of such places and, frustratingly, nothing is very recognizable. A few seconds of evocative footage shot at a Celtics home game in the days of John Havlicek and Don Nelson made me nostalgic for Section 41 of the old Boston Garden, though. Can you smell the spilt beer?

Diaries (1971-1976)'s status as a Boston film rests not so much in local color as it does in its reflection of the past and its impact on the future. Like Ed and Jane Pincus, I'm sure many people who blossomed in the 1960s struggled with such traditional institutions as marriage and parenthood in the 1970s (and not just in places like Cambridge, Berkeley and Ann Arbor). And the movie turned out to be a fountainhead that inspired an entire generation of Pincus' and Richard Leacock's filmmaking students at M.I.T., challenging documentary makers to search inside themselves for subjects for their movies. Some of *Diaries* can feel like a glorified home movie, especially the action with the kids; but this painfully intimate movie is also the start of a particularly Bostonian documentary genre.

The Dozens

1980. Directed by Christine Dall and Randall Conrad. Written by Marian Taylor, Christine Dall and Randall Conrad. With Debra Margolies, Edward Mason, Jessica Hergert and Marian Taylor. Cinematography by Joseph Vitagliano.

THE FIRST IMAGES YOU see in Christine Dall and Randall Conrad's movie are a long list of the foundations, institutions and government agencies that bestowed money upon their low-budget movie—the sort of list seen at the top of many a PBS documentary. It's an odd start for a feature, but not so surprising considering the husband and wife team have a background in documentaries. They had even originally conceived of *The Dozens*, their tale of a young female ex-con's uneasy transition back into society, as a non-fiction film before deciding to stretch into fiction.

The Dozens may be a dramatic feature, but don't expect glamour. Like Jan Egleson's *Billy in the Lowlands* and *The Dark End of the Street*—with which it shares two supporting cast members—it's as independent and off-Hollywood as you can get. The idea is to point the camera where Hollywood doesn't, with an eye for street-level realism movies generally avoid, as stories ask you to walk a mile in troubled characters' shoes. Everyone you see in it is either a newcomer or an untrained actor.

MCI Framingham inmate Sally (Debra Margolies, who had a tiny part in *Between the Lines*) has a female lover (Sumru Tekin) inside and, we learn after her parole, a husband, Sonny (Edward Mason), on the outside. After taking the rap for passing forged checks with him (he wasn't charged), she has little desire to reconcile. Reconnecting with Jessica (Jessica Hergert), the four-year-old daughter who's been living with her mother (Ethel Michelson) for the last two years, is more important to her.

In keeping with the movie's low-key, indie style, 21-year-old Sally's struggles come across on a very everyday level, thanks in part to the wounded determination Margolies gives the heroine. The effect of her limited budget on her apartment-hunting results in an amusing montage in which she reads apartment listings as we see each successive building; she ends up renting in a multi-family with, she says in mock-listing lingo, "a nice view of the projects." Meanwhile, the corrections system seems geared more towards finding ways to put Sally back in prison than to ensure she doesn't return there: the cosmetology training she takes is soon a casualty of budget cuts, and her parole officer (Jack Sheridan) acts eager to find an excuse to return

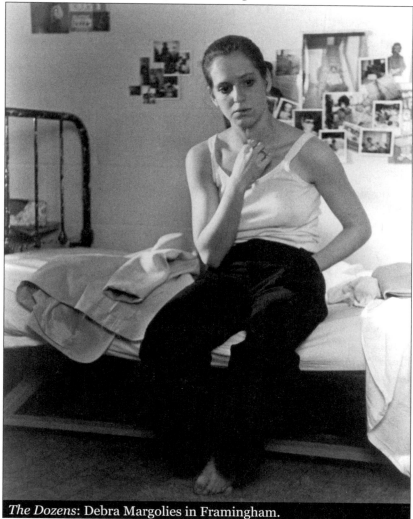

The Dozens: Debra Margolies in Framingham.

her to Framingham. Sonny, with whom she remains friendly, doesn't help, either. He takes advantage of her by using her new apartment to stash the cocaine he's dealing so he can buy a laundromat.

The Dozens' doesn't let its condemnation of "the system" overwhelm Sally's story. Although one damning scene of female inmates sewing American flags hits home, we generally follow Sally through ordinary days and nights—doing laundry, going to the handbag-factory job she holds for a spell, taking Jessica to the playground,

> It seemed like we'd be able to actually realize (the story) in more reality if we did it as a drama than if we tried to do it as a documentary.
> –Christine Dall

trying to get her friend Russel (co-writer Marian Taylor) to stop giving her grief and Sonny to get his coke out of her house. The script can be frustratingly vague at times (some have embraced Sally as a lesbian heroine, though her sexual preference is left open), but it pulls a nice swerve by *not* involving Sonny's coke in the climax.

Filmed at such locations as MCI Framingham, Cambridge, Somerville and Allston in 1978 and 1979, hence the out-of-fashion-by-1980 bellbottoms and disco songs, *The Dozens* shows the lingering impact that 1960s-era idealism held on 1980s independent film. Since Hollywood swung open its doors to a new generation following the success of *Easy Rider* and *Bonnie and Clyde*, independent film was almost dormant in the 1970s, and filmmakers like Dall and Conrad were helping to build it back up. Their movie was a hit on the then-small festival circuit, winning a Grand Prize at the 4th U.S. Film & Video Festival (later renamed the Sundance Film Festival) and running for nine weeks at Cambridge's Orson Welles Cinema. But, well-received as it was, *The Dozens* had little commercial impact nationally; few indie films did in the early 1980s. Its reputation as part of its era's cluster of humanistic Boston movies is secure, though.

▶ **Locations:** Cambridge; Somerville; Framingham; Allston, Boston.

▶ **Accents:** There's only the occasional accent. That's apparently just how things worked out with the casting. But it has little impact on the story or its authenticity.

▶ **Local color:** This story could take place in any urban setting. But the dense neighborhoods of Cambridge and Somerville convey the grimness of Sally's world. It seems as if the sun never shines during the entire movie. Her neighborhood is a hodgepodge of places—the exterior of her triple-decker is on Washburne Avenue, some of its interiors were done in the moviemakers' own Cambridgeport apartment and its view of the projects is actually a shot in Mission Hill. Sally is arrested on Sidney Street in Cambridge. There are also some fascinating glimpses of the city, circa late-1970s: Packard Square when the car dealers that fled to Route 1 were in their last throes (one is even boarded up); the Gore Street Playground, most of which, I believe, is now Twin City Plaza on the Somerville/Cambridge border, off of McGrath Highway; the outside of the long-gone Central Square Theater; the old Combat Zone; and a little farther up Washington Street, some old-school Christmas window displays.

Fever Pitch

2005. Directed by Peter and Bobby Farrelly. Written by Lowell Ganz and Babaloo Mandel. Based on the novel by Nick Hornby. With Drew Barrymore, Jimmy Fallon, KaDee Strickland, Ione Skye and Jack Kehler. Cinematography by Matthew F. Leonetti.

RHODE ISLAND-BORN PETER and Bobby Farrelly have long operated on the geographical edges of Boston moviedom: shooting bits of *Dumb & Dumber* and *There's Something About Mary* in their home state, filming portions of *Osmosis Jones* and *Stuck on You* in Massachusetts. But with *Fever Pitch*, the brothers finally made their Boston movie.

Some might approach it solely as a celebration of the Red Sox' 2004 victory and be disappointed to get a mere romantic comedy. Much was made at the time of how the romance between a workaholic Bostonian and a Sox fanatic had to be reworked when the team defied the odds and, finally, got more than *close* to winning. But it turns out the Sox' unlikely comeback is a small part of the movie, almost an afterthought. Win or lose, the main objective of the story, loosely based on Nick Hornby's soccer-fan-in-love novel, is getting its romantic couple back together, which it does rather convincingly. *Fever Pitch* has strong female and male perspectives at work, and the combination makes for a rare romantic comedy both men and women can like.

For most of the movie, we look at events through the eyes of Lindsey (Drew Barrymore), a mathematician at a business consulting firm who meets Ben (Jimmy Fallon) in October 2003, when the 9th grade math teacher brings his students up for a talk about what she does. Their relationship is fine, until spring training starts.

That's when Ben finally tells Lindsey just how obsessed he is with the Red Sox: season tickets near the Sox' dugout, not a missed game in 11 years, much Bucky Dent-Bill Buckner-Aaron Boone heartache, much accursed New England fatalism. She has to compete for his

Fever Pitch: Drew Barrymore and Jimmy Fallon at Fenway Park.

affection with the Sox. Their relationship survives the stress Ben's Sox devotion puts on it most of the time, except when he acts as if the Sox are more important to him than Lindsey, which is semi-regularly—especially if the Yankees are in town.

The story forces Ben to question whether his Sox jones is loyalty or arrested development, and forces Lindsey to ponder whether giving in to Ben's Sox fanaticism is betraying her own priorities (she's up for a big promotion at work). The issue of whether a man can grow up and commit to a woman is common fodder for a romantic comedy, but *Fever Pitch* endows it with enough realism to make it work. The two leads feel real, and their chemistry is palpable enough to make you care about what happens to them and to laugh along with them.

Lindsey takes to the Red Sox enough that most of the Fenway Park action takes place in the couple's box seats, not on the field. Despite occasional cut-ins to game action and cameos by local media personalities, the movie's true blue Bostonians are the Greek chorus of Sox fans around them. These include old-timer Al (Jack Kehler), who narrates the story, and another die-hard played by Jessamy Finet, from the Sox-doc *Still, We Believe*. The emotional bruises ailing Red Sox Nation add flavor to the romantic comedy, though I could have done without that most cringe-inducing Fenway custom, the "Sweet Caroline" sing-along. Reality is also a mixed blessing in the special *Fever Pitch* DVD that includes an "alternate Red Sox ending," since it's just the same resolution as the "regular" version that played in theaters, but with a little more playoff and World Series footage edited in (though the DVD's deleted scenes include Johnny Damon and Jason Varitek's cut restaurant scene in which they trade a bit of dialogue with Fallon).

> It was just killing me, the thought of someone else doing (this movie) with no allegiance to the Red Sox.
> –Bobby Farrelly

Budget constraints forced the Farrellys to film more of *Fever Pitch* in Toronto than they did in Boston. But the access the movie has to Fenway and the Sox, as well as its eye for local detail, makes it one of the most local movies Hollywood has ever made. In addition to the smattering of exterior scenes shot around the city—a Newbury Street café and the exteriors of Ben's North End apartment building and Lindsey's Marlborough Street apartment building—it's the state of mind that really makes this a Boston movie.

▶ **Locations:** The Fenway, Back Bay, North End, Boston.

▶ **Accents:** Jimmy Fallon's character was born in New Jersey and Drew Barrymore's doesn't have an accent. Plus, as usual, you don't necessarily want your stars dabbling in different voices. But such locals as Finet, Lenny Clarke and Brett Murphy (who plays one of Fallon's students and is in *Mystic River*) add realism, while Jack Kehler and Siobhan Fallon do well with their fake accents.

▶ **Local color:** Johnny Damon before he scrammed, Bob Lobel, Pesky's Pole, the Green Monster, Lenny Clarke, ticket scalpers, Tony C's black eye—I think you get my drift. Erin Nanstad and Dan Cummings, two other fans profiled in *Still, We Believe*, have non-speaking roles.

Floating

1999. Written and directed by William Roth. With Norman Reedus, Chad Lowe, Sybil Temchen, Will Lyman, Josh Marchette and Jonathan Quint. Cinematography by Wolfgang Held.

A HIGHLIGHT OF LATE-1990s local indie activity, William Roth's coming-of-age drama has a very appealing sense of restraint. That poise helps it to avoid clichés and develop into a quietly potent tale of youthful turmoil. Shot mostly on, in and around White Pond in Roth's hometown of Concord, *Floating* revolves around Van (Norman Reedus), a 19-year-old who, in keeping with the movie's water imagery, is a former high school swimmer now treading water in life.

"I had it, the white picket fence," he says in an early voice-over in which he describes the downward spiral that shrunk his ambitions before the movie even began: the car accident that caused his father (Will Lyman) to lose both legs below the knee; his mother's rejection of the invalid father, and her flight with most of the family's money; Van and his dad's move from their swanky home overlooking the pond to a rundown house across the water; and Van staying at home the year after high school to help his dad and try to figure out what to do while friends went off to school or just got out of town.

The start of another summer, and the return of those friends, pushes Van's uncertainties to the fore. His high school sweetheart (Sybil Temchen) has grown apart from him, and his pals (Sudbury's Josh Marchette, Jonathan Quint) are stuck in arrested adolescence. But a new friend arrives who is more sympathetic to Van's predicament than expected. He's Doug (Chad Lowe), and Van's friendship with him is an extremely well-written, unconventional movie friendship. At first, Doug appears to have the life Van thought was his—Doug's family moves into Van's old house and he's a college swimmer, just what Van thought he was going to be. But the initial resentment Van feels fades once he realizes Doug also has a strained relationship with his dad (Bruce Kenny) and feels anxious about an uncertain future.

As Van and Doug start swimming the pond together, there is all sorts of athletic and sexual tension between the two, even before Van learns Doug is gay. But *Floating* deals with the gay-straight gap between these men without the knee-jerk reactions of a Hollywood movie or the touchy-feely "understanding" of an art film. It's practically a non-issue, and totally convincing.

Roth's emotional realism isn't evident only in his writing. It carries over to his work with the actors, too. Reedus and Lowe both skillfully underplay their sometimes troubled characters. Reedus is especially expressive here. His good looks convince you Van was a high school hot shot, while his worried face carries the despair holding him back (although *Floating* took three years to reach theaters after shooting in the fall of 1996, Reedus' unaffected performance helped to get him a half-dozen lead movie roles in the ensuing gap, including in *Boondock Saints*). Although most of the casting choices are spot-on, there's an interesting casting what-if here: had Ben Affleck and Matt Damon not landed pre-*Good Will Hunting* lead roles in, respectively, *Going All the Way* and *The Rainmaker*, they were likely to join Casey Affleck as *Floating*'s pot-purchasing preppies.

> I didn't even think about shopping the script around. It was like, 'I'm going to raise the money and do it myself.' It wasn't a Hollywood script.
> —William Roth

In addition to its predominant Concord locations, including several private homes (Roth's parents' house among them), *Floating* also filmed at the Paradise in Boston (the interior of the music club scenes) and at the swimming pool at Lexington's Minuteman Regional High School.

▶**Locations:** Concord; Allston, Boston; Lexington.

▶**Accents:** Not that many. Marchette (on whom Matt Damon and Ben Affleck partially based Casey Affleck's *Good Will Hunting* character) sports one, as does Bruce Kenny, who plays Doug's hard-assed dad. But they, like everyone else, are just using their natural voices.

▶**Local color:** Very little—though there's an undeniable regional truth in the cold way Van treats Doug when the latter introduces himself and tries to make friends.

The Friends of Eddie Coyle

1973. Directed by Peter Yates. Written by Paul Monash. Based on George V. Higgins' novel. With Robert Mitchum, Peter Boyle, Richard Jordan, Steven Keats, Alex Rocco and Joe Santos. Cinematography by Victor J. Kemper.

ALL HAIL *EDDIE*. THE gritty film adaptation of attorney turned writer George V. Higgins' terse debut novel is the best movie ever made in Boston, a touchstone with a legendary status enhanced by the fact that it's never been released on any form of home video.

Director Peter (*Bullitt*) Yates' movie is one of the few post-1960 color thrillers to capture the desperation and doom of 1940s and 1950s film noir. Of course, it helps to have Robert Mitchum, who headlined such vintage noirs as *Out of the Past* and *Pursued*, playing the title character. Mitchum and his hangdog persona perfectly embody the weariness of Coyle, an aging, working-class crook awaiting sentencing for transporting stolen goods who reluctantly becomes a police informer in hopes that his tips to "uncle" will win him leniency.

Like Higgins' novel—which is almost experimental in its preferred use of two-character dialogues instead of conventional narrative—*The Friends of Eddie Coyle* atmospherically presents the workaday tug of war between crooks and cops. Seen through the movie's gutter's-eye view of the world, everyone's looking for a leg up on the other guy, a favor or some sort of insulation from jail (for the crooks) or bad work assignments (for the cops). Eddie Coyle is the common thread running among gun seller Jackie Brown (Steven Keats), bartender/hit man Dillon (Peter Boyle), federal agent Foley (Richard Jordan) and a group of robbers that's striking suburban banks.

As Coyle secures handguns from Jackie for the bankrobbers, Dillon keeps tabs on Eddie's travels and Foley fields tidbits of info from both men. These tips are cast out like fishing lines, hoping to return a nibble from Foley that might bring a desired favor. One such nibble comes after Eddie sees machine guns in Jackie's car trunk and hears him say he has to get to the train station at Sharon. He gets there, but so do Foley and a half-dozen other agents.

Still, Eddie's aid in Boston is not enough to get Coyle a break with a New Hampshire prosecutor, and you can feel the vice tighten around him. He's faced with a no-win situation: do jail time or fink on guys who, unlike younger Jackie, are his contemporaries and cohorts. In its own low-key, Eddie-ish way, *The Friends of Eddie Coyle* works to a tragic ending that, hard to believe, makes a change in the story that actually improves upon Higgins' plot.

> *Eddie Coyle* came out about the same time as *The Godfather*. I think people still prefer their criminals to be glamorized.
> —Peter Yates

Eddie Coyle is the first Boston movie with the guts to never be scenic (just look at the Quincy street Coyle lives on, with its row of drab, look-alike houses). It's a grey, grey movie, because Eddie is stuck in a grey, grey world, lacking the resources to go to sunny Florida (as he laments) or the traction to climb out of his place on the crime ladder. Yates shot the movie in late 1972, with winter approaching, and you can feel the chill in the air. You often see the breath exhaled by characters during the conversations on the Boston Common or outside a Quincy Red Line station. The other locations are grungy spots Thomas Crown would certainly never be

The Friends of Eddie Coyle: Robert Mitchum in the Kentucky Tavern.

caught at, including Dillon's bar (shot at the Kentucky Tavern at Mass. Ave. and Newbury Street), the cafeteria where Coyle and Jackie first meet (which appears to be on Boylston Street near Tremont), Boston Bowl and Dedham Plaza. A Weymouth bank, Memorial Drive, the old Boston Garden and even grim City Hall Plaza also serve the story very well. And rather than packing up back to Los Angeles for interiors, the production did everything here, even building sets, including the trailer belonging to robber Jimmy Scalise (hometown boy Alex Rocco), in Pier Five on the waterfront.

Apparently, Higgins did an uncredited polish on Paul Monash's script. When I checked with the Higgins archives at the University of South Carolina to see if the late novelist's papers contained any info on the movie's locations, the staff's perusal of his archival materials from that period turned up at least one reference in his letters to restoring dialogue from the novel to the screenplay. Thirty-five years after it was released to audience indifference, it's hard to watch *The Friends of Eddie Coyle* now and not think that it—the most essential movie Hollywood has made in Boston—deserves the awards, acclaim and popularity bestowed upon *Mystic River*, a lesser movie in the same vein. Oh, well. That's showbiz.

▶**Locations:** Back Bay, North End, Beacon Hill, Boston; Quincy; Sharon; Milton; Weymouth; Dedham; Cambridge.

▶**Accents:** Surprisingly good. Mitchum, originally eyed for Peter Boyle's role, manages to use a convincing Boston accent without losing his own distinctive voice. So Eddie comes off as an emotionally spent Mitchum character, and a neighborhood guy, too. Boyle and Richard Jordan use a light touch with their accents, too. Considering the strong sense of place the locations give the movie, thick accents might have been overkill. These guys sound right at home next to Alex Rocco.

▶**Local color:** "Numbah faw, Bobby Aw!" Eddie bellows from the Boston Garden balcony during a Bruins game featuring helmetless players and no ads on the ice or boards. Of course, Eddie and his "friends" would be into the big, bad Bruins (just as they'd be into the Pats today). The hockey sequence appears to have been shot during a real game, and that's the kind of authenticity you get here. It's not as if other movie productions were lining up to shoot at the Kentucky Tavern or fluorescent-lit cafeterias. The locations are so real I expected to see Eddie pop into a Zayre at some point, but no such luck.

▶**Aftermath:** Higgins fan Elmore Leonard borrowed the androgynous name Jackie Brown for the heroine of his novel, *Rum Punch*. When Quentin Tarantino made a film of Leonard's book, he renamed the story *Jackie Brown*, as did the movie tie-in re-release of the book.

Funny Ha Ha

2002. Written and directed by Andrew Bujalski. With Kate Dollenmayer, Christian Rudder, Myles Paige, Jennifer L. Schaper and Andrew Bujalski. Cinematography by Matthias Grunsky.

WRITER-DIRECTOR ANDREW BUJALSKI'S comedy-drama is a hit or miss affair. On the plus side are its no-gimmicks, documentary shooting style and doleful heroine Marnie (Kate Dollenmayer). On the minus are the sometimes dodgy sound and the fact that the male lead, Alex (Christian Rudder), the elusive college friend Kate has long had a crush on, is barely developed as a character.

Shot mainly in Allston—the *perfect* location considering the characters—*Funny Ha Ha* introduces Marnie's uncertainty about life ahead by putting her in a tattoo parlor (actually, it just looks like a room in an apartment, but that's OK). She doesn't know what kind of tattoo she wants and when the tattoo artist discovers she's drunk, he refuses to give her one. Mission: Not Accomplished. But that's not unusual for Marnie, we quickly learn. She soon tells a friend about how she asked for a raise at work, but got fired because of it. And she hears that Alex, who had been going out with someone else, is single again. But Marnie already got rejected by him once, and isn't even sure she wants to pursue him again.

Marnie is slouchy, all shrugs and raised eyebrows. Yet Dollenmayer gives her an almost endearing tentativeness, so we take some interest in her. Unfortunately, most of the other characters in *Funny Ha Ha* share her indecision and, in some cases, add a lack of commitment to it. That's certainly true of the men, including Dave (Myles Paige), the friend who's in seemingly the most stable relationship, yet who still makes a pass at uninterested Marnie, and Alex, who seems to toy with Marnie's affection.

The sheer sameness of these characters is numbing. Some have compared Bujalski's movie with the indie hit *Slacker* from a decade before, because both were made very independently and look at characters who are still clinging to the college experience, unsure of where life's taking them. But *Slacker* is an inspired tapestry of diverse characters poking around and looking for a niche to inhabit. Too often, *Funny Ha Ha* is just semi-dorky engineers clumsily socializing. Sometimes its little comic vignettes with peripheral characters score, like one with a friend (Anitra Menning) Marnie finds passed out in her car or another with Alex's roommate (Justin Rice), who's all dirty because of a scrape with neighborhood tykes.

The Marnie-Alex relationship is the most puzzling thing in Bujalski's movie. Alex's company pleases Marnie, as seen in a scene shot in Watertown's Deluxe Town Diner in which the two joke around. But the way Alex just wants to hang around with her and not address their "relationship" borders on the cruel, as do some of his later actions. It's hard to know whether to sympathize with Marnie because she keeps getting frustrated by her lack of progress with Alex or to sigh with relief because she's avoided becoming hurt even more by him.

In the hit-or-miss world of *Funny Ha Ha*, Marnie's intentionally awkward scenes with smitten, geeky Mitchell (Bujalski), the temp co-worker *she* just wants to hang out with, ring much truer. Although the movie has an admirably open-ended conclusion (there's no resolution at all), the sudden ending didn't exactly leave me satisfied, either.

▶ **Locations:** Allston, Boston; Watertown.

▶ **Accents:** None. But there's little sense these characters are natives.

▶ **Local color:** Not much. At one point, a supporting character mentions town-gown conflict between locals and students, but we never see a single townie. But then again, we get a lot of recent college graduates, of which Boston is full.

Fuzz

1972. Directed by Richard A. Colla. Written by Evan Hunter. Based on his novel. With Burt Reynolds, Raquel Welch, Tom Skerritt, Jack Weston and Yul Brynner. Cinematography by Jacques Marquette.

IT'S VERY COOL THAT someone decided to make an irreverent cop comedy in Boston in 1972. For a change, it wasn't tradition that moviemakers sought from the city, but of-the-moment hipness. Too bad the resulting movie is like a party that peters out too quickly. *Fuzz* fails to live up to its poster illustration, which features Raquel Welch in thigh-high boots and hot pants, gun drawn, references Burt Reynolds' *Cosmopolitan* centerfold and promises much more comic mayhem than the movie delivers.

Oddly enough, the first 20 minutes lay the groundwork for what might have been a very fun comedy. Starting with a memorable shot taken from the cockpit of a Cambridge-bound Red Line train as it rises onto the Longfellow Bridge, the mood is reminiscent of a Robert Altman ensemble comedy, with overlapping dialogue, an anti-authoritarian streak and Tom Skerritt, a veteran of Altman's *M*A*S*H*.

Fuzz: Burt Reynolds and Jack Weston in the Public Garden.

You immediately sense that this is a movie in which the police are not cardboard heroes, but jokers who are sometimes more concerned with horsing around than hunkering down with their work. Meanwhile, the look of the dingy squad room where its detectives work hints at TV's amiable *Barney Miller*, which would follow later in the 1970s.

But the hubbub of the early action is one of the few times *Fuzz* feels fully conceived. Generally, the comedy seems forced, as in the scene in which Reynolds' and Jack Weston's characters dress up as nuns for a Public Garden stakeout. This might have been funny if there were some sort of set-up (maybe a scene in which they find those are the only available costumes) or context (how about they dress up like nuns because there's a tour group of nuns with whom they try to blend?). Even more of a head-scratcher is the fact that Reynolds and Welch, who plays a detective brought in to lure the rapist who's been terrorizing the neighborhood, are in only one scene together (it's almost as if she's in an entirely different movie). And while the crime plot is not all that important, the one here—in which a gang led by a hearing-impaired mastermind (Yul Brynner) kills two politicians so it can *then* extort money by threatening to kill a rich businessman—is especially weak. You also get the feeling the movie started out as an R-rated comedy, and was toned down to PG in the editing room.

Starting with its opening Longfellow Bridge shot, this painless misfire actually uses its Boston locations very well. Director Richard A. Colla doesn't sprinkle the comedy into the thriller plot very successfully. But unlike most comedies, his movie adds grit with its locations. There are no pretty postcard views in scenes set in Copley Square, Park Square (where the pool hall is), the North End (where detectives trail a suspect home) and Charlestown, where the movie climaxes. Like *The Thomas Crown Affair*, this is also a Jack Weston movie that visits the North End's Copp's Hill Burying Ground.

Some sequences were clearly done on a studio backlot—including the scene in which Reynolds goes undercover as a bum and the longer liquor store stakeout—and one can only guess where the "mayor's mansion" exterior is (probably in California). At a time when New York crime movies were all over the screen (think *The French Connection* or *Shaft*), the makers of *Fuzz* bravely shifted one of Ed McBain's 87th Precinct novels from Manhattan to Boston (with McBain writing the screenplay under his given name, Evan Hunter). The movie is only so-so, but the locations definitely make it more interesting.

▶**Locations:** Back Bay, North End, Charlestown, Boston.

▶**Accents:** The shift of action from New York to Boston didn't carry over to the voices. Every once in a while, someone tries to say something "Bostonian," but no one does a bona fide accent. With the cast talking in their own voices, there are more Noo Yawk accents than Boston.

▶**Local color:** *Fuzz* is not the sort of movie in which geographical accuracy is important. Check out the scene in which a suspect being followed by detectives exits the Green Line's Auditorium Station (now Hynes/ICA) on Mass. Ave., walks towards Newbury Street and is suddenly in the Haymarket, checking out fruit stalls. The movie supplies a good cross-section of local sights, though, and the passage of time has only enhanced their value, especially the old elevated Orange Line, complete with its perfectly dingy stations.

Girltalk

1987. Directed by Kate Davis. Cinematography by Alyson Denny.

THIS IS THE BOSTON movie guaranteed to break your heart. Former Harvard students Kate Davis and Alyson Denny, who both worked as editors on Ross McElwee's *Sherman's March*, take their documentary camera and sound recorder to places movies rarely dare to travel, focusing on three Boston teen runaways. Rather than damning its troubled teens to hopelessness or glazing them in simple solutions, *Girltalk* humanizes all those statistics about runaways, teen pregnancies and abused children. The result is an engrossing combination of heartbreaking tragedy and life-affirming resilience.

Each girl is in a different stage of her teen years and a different stage of her troubles. Pinky is a 14-year-old Roxbury truant who's run away in the past. After living in two foster homes briefly, she's now back with her mother in a no-questions-asked situation. Mars left home at 13, after being raped by her stepbrother. Years later, she's still numbed by the experience, and works as a stripper in the Combat Zone. And Somerville's Martha—19, single and pregnant—is using motherhood as a reason to put a past of sexual abuse and self-destructive behavior behind her.

> I began to realize how little attention had been paid to the troubles of female teens. The juvenile police and social workers were open to helping (filmmakers), and the city was layered with obscure yet visually striking backdrops for wayward kids.
> –Kate Davis

Combining interviews and footage that follow each in day-to-day activities, *Girltalk* deftly avoids pigeonholing or exploiting the girls. These girls are here because of their troubles, yet they're not simply victims in a "case study" movie. Mars and Martha both talk about the sexual abuse they suffered, yet Davis resists sensationalism. The movie never acts with moral superiority or pity, and it never looks down on its "girls."

Girltalk: Mars in the South End.

It also never weighs itself down with self-importance. Pinky, Mars and Martha appear to be so comfortable on camera that the movie is unusually intimate and they speak very freely. Director Davis, who'd previously co-written *Vacant Lot*, a documentary-style short about Somerville project kids, obviously made them at ease. *Girltalk*'s greatest achievement is blending a variety of emotions into a thoroughly captivating, bittersweet mood. Such a mood accommodates a funny-sad line like Pinky's half-optimistic, half-pessimistic "The first time I get married I'm gonna wear white, the second time I'm gonna wear pink," and makes you feel for Martha at the same time you want to chew her out for smoking while pregnant.

The tone also informs the sequences filmed at the bar where Mars strips in a schoolgirl's uniform, the Combat Zone's Pussycat Lounge (which had already closed by the time the movie opened at the Brattle Theater in May 1988). She usually performs her act in a schoolgirl outfit, the energetic music to which she disrobes mixing with the sad irony of what grown-up-too-soon Mars is doing.

Such a mood makes *Girltalk* unusually dramatic. Mars' final dance, in which she's bathed in red light and wears a diaphanous cape, is set to Janis Ian's "Bright Light and Promises" and has the sad beauty of the Rolling Stones' "Love in Vain" sequence in Albert and David Maysles' *Gimme Shelter*. There's a split-second when the camera catches the expression of weary despair on Mars' face as she finishes, and there's more emotional tension in it than most fiction films ever muster.

Though all three girls complain of inattentive parenting, *Girltalk* doesn't merely point fingers. It looks more towards the future. With Mars and Martha, the movie seems to say, we're watching survivors (though Martha's baby has a worried face that makes you think he knows the struggle he's in for). In Pinky's case, there's the foreboding of someone who seems headed for more trouble. *Girltalk* is not conventionally entertaining, but it is incredibly engaging. Like the best documentaries that have taken a similar path—from *Streetwise* and *Hoop Dreams* to *Love and Diane*—you'll never forget it.

Gone Baby Gone

2007. Directed by Ben Affleck. Written by Ben Affleck and Aaron Stockard. Based on Dennis Lehane's novel. With Casey Affleck, Morgan Freeman, Ed Harris, Amy Ryan, Michelle Monaghan, Titus Welliver, John Ashton and Amy Madigan. Cinematography by John Toll.

BOSTON MOVIES COME FULL circle in Ben Affleck's impressive directorial debut. The circle starts with the homegrown "Beanstreets" films of the late 1970s and early 1980s, continues through the 1990s indie films they inspired (including *Good Will Hunting* and *Squeeze*) and then on to Hollywood-produced Boston neighborhood movies such as *Mystic River* and *The Departed*.

Thanks to its director, *Gone Baby Gone* has a more intimate relationship to its cinematic predecessors than *Mystic River* and *The Departed* do. Affleck made his movie debut with a tiny role in Jan Egleson's 1981 Cambridge drama, *The Dark End of the Street*, and 15 years later channeled some of that movie's class consciousness into his and Matt Damon's *GWH* script. The success of this dark, character-driven thriller—like *Mystic River*, an adaptation of a Dennis Lehane novel—hinges on its mix of Hollywood gloss and local flavor. You don't have to be from Boston to "get" it, that's for sure, or to get wrapped up in the story. But if you are, there are plenty of between-the-lines details to savor.

The child-kidnapping tale here shares elements with *Mystic River*— a daughter in danger, a criminal investigation, a white working-class neighborhood, an emphasis on moral choices and their aftermath. Like novelist George V. Higgins (*The Friends of Eddie Coyle*) before him, and *The Departed* screenwriter William Monahan, Lehane sees how

Boston's tribalism cuts in positive and negative ways. There are tightly knit family and neighborhood loyalties on the positive side, a chip-on-the-shoulder suspicion of the world beyond that neighborhood on the other. Not only that, he also sees how entwined the provincial and paranoid sides of the Boston soul are—that's what makes Boston crime movies (and sometimes Boston *life*) so chilling at times.

GBG doesn't have a scene as probing as the one in *The Departed* in which Mark Wahlberg's character peels back the layers of Leonardo DiCaprio's to reveal the latter's insecurity from being of *two* tribes (poor Irish-American and lace-curtain Irish-American) and feeling at home in neither. Nor does it nail blue-collar melancholy as consistently as *The Friends of Eddie Coyle* does. But it's not without such moments, primarily due to Affleck casting more locals (many of whom hadn't acted before) than any similar movie has.

As Dorchester private detectives Patrick Kenzie (Casey Affleck) and Angie Gennaro (Michelle Monaghan) scour the city's underbelly to find missing four-year-old Amanda McReady (Madeline O'Brien), they cross paths with a number of ornery folks who operate in the shadows. But it's their trip to The Fillmore—the rough-and-tumble bar where negligent mother Helene McReady (Amy Ryan) regularly plastered herself with drink and drugs—that stands out. It's a descent to the ninth circle of Dorchester because, to play the scary barflies, Affleck cast—there's no other way to put it—scary locals. The characters played by toughs-turned-actors William Lee (who plays the belligerent bartender) and Brian Scannell (as the hothead who'd like to literally tear Patrick and Angie apart) are true Massholes.

The character who makes even more of an impression than the bar thugs is Helene's foul-mouthed friend Dottie, played with in-your-face gusto by another non-actor, South Boston's Jill Quigg. Like the thugs, Dottie can't *not* seem aggressive. She's the angry young mother yelling at her kids in Target, the chain smoker muttering in anger on the subway platform, the woman who looks at you like she wants to kick your ass after you beat her to a parking space in the Market Basket parking lot. Ryan does a flawless job with her accent and her demeanor as Amanda's lax mother, but her performance also gains authenticity just by putting Dottie next to her. If Dottie were a cartoon character, there'd be steam shooting out of her ears. Quigg's emotion just jumps off the screen.

As the kidnapping case pinballs the detectives into conflicts with drug dealers, child molesters and, eventually, unexpectedly guilty parties, such doses of local grit regularly enrich the plot. Certainly, Patrick's idealistic morality colors the story, too, a consequence of

Gone Baby Gone: Casey Affleck in South Boston.

his Boston Irish Catholic upbringing (this is where Casey Affleck's boyishness works so well). But more everyday Boston concerns also figure in the story. There's an interesting aside in which older police detective Remy Bressant (Ed Harris), born in New Orleans, needles younger Patrick by arguing that he's more "local" than the homegrown private eye. Maybe Bressant is right. He later claims that you should "die with your secrets," showing that this cop has adopted the tight lips of a local.

Gone Baby Gone is not without minor problems. I'm puzzled why Affleck and co-writer Aaron Stockard jettison some of the background info that builds up Patrick and Angie's credibility as finders of lost children (specifically, mention of a big, publicity-drawing case they'd cracked); similarly, the movie's Angie is a less active, formidable participant than the book's version. Perhaps the biggest liberty the screenplay takes is making police higher-up Jack Doyle black, with Morgan Freeman in the role. Freeman is as sturdy as ever, but making Doyle an African-American comes off awkwardly. The script supplies uneducated bigots such as Helene McReady and her glorious friend Dottie, and then makes Amanda's rescue dependent on a powerful black man. To never have that dependence be a source of conflict—even unspoken conflict—comes off as wimpy wishful thinking.

That wishful thinking reflects Affleck the Cambridge liberal more than his Dorchester townie characters. But his movie creates a lived-in mood through its locations. Lehane's story lifts up a metaphorical rock to find many of his characters, and in that spirit the movie uses out-of-the-way, very unglamourous locales. The McReadys' triple-decker is outside Fields Corner, Uphams Corner's Cataloni's "plays" the scary dive bar The Fillmore and Patrick and Angie meet with the police detectives at Roxbury's Silver Slipper Restaurant. Other locations range from The Chart House restaurant on the waterfront, Southie's Murphy's Law pub for the climax, Mount Auburn Cemetery and the Quincy quarries, among others. Fittingly, the quarries are also a location in *The Dark End of the Street.*

►**Locations:** Dorchester, South Boston, Roxbury, Allston, Boston; Cambridge; Quincy; Sherborn; Medford (interior sets).

►**Accents:** Such locals as Jill Quigg give *Gone Baby Gone* more authentic accents than any "major movie" has ever had. But let's not forget what a good job Amy Ryan does. Casting a genuine blue-collar Bostonian like Quigg could have made Ryan look phony by comparison. But these two could go bar-hopping together on Dot Ave., and few would know one was really an out-of-town actress.

►**Local color:** *Gone Baby Gone* is indicative of how increasingly gritty Boston neighborhood movies have become. Ten years earlier, *Good Will Hunting*'s Southie action seemed rough-hewn, because few movies had traveled to Boston's neighborhoods. *GBG* is infinitely skeezier. There are no trips to the Public Garden this time; just bleak apartments, barrooms and greasy spoons, with few exceptions. The movie also passes Boston Vocabulary 101 with flying colors. The tense scene in The Fillmore uses the particularly Boston working-class-Joe term "guy" to great effect—a designation that often blends begrudging politeness and underlying hostility. In this case, the hostility isn't even veiled. Patrick understands the lingo and calls the antagonistic barkeep "guy" in return, a means of telling him he's not backing down.

The Good Mother

1988. Directed by Leonard Nimoy. Written by Michael Bortman. Based on Sue Miller's novel. With Diane Keaton, Liam Neeson, Asia Vieira, James Naughton, Jason Robards and Ralph Bellamy. Cinematography by David Watkin.

WEST END NATIVE LEONARD Nimoy returns home—briefly—for the adaptation of local author Sue Miller's novel. I don't think the words Boston or Cambridge are ever uttered. But a stroll or two through Harvard Square, a visit to Quincy Market and a night out at the 1369 Jazz Club make it clear the story takes place here, even though Nimoy filmed most of it in Ontario.

Starring Diane Keaton as Anna, a single mother who becomes embroiled in a custody battle, *The Good Mother* is a story of punished female sexuality. The movie sets up its context of punishment in an unwieldy 10-minute prologue set circa 1960, detailing the fall from grace of Anna's young aunt (Tracy Griffith), who gets pregnant and is sent away by Anna's domineering grandfather (Ralph Bellamy).

Cut to present day, and Anna is recently divorced and living with her six-year-old daughter (Asia Vieira). Her marriage was sexually unsatisfying, but her sensuality blooms when she meets outgoing artist Leo (Liam Neeson). She starts to lose the shame over her body and sexuality ingrained in her by her family. And she starts to act in ways designed to let daughter Molly feel nudity and sexuality are natural.

Of course, it's hard for a movie to get that across when it *doesn't* act as if nudity and sexuality are natural. Although *The Good Mother* is rated R, it hardly feels it. That rating is only because of talk about sex, which happens after Molly goes for her regular visit with her remarried father (James Naughton) and starts acting curious about *his* body. He learns about the new permissiveness at Anna's, and soon files a custody suit to remove Molly from her Somerville apartment.

The Good Mother then bogs down in court proceedings (filmed at East Cambridge's Probate Court), with Jason Robards as the lawyer who advises her to betray all of her ideals about demystifying sexuality for her daughter, and to essentially chuck Leo under a bus and testify that any indecent behavior was all his fault. The hearing and the run-up to it play very badly, with the lack of communication among Anna, Leo and the lawyer feeling contrived, as does the virtual non-participation of the judge during the courtroom action.

All of which renders *The Good Mother* surprisingly inert. There's more potential resonance to the story if you see it in the context of the baby-boomer generation, of which Anna is a member, and consider their ideals of the 1960s slipping away during the 1980s (if not sooner). The progressive ideals of a liberal hot spot such as Harvard Square and the old-fashioned conservatism of New England, represented by Anna's patriarchal family, butt heads here, but Nimoy and screenwriter Michael Bortman fail to put such elements together very dramatically. Ultimately, for a movie about passion, it's awfully flat. Nimoy came to this after scoring a big hit by directing the fluffy *3 Men and a Baby*, and he seems unable to handle the jump to straight drama.

▶**Locations:** Cambridge; Somerville; Boston.

▶**Accents:** James Naughton's Brian *sometimes* seems to have a Boston accent—particularly in the scene where he lashes out at Keaton's Anna—but then again he doesn't in his most sustained scene, during the hearing. You hear a little from Anna's neighbors, though. And Neeson provides the near-obligatory Irish or English accent thrown into most every Boston movie.

▶**Local color:** Barely a taste in the few scenes filmed locally, but they're probably here only because Nimoy fought for the chance to film at least that much in Massachusetts. Rhode Island band Roomful of Blues appears in the club scene, too.

The Good Son

1993. Directed by Joseph Ruben. Written by Ian McEwan. With Elijah Wood, Macauley Culkin, Wendy Crewson, David Morse, Daniel Hugh Kelly, Jacqueline Brookes and Quinn Culkin. Cinematography by John Lindley.

CASTING CONTINUES TO BE the main draw of Joseph Ruben's flimsy 1993 thriller. But the reasons have changed over time. Back then, it was because Macauley Culkin, the All-American kid of the moment from John Hughes' inescapable *Home Alone* and its sequel, plays *The Good Son*'s "bad seed" villain. Now, it's more because the film also stars Elijah Wood, when he was a similarly prolific child actor, but years before he became better-known in the equally inescapable *Lord of the Rings* movies.

Thanks to the economic benefits of shooting close to Boston (and to Teamsters regional headquarters), much of *The Good Son* uses Cape Ann locations, even though the story takes place mainly in Rock Harbor, Maine. That's where Mark (Wood), the Southwestern kid whose mother dies at the story's start, goes to temporarily stay because his dad (Beverly native David Morse) has to leave on an important business trip. Plucked from the arid desert and dropped into a coastal New England winter, Mark also has to get comfortable with his aunt (Wendy Crewson), uncle (Daniel Hugh Kelly) and cousins Henry (Culkin) and Connie (Quinn Culkin).

The Mark-Henry relationship is, of course, the central one. The two pre-pubescent boys get along fine at first, but Henry starts showing more of his considerable dark side to Mark. This dark side swells from boyishly mischievous (Henry has a homemade crossbow of sorts that fires bolts) to majorly dangerous (he starts a highway pile-up by dumping a life-sized dummy off of an overpass) and murderous (he hints that he killed the younger brother who drowned in a bathtub). But Henry shrewdly silences Mark by implicating his cousin in some of his malice and threatening to say such deeds were *Mark's* idea. When Mark finally can't bite his tongue anymore and tells his aunt what's happened, he is, of course, not believed.

The combination of too-creepy-for-kids misdeeds (such as a skating "accident" in which Connie plunges though the ice) and kid-friendly adults-don't-believe-me outbursts makes *The Good Son* an odd film. At 80 minutes from opening titles to end credits, it's a bit cartoonish and, consequently, a little cheesy, too. That's not necessarily a bad thing. When Henry finally cops to his evil nature, he tells Mark, "Once you realize you can do anything, you're fine." Not only is it silly to hear a runty 12-year-old say such a thing. It also immediately makes the story more interesting. Hey, if a Macauley Culkin character visually "quotes" Edvard Munch's *The Scream* in *Home Alone*, why not some Nietzschean philosophy in *The Good Son*? Of course, this being Hollywood, the whole thing ends with a battle between good and evil and a fight to see who really is the title character.

In similar Hollywood fashion, the movie mixes together many, many disparate locations for its fictional setting—in fact, the rock cliff where the climax occurs is actually in Minnesota, and overlooks Lake Superior, not the Atlantic Ocean. Closer to home, Annisquam in Gloucester is the backdrop for some of the boys' shenanigans (the Lobster Cove footbridge figures prominently and you can see the Annisquam Lighthouse off the shore), Marblehead's Old Burial Hill Cemetery helps keep death on the minds of viewers (as it is on Mark's), the huge house where he goes to visit his relatives is the so-called Pyle House in Manchester-by-the-Sea and Rockport's Peg Leg Inn is here, too. The production spent nearly two months filming in the area.

▶**Locations:** Manchester-by-the-Sea; Gloucester; Marblehead; Rockport; Beverly; Danvers.

▶**Accents:** The factory worker who chases Mark and Henry away after the kids break windows is the only accent here. For a movie so unconcerned with New England lingo, the guy's line ("Come back heah, ya little baaaastahds!") is surprisingly perfect.

▶**Local color:** As is usually the case with Cape Ann films, this is more a regional movie than a local movie. The story needed a wet, wintry setting to contrast with the dry, summery setting where Mark lives, and New England is it. So the water and the winter *are* the local color.

▶**Off the set:** *The Good Son* is an early-1990s relic of the crash-and-burn run of both Macauley Culkin and his manager/dad Kit. When the two felt that Macauley should play nasty Henry, they reportedly told Twentieth-Century Fox that he would not do *Home Alone 2* unless he could. Director Michael Lehman, who had reservations about Culkin in the role, was soon out and, following the filming of *HA2*, Joseph Ruben was in when the movie shot locally in the winter of 1992-93. It all seems so silly now—as it did then.

Good Will Hunting

1997. Directed by Gus Van Sant. Written by Ben Affleck and Matt Damon. With Matt Damon, Ben Affleck, Robin Williams, Minnie Driver, Stellan Skarsgård, Casey Affleck and Cole Hauser. Cinematography by Jean Yves Escoffier.

IT'S NOT QUITE THE best Boston movie, but it is easily the best Cinderella story of *all* Boston movies: young Cambridge-born actors Matt Damon and Ben Affleck write a script as a vehicle for themselves, fight to get it shot in their hometown with them headlining, agree to some concessions to make that happen, do great work and then find the movie turn into a surprise hit. Oh yeah, they also win an Oscar for their screenplay and become big stars.

If you think about it, *Good Will Hunting* could have come off as an overly simple, emotionally sketchy movie. Twenty-year-old M.I.T. janitor Will Hunting (Damon)—a math genius with a chip on his shoulder and a stereotypical South Boston beer-'n'-brawls townie lifestyle—is not exactly an immediately believable character. It's a credit to Damon's charisma and acting chops that he can encapsulate such extremes within Will, and make us accept the bruised brainiac without a second thought.

Similarly, there's a conveniently diverse cross-section of people vying for Will's affection: a best friend, Chuckie (Affleck), without the talent to get out of Southie; a new girlfriend, Skylar (Minnie Driver), pushing him to take a chance on love; Professor Lambeau (Stellan Skarsgård), an M.I.T. math teacher who discovers Will's talents and wants him to fully use them; and Sean (Robin Williams), a Southie-born psychologist who starts counseling tightly-wound Will after he gets into his latest scrape with the law.

But the writing and acting keep the premise from being as schematic as it might have been. Director Gus Van Sant (*To Die For*) treads the line between comedy and drama like the master of tone he could sometimes be in the 1990s, a dialed-down Williams leaves his schtick behind, and *GWH* emerges as both a very moving and very entertaining picture.

The reason why everything works well together is because everything works well separately. The scenes with Will and his buddies (Casey Affleck and Cole Hauser play the other two) are bawdy fun, those with Skylar capture the romantic boost Will feels and those with his math mentor give us an idea of the smarts with which Will was born. Will's sessions with Sean, while often funny (especially when Will ruthlessly cuts down the painting in Sean's office during their first meeting), also get at the deep pain that emotionally shut-down Will repeatedly suffered as a physically abused foster child.

> The idea was we'd do it really low-budget here in Boston. We'd somehow beg the film commission to give us permits to do it really cheaply. To try to get someone relatively famous, we wrote a middle-aged role for an older guy. Our acting agent said, 'Hey, we can sell it.' And we did, and got lucky.
> —Ben Affleck

Alert moviegoers had already noticed Affleck and Damon in the year before *Good Will Hunting* came out. Although their frustration as actors motivated their writing of the script (which Damon had started as a student at Harvard), each had already graduated to starring roles by the time they made "their movie": Affleck in *Chasing Amy* and Damon in *The Rainmaker* (Damon had also made a strong impression in featured supporting roles in *Courage Under Fire* and *School Ties*). But *GWH* was their genuine coming out, with Damon oozing star power and Affleck also shining, despite playing the best friend instead of the hero. Affleck's contribution shouldn't be overlooked. The scene in which his Chuckie tells Will that it would depress him if his gifted friend *didn't* apply himself is one of the movie's dramatic highlights, as well as a turning point in the story. (A deleted scene on the movie's DVD, in which Chuckie talks about seducing a girl from Roslindale by telling her he was a cosmonaut, is hilarious.)

Good Will Hunting: Ben Affleck and Matt Damon in the L Street Tavern.

Like the stars, the movie boasts so much heart and energy that it just sails along. And one of the things that makes *Good Will Hunting* an essential Boston movie is that, despite the fact that more than half of it was shot in Toronto, the city (not just Boston; Cambridge, too) becomes a player in it and a source of its characters' heart. Rough and tumble Southie and academic Cambridge embody the two sides of Will's personality, and two possible paths for him in life. That's the ultimate "Boston movie" quality—that the film would have lost something had it not been at least partially shot here.

Despite the mix of Toronto and Boston, local spots get most of the big moments. Southie's L Street Tavern and Harvard Square, including the oft-mourned The Tasty, are characters' favorite hangouts, while the corner of Mass. Ave. and Bow Street, just outside the square, also figures heavily. Some of the less recognizable Southie locales: Will's house is on West 6th Street (though we see it from the back, on Bowen Street); Sean's is on D Street; the Little League game is at Foley Field (which turns up more recently in *Black Irish*); and the playground fisticuffs that land Will in court take place on the basketball courts on West 5th Street between D and E Streets. The payphone from which Will calls Skylar, which many have tried to find, doesn't exist. It's a prop phone temporarily installed across the street from the L Street Tavern for the scene.

> (Winning the Oscar) was incredible, but it was not the answer. We woke up the next day, and got on a plane to Pittsburgh and rehearsed *Dogma*. That was an eye-opener, in the sense that things didn't change. Internally, there was not some massive shift.
>
> –Matt Damon

Outside of Southie and Cambridge, Will sits and talks with Sean at the Public Garden (which the movie's fiction puts within walking distance of Charlestown's Bunker Hill Community College), while he bets on the dogs with Skylar at Wonderland in Revere. Like the "quick" walk from Charlestown to the Public Garden, the movie cheats by putting some of Will's Red Line journey from Southie to Cambridge in the opposite direction that he would really travel.

▶**Locations:** South Boston, Charlestown, Back Bay, Boston; Cambridge; Revere.

▶**Accents:** Damon and the Afflecks are locals. Williams' accent is passable at best, but he fortunately uses a light touch; although his character was born and still lives in Southie, you have to figure maybe his character has traveled widely and lost some of that accent.

▶**Local color:** Off the chart. Any movie with passing mentions of Kelly's, T passes and Howard Zinn's *A People's History of the United*

States (yes, that book *will* knock you on your ass) is Boston, even if most of it was shot in Canada.

▶ **Off the set:** Robin Williams introduced Matt Damon to Steven Spielberg, who was in town briefly to shoot a scene for his *Amistad* at the State House. The result: Damon gets cast as the title character in *Saving Private Ryan*. How do you like *them* apples?

▶ **Don't blink!:** Wellesley's Alison Folland, who co-starred with Casey Affleck in Van Sant's *To Die For*, plays the student who tells Prof. Lambeau (Skarsgård) someone has solved the proof he posted.

Harvard Man

2001. Written and directed by James Toback. With Adrian Grenier, Sarah Michelle Gellar, Joey Lauren Adams, Rebecca Gayheart, Ray Allen and Eric Stoltz. Cinematography by David Ferrara.

IT'S NOT UNCOMMON FOR the story *behind* a movie to be more interesting than the story *in* that movie. But rarely has the backstory been so much more intriguing than in the case of writer-director James Toback's long-in-gestation *Harvard Man*. Set and partially filmed in Cambridge (but mostly in Toronto), the movie is semi-autobiographical, working in a misadventure of Toback's as a Harvard student in the mid-1960s—when he took 100,000 micrograms of LSD and flipped out for eight days, eventually getting an intravenous antidote from Max Rinkel, one of the scientists who invented acid and who, fortunately for Toback, lived in Brookline.

After 25 years of trying to get *Harvard Man* made, *Bugsy* writer Toback was ready to go ahead in the mid-1990s with Leonardo DiCaprio in the lead role of the Harvard basketball star whose problems include not just acid, but also point-shaving, love triangles and the mob. But the actor decided to play hoops in another film, *The Basketball Diaries*. Toback then had Skeet Ulrich lined up. He was offered financial backing from producer Don Simpson (for whom Toback had script-doctored *Bad Boys*), but turned it down due to Simpson's intrusive reputation; two years later, in 1996, he and Simpson came to an agreement, but Simpson dropped dead minutes after their phone call. Later, Barry Levinson was set to produce the movie with a $7 million budget. It eventually came out in 2001, without Levinson producing and with what looks to have been a much skimpier budget.

At least we have Toback's obsessive personality to thank for finally getting the movie made and shooting some of it in Cambridge. Harvard

Square, both the Cambridge and Boston banks of the Charles (site of an Al Franken cameo), the Weeks Footbridge and Mount Auburn, Holyoke, Bow, Linden and Winthrop Streets are all here. There's even a quick visit to Harvard Yard that was probably "stolen" without having a permit to shoot there.

Toback twisted his acid-OD incident into the coming-of-age story of Alan (pre-*Entourage* Adrian Grenier), the starting point guard of Harvard's basketball team and a philosophy major dying to get in touch with his inner self. Alan is also dying to get in touch with money. When a tornado demolishes his parents' Kansas house, he tries to help them by putting the touch on Cindy (Sarah Michelle Gellar), the Holy Cross cheerleader and Mafia princess he's shagging at every opportunity, even during the opening minutes of the Harvard-H.C. game. This Meadow Soprano pushes Alan into a deal whereby her father (Gianni Russo) will give him the money if he'll shave points in Harvard's next game. She'll take the points and bet a bundle on Dartmouth, and no one will be the wiser.

That is, except for the bookies (Eric Stoltz, Rebecca Gayheart) who think something is fishy and have their own agenda. Except for the slinky philosophy professor (Joey Lauren Adams) with whom Alan is also sleeping. And except for Alan, whose reaction to the stress is to take a triple dose of LSD (time for the funhouse-mirror visuals).

Harvard Man may obsess over "big things" like the nature of personality and self-knowledge, but it trips over storytelling details as if they were skyscrapers. Credibility is the casualty. So, despite his increasingly complicated life, Alan flies from Boston to Kansas and back twice in a week, showing no concern over money, missed classes or team practices. Meanwhile, Toback's jump-cut editing, which sometimes switches shots between every one or two words of dialogue, is enormously distracting, as well as a terror on continuity (watch a basketball magically go back and forth between Grenier and Gellar without ever being passed). And what can you say about a movie that's set during college basketball season but takes place—by all indications—in the middle of summer, with shorts and open-toe shoes being the norm?

> The average studio executive can't get through a newspaper article and figure out what's going on. (This movie) deals with an LSD flipout, it deals with Harvard basketball fixing, it's very sexual, it's very philosophical.
>
> –James Toback

▶**Locations:** Cambridge; Allston, Boston.

▶**Accents:** Only if you want to count the Noo Yawk dems-and-dose of the mob guys.

►**Local color:** Little to really speak of. Aside from the early stroll through Harvard Square, this is a fairly insular story. Toback's budget probably also prevented any really public scenes that would have involved blocking off streets and the like.

Home Before Dark

1958. Directed by Mervyn LeRoy. Written by Eileen and Robert Bassing. Based on her novel. With Jean Simmons, Dan O'Herlihy, Rhonda Fleming, Efrem Zimbalist, Jr. and Mabel Albertson. Cinematography by Joseph Biroc.

NEW ENGLAND IS CENTRAL to the wave of melodramas layered with scandal and social commentary from the 1950s. New Hampshire's Grace Metalious wrote *Peyton Place*, the blockbuster 1956 novel that helped to spur that wave (its movie adaptation came out the next year). But her tale is hardly the only one of its time to pry off the façade of Puritan New England propriety and find hypocrisy beneath. Like Douglas Sirk's better-known *All That Heaven Allows*, *Home Before Dark* unfurls a tale of intolerance in autumnal New England as it follows one small-town woman's struggle.

In veteran director Mervyn (*Little Caesar*) LeRoy's glossy film, the typical New England coastal town of Cape Marble, represented by Marblehead in several exterior shots, is a prison for heroine Charlotte (Jean Simmons). We first see her as she's released from a state asylum a year after suffering a nervous breakdown (the asylum is the old Danvers State Hospital).

It's easy to see what might have driven Charlotte mad, and how coming home is not so freeing. Her husband Arnold (Dan O'Herlihy), a professor at the local college, has no ideals, just an eye for the internal campus politics that might gain him a promotion. He's friendlier with Charlotte's stepsister Joan (Rhonda Fleming) than he is with Charlotte, and shows no interest in having a physical relationship with his wife, even lying to Charlotte by saying her doctor recommended they sleep in separate bedrooms. Charlotte's kin take even more advantage of her—Arnold, Joan and Charlotte's stepmother (Mabel Albertson) all live cozily in the house her dead parents left her.

Nestled somewhere between the lurid sin of *Peyton Place* and the subversive subtext of *All That Heaven Allows*, Eileen and Robert Bassing's script, based on her novel, seems afraid to totally indict those around Charlotte. These relatives smother Charlotte with "care" that feels designed to keep her dependent on them, yet the movie never comes out and says whether they're scheming or just misguided. Much is made of Charlotte's obsession over whether Arnold and Joan are carrying on behind her back, yet—like her husband and stepsister—the movie never answers the question of whether they are. It also never makes it clear that a marriage without a sexual relationship is troubled. In short, although *Home Before Dark* wants us to root for Charlotte to escape her relatives, it's often scared to offer any reason more concrete than that she's unhappy with them.

So, even though the movie earns a place alongside other melodramas that pry at the cracks in 1950s conformity (there are more of them than you might think), it's only partially successful. It's a little too glossy (complete with lush theme song crooned by Mary Kaye) and a little too long (136 minutes), yet Simmons is wonderful at portraying Charlotte's fragility without being whiny.

Although *Home Before Dark* uses location shooting less than *Walk East on Beacon!* or *Six Bridges to Cross*, it's a rare pre-1968 movie that bothers to enhance its soundstage sets with a smattering of shots in authentic Greater Boston locales: the old Danvers State Hospital for the introductory sequence, a walk through the center of Marblehead, scenes outside R.H. Stearns on Tremont Street and Bonwit Teller on Berkeley Street (where Louis Boston currently is). The exterior of Charlotte's house is Marblehead's well-known Lafayette House (from which, legend says, the lower corner was lopped off to allow the coach of the Marquis de Lafayette to pass during an 1824 visit), while Tufts University doubles for Cape Marble's unnamed college.

The location shooting is not without awkard moments. There is frequent use of back projection for scenes in cars and trains, while a quick shot of Charlotte looking toward the ocean and waving actually puts her in front of a *mural* of a coastal village. There's a good chance such scenes near the beach were done in California.

▶**Locations:** Marblehead; Danvers; Boston; Medford/Somerville.

▶**Accents:** With English Simmons and Irish O'Herlihy in the leads, this is one of those movies that equates cultured New Englanders, or at least those trying to be cultured, with a general mid-Atlantic English. It fits.

▶**Local color:** As is typical with movies shot in Cape Ann, there's a generic New England coastal feel the movie strives for, and achieves. The characters' forays into the city provide much more specific color, though: the Boston and Maine railroad, the intersection of Boston's Washington, Winter and Summer Streets before it was closed to traffic and christened Downtown Crossing, plus exteriors of R.H. Stearns and

Jordan Marsh, the latter at Christmastime. The wintry surroundings enhance the chilly feeling Charlotte gets from her relatives.

▶**Local celeb alert!:** Future newsman (and *The Boston Strangler* bit player) Jack Hynes is an extra.

Home Before Dark

1997. Written and directed by Maureen Foley. With Stephanie Castellarin, Patricia Kalember, Brian Delate, Helen Lloyd Breed, Katharine Ross and Jamie Dunphy. Cinematography by Brian Heller and Mark Petersson.

MAUREEN FOLEY'S MOVIE FLIRTS with danger. It starts with a pensive voice-over from a young female character—the kiss of death for 101 overly earnest independent films before it. But the first-time writer-director's well-observed, bittersweet coming-of-age tale is the exception to the rule. Like a rare 1980s comedy that actually gets away with its freeze-frame ending, *Home Before Dark* (no relation to its 1958 predecessor of the same name) earns its adolescent voice-overs and turns usually trite story devices into involving drama.

Set in 1963 and 1964, its pensive adolescent is Nora (Stoughton's Stephanie Castellarin), a seemingly average central Massachusetts 11-year-old. The semi-autobiographical movie does a seamless job of blending the universal and very specific problems that mark Nora's days. At her Catholic school, she deals with the onset of puberty and teacher troubles (recalling the flashback sequences in Beth Harrington's *The Blinking Madonna and Other Miracles*, Foley's movie steeps itself in JFK-era Boston Catholicism). But, at home, Nora faces much different challenges: her mother (Patricia Kalember) is still traumatized from the car accident that took her first set of kids, before Nora was born. About the only thing that keeps her mother semi-functional is the memory of meeting John F. Kennedy outside Filene's when he was a young, campaigning politician.

When JFK dies, one more link to a happier time severs. The mother tries to kill herself and ends up in a Brighton hospital. Nora's carpenter father (Brian Delate) ships Nora off to icy aunt Rose (Katharine Ross) and her younger siblings to other relatives.

As Nora struggles to, in her own way, patch her family back together, *Home Before Dark* continues to mix in such adolescent concerns as Nora's first boyfriend and the arrival of her first period. But there's no great secret to why Foley is able to balance the everyday and the extreme. It's because every segue from one concern to the other, and back, is so assured. The really standout thing about *Home Before Dark* is that it's a low-budget movie that never strains to create an emotion and never fudges something because its inexperienced filmmakers didn't get all the shots they needed. Foley keeps things very low-key, and it's the right move. The movie never acts as if the family drama is "important" and the adolescent action is frivolous; to Nora, through whom we see events, they're equally important.

> This movie is not fashionable at *all*. It's not edgy. It's not the right demographic. Everything that film festival and (arthouse) programmers favor is 180 degrees away from what this movie is.
> –Maureen Foley

The low-key mood also suits the performances, and the characters really connect in their conversations. They talk to each other, not at each other. Castellarin is adorable without being cute, Delate seems incapable of a phony moment and Kalember and Ross play their troubled women with a convincing weariness. Helen Lloyd Breed is also very memorable as the imposing nun who occasionally reveals the self-knowledge that her intimidating personality is just an act.

Much of the action in *Home Before Dark* takes place in Northampton, though it was all shot closer to Boston. The aunt's super-modern house is on Commonwealth Avenue in Newton, and the Northampton house, as well as the "country" woods where Nora likes to ride her bike, is actually in the Stony Brook Reservation bordering Hyde Park, West Roxbury and Milton. Her Catholic school is a composite of two schools: the exterior, a former parochial school, is now the Benjamin Banneker Charter Public School in Cambridge; the interior is a school in Waltham. Waltham is where the beauty parlor and dress shop scenes were filmed, too.

▶**Locations:** Newton; Waltham; Hyde Park, Boston; Cambridge.

▶**Accents:** Aside from Castellarin, the leads are not local, and she has no accent. But every so often an accent pops up, like that of a briefly seen bus driver.

▶**Local color:** As is almost always the case with a low-budget period piece, recreating older Boston was not a possibility. There are no crowd scenes or scenes in very public places. There's more of an effort to recreate time rather than place, by shooting at old buildings.

Housesitter

1992. Directed by Frank Oz. Written by Mark Stein. With Steve Martin, Goldie Hawn, Dana Delany, Julie Harris and Donald Moffat. Cinematography by John A. Alonzo.

I GUESS MEG RYAN was right. The actress had been set to star in this romantic comedy, then the most substantial made in Greater Boston in terms of time and money spent here. Instead, she dropped out of the Steve Martin project due to proverbial "creative differences" and the part of overimaginative Gwen went to Goldie Hawn, the person to whom Ryan had so often been likened. Maybe the reason behind the differences was that, like so many romantic comedies, *Housesitter* has a strong premise but an undernourished script. Hawn's replacement of Ryan gives the movie an interesting twist, though: for once the couple in a romantic comedy is actually the same age.

Gwen is the pathological liar who strays into the life of more tightly wound Newton (Martin), a Boston architect who opens the movie by

Housesitter: Goldie Hawn and Steve Martin in Cohasset.

proposing to his hometown sweetie Becky (Dana Delany)—in front of the dream house he's built for them—and getting turned down. Ouch.

A misery-driven one-night stand follows with opportunistic waitress Gwen, who hears all the gory details, then heads to fictional Dobb's Mill, moves into the house and tells locals she's Newton's new wife. When Newton finds out what's going on, he flips, but he soon discovers his "marriage" might help him win back Becky.

So it goes in *Housesitter*, which, at the time of its filming, was pitched as a sort of comic *Fatal Attraction*. The premise of an adventuress and the strait-laced man she draws into her crazy world may recall classic screwball comedies of the 1930s and 1940s, such as *Bringing Up Baby* and *The Palm Beach Story*, but while those movies brimmed with comic energy, *Housesitter* just feels strained. Gwen is a convincing enough comic character, but Newton seems only a screenwriter's tool, not a real man. There's little chemistry between them. And Becky wears such unflattering preppie clothes that you wonder how he, or anyone else, could have a thing for her. Although there are a few amusing moments—when Newton is forced to lie to avoid the embarrassment caused by *Gwen's* fibs, when he and Becky clumsily *almost* make love—the comedy simply never gathers momentum. The direction by Frank Oz is neither deadpan nor very active, operating in an ineffective middle ground.

> You have to figure out a way to get the spirit of an old-fashioned comedy, and bring it forward. To me, (this) is 'new-fashioned' or 'new old-fashioned.'
> –Steve Martin

Oz and company chose Boston for the contrast between the stressful city where Newton works and the quaint hometown in which he wants to rejoin Becky. They get that contrast from the locations they chose—Dobb's Mill is supposed to be 50 miles from the Boston, but the Concord, Cohasset and Sudbury locations they used for it are, of course, much closer (the mill is in Sudbury, and some of the Cohasset spots, including the hardware store, had already been seen in *The Witches of Eastwick*). An award-winning Connecticut house, consisting of a pair of neo-Colonials joined by an atrium, inspired the dream house here, which was built off a winding Concord country road near where the Acton Minutemen marched in 1775 (the house, which didn't have plumbing, was demolished after filming). Concord's Emerson Umbrella Center for the Arts doubles as the school where Newton's dad is principal. In the city, Newton's office is at One Beacon Street, and *Housesitter* also captures Café Budapest, the since-closed Copley Square fixture. The restaurant interiors are the real thing, but its movie exterior was built in the Financial District's Liberty Square.

Hawn and Martin reteamed for 1999's remake of Neil Simon's *The Out of Towners*. Like the Jack Lemmon original, it includes a segment set in Boston but, ironically, the *Housesitter* stars filmed none of that Boston sequence here.

► **Locations:** Concord; Cohasset; Back Bay, Financial District, Boston; Sudbury.

► **Accents:** Not a single one, not even a crusty shopkeeper. At least we get veteran sportscaster Heywood Hale Broun (since passed) behind a shop counter.

► **Local color:** *Housesitter* offers the mix of old and new, city and country, that keeps Hollywood periodically returning to Greater Boston. It's not a very specific or intense local color, though, and as with the accents there's little Boston pop culture on display here, unless you count Plymouth & Brockton buses.

► **Don't blink!:** Comedian Tony V. plays the bus driver bringing Gwen to Dobb's Mill.

Lift

2001. Directed by Khari Streeter and DeMane Davis. Written by DeMane Davis. With Kerry Washington, Lonette McKee, Eugene Byrd, Todd Williams and Barbara Montgomery. Cinematography by David Phillips.

A SURE NOMINEE FOR most unjustly overlooked Boston independent movie, *Lift* is indicative of how the 1990s indie-film boom had crashed by the turn of the new decade. Although well-received on the film festival circuit—including the Sundance and Boston fests—DeMane Davis and Khari Streeter's meaty character study had trouble finding theatrical distribution and ended up being sold to Showtime as a cable premiere (another remarkable indie movie from that period, Allison Anders' *Things Behind the Sun*, took the same exact path).

As *Good Will Hunting* does, *Lift* uses local geography to illustrate its protagonist's dilemma. Niecy (Kerry Washington) hails from Roxbury, but has her sights set on department stores in town and boutiques on Newbury Street. She works at a fictional department store, Kennedy's, and chases her champagne dreams by being a booster, a shoplifter who, through stolen credit cards and old-fashioned five-finger discount, not only keeps herself in designer duds but also sells her ill-gotten *couture* around town. The thievery also lets Niecy impress her hardened mother (Lonette McKee) with luxurious gifts.

Crime story and domestic drama mesh extremely well here, as both the addictive rush of boosting (represented at one point by a ballet-like shopping fantasy) and the hunger to connect with an emotionally stingy mom come across strongly. Niecy's drive might have made her cold and unsympathetic, but Washington's charismatic performance easily overcomes that. Niecy's relationship with Angelo (Eugene Byrd) also shows us her more sensitive side. The push-and-pull between Niecy and Angelo—each angered by the other's flaws but drawn to a life together—makes theirs an unusually mature screen relationship, while Washington (seen more recently in such movies as *The Last King of Scotland* and *I Think I Love My Wife*) portrays Niecy's slick surface and troubled core with genuine ease and histrionics-free depth.

Niecy's ability to contain her inner turmoil within a deluxe wrapping unravels over the course of *Lift*. Such scenes as a tense birthday party for Niecy's grandmother (Barbara Montgomery) provide a fuller sense of our heroine's difficulties with her mother, while Niecy's plan to get her mom a swanky necklace leads to an ill-fated alliance with Christian (Todd Williams), who runs a gang-like crew of boosters. A surreal touch during a funeral misfires, but *Lift* closes powerfully, as Niecy's realization that her life of crime won't bring her satisfaction takes hold and she becomes increasingly desperate.

Cambridge's Streeter and Roxbury native Davis, who had segued from advertising to moviemaking with *Black & White & Red All Over*, use a wide variety of locations to show the economic gulf Niecy hopes to travel (including the offices of their old employers, Hill, Holiday, in the John Hancock Tower). The opening credits smartly establish this contrast between the fashionable and unfashionable, as aerial images from the Financial District and the Back Bay to give way to street-level views of Dudley Station.

On the deluxe side, there are Suzanne and DKNY on Newbury Street and Lux Bond & Green on Boylston, with the exterior of Lord & Taylor (further down on Boylston) for the exterior of the jewelers and Broad Street's Maksou for the salon. More down to earth are Niecy's apartment on The Fenway, Angelo's on Blue Hill Avenue and Niecy's grandmother's in Roxbury's Warren Gardens Housing Cooperative. Amazingly, the interior of Kennedy's, the fictional store where Niecy works, is actually the prop-dressed lobby of the 100 Summer Street office building. Outside the city, a Carlisle home doubled as Christian's place and Davis and Streeter filmed the movie's final sequence at the Newton city jail.

▶**Locations:** Roxbury, Fenway, Back Bay, Boston; Carlisle; Newton.

▶**Accents:** Hallelujah—black folks with Boston accents! Outsiders probably think they don't exist, but locals like Davis and Streeter know better. Just listen to Niecy's Aunt Lily (Jacqui Parker) or the beauty salon owner.

►**Local color:** After making a movie that takes place entirely indoors (*Black & White & Red All Over*), Davis and Streeter turn out a much livelier story here, thanks to *Lift*'s strong sense of place. There aren't many specific references to local things in the dialogue and you could easily move its events to another city (in fact, *Lift* almost shot in Baltimore). But Boston locations more than fulfill the needs of the story. That story hits home even more for those who know how short a geographical journey it is between the rich and poor sections where its events take place.

The Little Sister

1984. Written and directed by Jan Egleson. With John Savage, Tracy Pollan, Richard Jenkins, Roxanne Hart and Henry Tomaszewski. Cinematography by Ed Lachman.

THE THIRD PART OF Jan Egleson's "Boston trilogy" veers more towards "professional moviemaking" than its predecessors. Like *Billy in the Lowlands* and *The Dark End of the Street*, it developed from real situations—a probation-officer friend telling Egleson that more girls were committing crimes and ending up "in the system" than before, and another friend, Judith Herman, writing an eye-opening book on father-daughter incestual abuse. But in the climate of mid-1980s independent filmmaking, with new distributors hoping to release alternative hits, it was hard to find funding to make a grass-roots movie like Egleson's first two. Instead, he found partial funding from PBS' new *American Playhouse* series—much more than the budget of the first two combined—but with it came the obligation to make a more polished film.

So *The Little Sister* features a name performer in the lead—John Savage, still riding the wave of acclaim from *The Deer Hunter*—and more of a dramatic arc. Not that anyone would ever mistake it for a slick mid-1980s Hollywood movie, though (there's even a funny line mocking *Flashdance* at one point). The pivotal characters are still at-risk youth, the style is still down to earth and the Boston and Cambridge locations still add grit.

Egleson had focused on a juvenile offender in *Billy* and project kids in *Street*. His *Little Sister* script expands his scope by broadening its economics. If it had a subtitle, it might be *Even a Rich Kid Can Be Messed-Up*. Nicki (Tracy Pollan) is that rich kid, the 18-year-old daughter of an upstanding father (Richard Jenkins), who has started hanging around with the sort of disadvantaged youths familiar from Egleson's previous films (literally, as they're played by many familiar faces, especially Henry Tomaszewski, as a character not unlike his Billy from the other two movies; his Kevin here shares the last name Shaughnessy with Billy).

Why a "nice girl" like Nicki would hang around with people like Kevin, who has little of the opportunity she does, is the question that puzzles Tim Donovan (Savage), the probation officer who struggles to put kids like Kevin on the straight and narrow. When Nicki tussles with a cop after she and Kevin get in a fender bender, Tim asks the judge handling the case for her to be put under his watch. Although his dedication in trying to get his kids to "see the light" is downright priestly, there's something more carnal to his attention to Nicki—35-year-old Tim is obviously attracted to her.

Tim's interest in Nicki collides with that of her father. He wants Tim's nose out of his family's business but, as with Tim, there's something a little creepy beneath his concern. Just how creepy the father is to Nicki and her sister Rachael (Lauree Berger) becomes increasingly important as the movie progresses. Although it's a much more common dramatic topic now, exposing Nicki's dad as an incestuous molester of his daughters was a rare thing in the 1980s, and Nicki's monologue about the girls' suffering at the hands of their dad is still very powerful.

But father-child relationships of all sorts are at the heart of *The Little Sister*. The surrogate-parent role Tim takes towards Nicki and his other "kids" mirrors the real father-child relationship of Nicki and her dad. There's also Tim's relationship with his late father (a dockworker who dies in the first scene) and with his little daughter (Vanessa Hill), of whom he shares custody with his ex-wife. The script seems to say there's a fine line between dangerous men like Nicki's father and men like Tim, who eventually tries to initiate a sexual relationship with Nicki but whose libido is, fortunately, derailed when he sees the emotional damage her father has inflicted. As in *Billy in the Lowlands* and *The Dark End of the Street*, the solution is for people to treat each other with

> It was a double-edged sword. I had a crew of 50 and all the trucks and unions and equipment. Yeah, you could make some beautiful images, but you lost a lot of the spontaneity and a lot of what made the other (movies) special.
>
> –Jan Egleson

The Little Sister: John Savage in the South End.

respect, an ideal that isn't always reached in the hard-knock settings of Egleson's Boston trilogy.

The Little Sister—which had only spotty theatrical play before its PBS airing (there was no Boston run)—offers a new set of locations for Egleson, including the docks of East Boston, Harvard Square and the Combat Zone. Although Tim regularly drives down Washington Street in the Zone to find Nicki hanging out with Kevin and his friends, the sidewalk where Egleson shot the group is actually on East Berkeley Street across from longtime retail fixture Harry the Greek's, by the old Dover elevated Orange Line stop. Action was also filmed in and around the Boston Ballet headquarters in the South End, Buckingham Browne & Nichols School in Cambridge, Brookline (where the family's home is) and the Somerville Boxing Club in its old East Somerville location. The strip joint Nicki and Kevin hang out in is not in the Combat Zone, as implied. It was created inside Central Square's music spot The Club, which later become Nightstage.

An unexpected outgrowth of *The Little Sister* was the formation of Collinge-Pickman Casting. Egleson's wife Patty Collinge (who plays Nicki's mom) and Carolyn Pickman (who, like Egleson, appears in *The Friends of Eddie Coyle*) had helped to cast this movie and were then asked to do the same for the visiting production *Billy Galvin* (another film that PBS' *American Playhouse* had partially funded). Their agency then became a regular collaborator throughout the 1990s on big and small productions that shot locally (Carolyn Pickman carries on today with her CP Casting).

And, yes, that's Ben Affleck's dad Tim in the credits as "swing man." Ben made his movie debut in Egleson's *The Dark End of the Street*, while the director, with whom Tim had acted in Theater Company of Boston, used the elder Affleck on the crew this time.

▶**Locations:** East Boston, South End, Boston; Cambridge; Brookline; Somerville.

▶**Accents:** Kevin Bacon, in an uncredited role as Tim's coworker, uncorks an iffy one (Bacon was star Tracy Pollan's boyfriend at the time). Not even the Brigham's cup he sips from can put *that* accent over, though Bacon did better years later in *Mystic River*. Surprisingly, there's no accent from Roxanne Hart, as another of Tim's coworkers (and his increasingly neglected girlfriend); she later did a very convincing one in *The Verdict*. John Savage (brother of longtime Boston broadcaster Robin Young) drops an R here and there, but generally everyone speaks in his or her regular voice, with Henry Tomaszewski providing the most prominent local voice.

▶**Local color:** There's less of a taste of pop culture Boston than in Egleson's previous movies. The economic gulf between rundown locations like the docks or the Combat Zone and tonier spots like Nicki's private school or her family's house is the main value of the locations here. You could find such a gap in many cities, but the Greater Boston sites convey it very well. The East Cambridge courthouses where both Tim works and Nicki's father serves on a licensing board are a sort of demilitarized zone in society's class wars.

The Love Letter

1999. Directed by Peter Ho-Sun Chan. Written by Maria Maggenti. Based on Cathleen Schine's novel. With Kate Capshaw, Tom Selleck, Tom Everett Scott, Ellen DeGeneres, Geraldine McEwan, Julianne Nicholson and Blythe Danner. Cinematography by Tami Reiker.

HOLLYWOOD MAKES ONE OF its semi-regular trips to Cape Ann for this adaptation of Cathleen Schine's novel, and captures the requisite cozy shops, shingled houses, wainscoting and boats bobbing in a sun-dappled harbor. The name of the fictional town in *The Love Letter*, Loblolly-by-the-Sea, hints at the kind of whimsy the movie is going for. And the way in which that name tries a little *too* hard to sound quaint is indicative of how the this painless misfire never quite nails that whimsy.

The setting—the sort of set-in-its-ways small town where you find cranky old locals and antique stores—is fitting for a story focusing on a heroine who's older than usual for a romantic comedy. Forty-ish Helen (Kate Capshaw) is a divorcée who owns a bookstore, and finds the letter in question there. It's a passionate missive that appears to come to her through the mail, without an envelope and lacking an addressee and a signature.

Assuming it's meant for her, lovelorn Helen becomes obsessed with who wrote the letter. Her silent quest to find her secret admirer ripples through the shop. It makes Helen more open to the advances of Johnny (East Bridgewater native Tom Everett Scott), the impulsive college student who's working for her during his summer vacation, at the expense of neglecting Walter (Tom Selleck), the thoughtful fireman and high-school classmate who wants them to become a couple, now that each is divorced.

The fact that Helen doesn't actually mention the letter to her possible admirers is a stretch, as is the fact that, despite her secrecy, she carelessly leaves it around so that others see it and, naturally, assume it's meant for *them*. These letter readings, including one by store manager Janet (Ellen DeGeneres), as well as a crush harbored by the other store employee, Jennifer (Medford native Julianne Nicholson), complicate the cluttered plot. The relaxed performances are appealing, but they don't quite mesh with the overreaching, near-farcical story.

The Love Letter also doesn't want to do the work it needs to do to succeed. For instance, Helen's bookstore (built in a closed Rockport bank) has more employees than customers and, despite the movie being set during the summer, Loblolly seems to be the only picturesque coastal town without a tourist season. The lack of incidental people like tourists and townies is why the locations in Rockport and its vicinity (one of the houses—Johnny's, I believe—is in Gloucester) lack personality. The movie can also just be off-putting. How else to explain a scene in which Johnny and Jennifer walk out of a Buster Keaton movie at Rockport's Little Art Cinema, and you're *not* supposed to think badly of them because of it? (As if this movie could even hope to compare with *Sherlock, Jr.*, the Keaton movie they reject.)

What's most interesting about *The Love Letter* has nothing to do with the locations or even Helen's predicament. It's when the letter turns out to not be what she thinks, but a misplaced love note from one woman to another. Director Peter Ho-Sun Chan (who'd previously made the gender-bending Hong Kong comedy *He's a Woman, She's a Man*) and screenwriter Maria Maggenti (who'd previously written and directed the self-explanatory *The Incredibly True Adventure of Two Girls in Love*) have smuggled an ode to lesbian love inside a mainstream, heterosexual romantic comedy, and that's a rare thing. The movie plays with gender roles by casting famously gay DeGeneres as a promiscuous straight woman and he-man Selleck as a passive guy. So there are certainly interesting things going on beneath the surface in *The Love Letter*, but the surface remains rather routine.

▶ **Locations:** Rockport; Gloucester; Manchester-by-the-Sea.

▶ **Accents:** A couple of locals, the cop (Bill Buell) and the postal clerk (Alice Drummond), utter New England's flat vowels, while the wonderful Geraldine McEwan slightly modifies her natural English accent as crusty Miss Scattergoods. But, beyond that, bupkis, and it's not really an important factor. After all, the cast's Massachusetts natives, Scott and Nicholson, talk in their natural voices and they don't have accents.

▶ **Local color:** Most of what we see here is pretty generic New England coastal stuff. It's effective, but being any more specific than that was clearly not an objective. Just look at the old postcard from Walter that Helen unearths—its address doesn't even contain a state in it, though Loblolly's zip code, 01930, is Gloucester's (the fact that a postcard actually figures in the plot makes the superficial postcard views here easier to take). But if you step back a bit, you'll realize just about everything in the movie is old and just about everyone in it is miserable. Yup, that sounds like Greater Boston, doesn't it? And the movie manages to do this without even bringing up the pre-2004 Red Sox. So *The Love Letter* scores local color points, after all.

Love Story

1970. Directed by Arthur Hiller. Written by Erich Segal. With Ryan O'Neal, Ali MacGraw, Ray Milland and John Marley. Cinematography by Dick Kratina.

REMEMBER THE *OLD* HARVARD Square, the one with lots of colorful local businesses and only a few national chains? It's captured in a small way in *Love Story*, and its presence is a large part of the movie's success.

What can you say about this unabashedly romantic drama that became a monster hit? That it's about as square as a movie about young people could be in 1970? That it's sometimes laughable, like when a bawling Ali MacGraw babbles "Love means never having to say you're sorry," which snowballed into one of the decade's more inescapable catch phrases? That, despite it all, it somehow works?

It would be so easy to knock *Love Story* for being uncool, which it decidedly is. But, nearly 40 years later, that's part of the boy-meets-girl, boy-gets-disowned-for-marrying-girl, girl-drops-dead melodrama's charm. It's cheese, that's for sure. But, in a way, it's well-crafted cheese (and it definitely outrates other deathbed romances, such as 2000's *Autumn in New York*). Ryan O'Neal and MacGraw aren't the most expressive or graceful performers, yet as the college-student lovers—he's a rich hockey star, she's a poor pianist—they have a certain chemistry together.

They're like two tennis players who are at the same level and can volley well with each other. You couldn't have put Dustin Hoffman in *Love Story* and expected his more emotional style of acting to mesh with flatter MacGraw. But with O'Neal, she found a fitting tennis partner of sorts (O'Neal got the part after Beau Bridges and Michael York turned it down). Their characters come from different classes—Jenny is the daughter of a baker, his to-the-manor-born name (Oliver Barrett IV) says it all—and Erich Segal's screenplay (which he fashioned into the best-selling novel only *after* the movie was shot) offers a semi-enlightened *Romeo & Juliet* for a changing society. This time, only *his* stern, imposing father (Ray Milland) is against the union, while her earthier dad (John Marley) tolerates his daughter's wishes.

The "enlightenment" in *Love Story* is a little suspect all these years later. It's certainly there in Jenny's wisecracking and her distaste for sugarcoating things. But the fact that this "modern woman's" doctor would discover that she's terminally ill and then dutifully tell her husband, but not her, is about as patriarchal and boneheaded as can be. And no one questions this withholding of information for a second—not even Jenny once she finds out she's sick. The entire illness plot turn comes off very poorly, since Segal and director Arthur Hiller's way of showing Jenny being strong is to give her an unnamed condition with no visible symptoms, so Jenny becomes a stereotypically Hollywood beautiful corpse.

Yet you do feel the sense of loss in *Love Story*, as the happy Cambridge couple becomes a tragic Manhattan couple. But maybe that's the problem. Maybe the couple should have never left Cambridge: they obviously enjoy meals at The Tasty, walks to the Weeks Footbridge, their Oxford Street apartment and lunches across the river outside Harvard Stadium. *Love Story* received rare access to Harvard Yard, and at one point the lovers enjoy a leisurely chat as they traverse it. The movie also has time-capsule vistas to behold as Jenny and Oliver drive down Soldiers Field Road and then off of the old elevated expressway and towards the Tobin Bridge; later, there's a small glimpse of the corner of State and Congress Streets in the Financial District. Of course, the reputation of *Love Story* as a Boston movie jumps mightily thanks to one line of dialogue: "This is Boston. Everybody drives like a maniac." Say what you will about *Love Story*, but at least it gets *that* much right.

▶**Locations:** Cambridge; Allston, East Boston, Boston; South Hamilton.

▶**Accents:** Not a single one. Unless you want to count Ray Milland's generically patrician New England voice, but it's just the transplanted Brit's faded English tones. In real life, there are local accents inside Harvard Yard—just ask *The North End*'s Frank Ciota, a Crimson grad—but not many, so it's not a glaring omission.

▶**Local color:** I'm sure at the time a little taste of the normal sights and sounds of Harvard Square didn't seem like much. But it sure does now. O'Neal and MacGraw eat at The Tasty 27 years before Matt Damon and Minnie Driver do so in *Good Will Hunting*, there's a cool high shot overlooking the exit of the Harvard Square Station bus tunnel (there was a gas station in Brattle Square!?) and there's a quick peek at The Midget Restaurant, which was at the corner of Mass. Ave. and Holyoke Street before Yen Ching, the Chinese restaurant that's *still* there, replaced it. This view also includes one of my favorite things in "old Harvard Square": the unmarked back exit from the pre-renovation Red Line station, opposite Holyoke Street. And I'm sure there are some Ivy Leaguers who get a kick out of seeing Harvard's old Watson Rink here.

▶**Don't blink!:** That's Tommy Lee Jones—Harvard '69, linebacker, college roommate of Al Gore, and the first house manager at Cambridge's late great Orson Welles Cinema—as one of O'Neal's roommates. He'd be back in town 23 years later, as the mad bomber in *Blown Away*.

Mermaids

1990. Directed by Richard Benjamin. Written by June Roberts. Based on Patty Dann's novel. With Cher, Winona Ryder, Bob Hoskins, Michael Schoeffling and Christina Ricci. Cinematography by Howard Atherton.

MERMAIDS, SET IN THE early 1960s, might be best remembered today for Cher's tie-in hit version of Betty Everett's "The Shoop Shoop Song (It's in His Kiss)," with co-stars Winona Ryder and Christina Ricci chipping in on the song's video.

But the movie's production was more about kiss-offs than kisses. The Cape Ann comedy-drama, about a single mother and her two daughters, went through two directors (Lasse Hallström, Frank Oz) before settling on Richard Benjamin, while Emily Lloyd was originally cast as the older daughter ultimately played by Winona Ryder (Lloyd, an all-but-forgotten English actress who'd given a dynamite performance in *Wish You Were Here*, later earned a settlement from Orion Pictures over her dismissal).

The amount of comedy in the movie was reportedly a point of contention between the departing directors and Cher, in her first role following the very popular romantic comedy *Moonstruck* (and five years after she made *The Witches of Eastwick* on the South Shore). In any case, *Mermaids* is a tricky blend of drama and comedy dependent on quirky characters and on tragedy. Rachel (Cher) and daughters Charlotte (Ryder) and Kate (Ricci) come to Cape Ann the same way they arrive anywhere—Rachel's life takes a troubled turn and she packs up the girls and moves somewhere new.

The story filters through the eyes of 15-year-old Charlotte, who's mortified by her mom's tight dresses and eye-turning shimmy. Charlotte also overflows with internal conflict, as her fascination with Christianity and becoming a nun (despite the fact that she's Jewish) soon bumps up against the lust she feels for Joe (Michael Schoeffling of *Sixteen Candles*), her hunky new neighbor.

Charlotte's frequent and increasingly annoying voice-overs might be a symptom of the tweaking and retweaking of the movie's tone. Too often, they convey thoughts and emotions that images should communicate. It's this very uncinematic storytelling that most hurts the comedy. *Mermaids* seems to have no desire to be anything more than a light comedy with dramatic undertones. It generally delivers on that desire, its main failings—the voice-overs and a near-death that occurs late in the movie and feels as if it's almost from a different film—come when it overreaches with its drama.

You certainly can't fault the performances. As in *Moonstruck* and *Stuck on You*, Cher's performance benefits from the streak of self-deprecation she injects into it. Up-and-coming Ryder is a more adept actress than you usually get in a mere "daughter role," while Ricci, in her movie debut, provides comedy as the swimming-obsessed youngest daughter. And Bob Hoskins is a warm presence as Lou, the

Red Sox-loving shoe salesman who woos Cher's character and tries to get her to commit to their relationship (minor script quibble: would a Sox fan really want to go to the Baseball Hall of Fame to touch *Lou Gehrig's* glove?).

For all its intermittent clumsiness, *Mermaids* uses its Cape Ann locations well. Despite shooting large sections of the story on Rockport's Main Street, it's not exactly interested in using such locations specifically (an art gallery was turned into the movie's shoe store). That's evident from the use of a fictional town name—Eastport, Massachusetts. Still, these and other Greater Boston locations provide the scenic coastal imagery necessary to serve the movie's title and an autumnal feel that only *The Cider House Rules*, shot in western Massachusetts and Maine, can match. The swimming pool young Kate loves so much is closer to the city, in Cambridge.

Interestingly enough, each of the departed directors returned to the area for other movies. Hallström directed *The Cider House Rules* and Oz soon made *Housesitter* with Steve Martin and Goldie Hawn. Richard Benjamin came back, too, for the lesser *Mrs. Winterbourne*.

▶**Locations:** Rockport; North Easton; Cambridge; Ipswich; Essex; Manchester-by-the-Sea; Waltham.

▶**Accents:** Not here. The female characters are not local, Hoskins uses his standard accent for American roles and, despite playing a townie, Schoeffling eschews an accent. The only local inflection comes from the margins: the "on your mahks" of the starter at young Kate's swim meet and a mention of "noisemakahs" at the New Year's Eve party.

▶**Local color:** Like Beth Harrington's *The Blinking Madonna and Other Miracles* and Maureen Foley's *Home Before Dark*, the movie mines the early-1960s crossroads of Catholicism and JFK-led America that was most strongly felt in these parts. And the New England foliage is a colorful backdrop.

▶**Off the set:** Winona Ryder took Cher to see Steven Soderbergh's indie hit *sex, lies and videotape*, which was playing near their Harvard Square hotel. But their planned quiet outing wasn't so quiet when fans mobbed Cher.

▶**Local celeb alert!:** Boston TV legend Rex Trailer plays Charlotte's gynecologist. Sans cowboy hat, or Goldrush. Howdy Rex!

Mr. Death

1999. Directed by Errol Morris. Cinematography by Peter Donahue and Robert Richardson.

CAMBRIDGE-BASED ERROL MORRIS is one of the influential documentary directors who make movies in Greater Boston, but don't necessarily make movies *about* Boston. After the quirky Americana of his *Gates of Heaven* and *Vernon, Florida*, he broke through with 1988's *The Thin Blue Line*, in which one-time private detective Morris unravels the murder case that landed innocent Randall Adams in a Texas jail. Completed a decade later, his fascinating though overextended *Mr. Death: The Rise and Fall of Fred A. Leuchter, Jr.* is, in a sense, a companion piece to *The Thin Blue Line*. Both are about people deluding themselves into ignoring the truth (as was the movie that scored Morris an Oscar, 2003's *The Fog of War*).

As always, Morris' focus reaches far beyond the regional or even the national. But *Mr. Death* is also the movie that keeps Morris closest to home. Fred Leuchter is a Malden resident who, we immediately learn, designs death machines. The son of a Massachusetts prison employee, he got into the business of updating and designing execution machines: electric chairs, lethal-injection systems, the odd gallows or gas chamber. To hear Leuchter tell it in the movie, he does such a good job

> People are put in an uneasy position by Fred, because they don't quite know how to view Fred. Which I think is a good thing. I think it's another way of saying we don't quite know how to view ourselves.
> —Errol Morris

of designing execution hardware because he cares so much about not hurting the inmates who'll be strapped into them.

The need to execute people in the most humane fashion is a valid notion, for sure, but it's just the first of Leuchter's ironic views. The initially amusingly creepy Leuchter, with his bizarre habit of drinking 40 cups of coffee a day and his basement workshop of death, turns out to be just creepy. Because he helps renovate prison gas chambers, he's asked to go to Auschwitz by the defense lawyers for Ernst Zündel, a Holocaust denier on trial in Canada, to determine whether any people died in the chambers there. Leuchter—who had earlier marveled over getting hired to build a lethal-injection machine despite having only refurbished old electric chairs—somehow doesn't question his qualifications for *this* task (his next ironic view).

So Leuchter goes to Poland, secretly chips and scrapes away samples from the then-45-year-old structures at Auschwitz, apparently does no research at the museum there, smuggles his samples out of the country, sends them to a lab without providing any contextual information and gets back results saying no cyanide traces are evident. Then he goes to Canada and testifies that there were no gas chambers at Auschwitz and, by implication, the Holocaust is a myth. (Meanwhile, historian Robert Jan van Pelt shows us the voluminous evidence to the contrary sitting in the Auschwitz museum's extensive archive.)

The ironies continue for Leuchter. When he becomes the darling of Holocaust deniers and business cools off following the trial, he doesn't seem to understand why. His wife, whom he'd taken to Auschwitz in lieu of a honeymoon a month after they'd married, leaves him, too.

As intriguing an oddball as Leuchter is, even at 91 minutes the movie is too long. Since we don't actually feel sorry for him, the drama seeps out of *Mr. Death*. Apparently Morris originally had intended to feature Leuchter in an anthology film he'd talked of following *The Thin Blue Line*, which eventually morphed into his *Fast, Cheap & Out of Control*. He occasionally devotes too much time to his subjects, as he does here, which is why *First Person*, his 1990s TV series of lean half-hour profiles, is among his best work. Like *First Person*, *Mr. Death* features the Interrotron, Morris' invention that, through the use of two cameras and two TelePrompTers, lets Morris and his interview subjects look at each other and into cameras at the same time.

Mrs. Winterbourne

1996. Directed by Richard Benjamin. Written by Phoef Sutton and Lisa-Maria Radano. Based on Cornell Woolrich's *I Married a Dead Man*. With Ricki Lake, Brendan Fraser and Shirley MacLaine. Cinematography by Alex Nepomniaschy.

MASTER OF DOOM CORNELL Woolrich's melancholy 1940s novel *I Married a Dead Man*—previously filmed in Hollywood as *No Man of Her Own* and in France as *I Married a Shadow*—turns into a soggy, post-*Pretty Woman* 1990s Cinderella-story, chick-flick romantic comedy. Yicch.

Just about everything in director Richard Benjamin's *Mrs. Winterbourne* is more cartoonish than it should be, from the story to the use of Boston. First off, Ricki Lake, moonlighting from her 1990s talk show, overacts as Connie Doyle. Connie is the homeless, very pregnant New Yorker who's befriended on a Boston-bound train by rich Hugh Winterbourne (Brendan Fraser). After machinations involving his equally pregnant wife's (Susan Haskell) wedding ring and a horrific derailment that kills the married couple, she is then mistaken for Mrs. Winterbourne. Before she regains consciousness, she has given birth to a baby boy and been installed in the hoity-toity mansion of the dowager (Shirley MacLaine) who thinks Connie and her child are the daughter-in-law she'd never met and her new grandson.

MacLaine fails to give the imperious but fragile older woman much depth, though the script doesn't exactly give her or anyone else much to work with. Benjamin (*Mermaids*) is content to wallow in the script's greeting-card superficiality, and the best he has to add is a small part by his wife, Paula Prentiss (*Where the Boys Are*), a talented comic actress who's acted only sporadically since the early 1970s. The gimmicky casting of Fraser as his dead character's still-kicking brother, who starts to fall for his late brother's widow (and vice versa), only adds to the movie's cutesy quotient.

Gimmickry is about the last thing the movie needs, as it tries to blend romantic comedy into the darker last third of the movie in which the boyfriend (Loren Dean) who got Connie pregnant (and then dumped her) shows up in Boston, with blackmail in mind. It's a little disconcerting to see Lake, who played such brash young women in the movies of John Waters (she's spunky, chunky Tracey Turnblad in the original *Hairspray*), play such a fret-filled character this time. She just doesn't portray worry as convincingly as she does cheekiness.

Considering the glossy aims of the feel-good story, in which Connie discovers she has a place in her new family's world, whatever her name might be, it's not surprising that *Mrs. Winterbourne* offers a purely tourist's-eye view of Boston. I'll admit the shots of the pre-Big Dig Southeast Expressway and of the longtime (and now former) location of Shreve, Crump & Low at Boylston and Arlington Streets are nice snippets for the time capsule. And there are a few locations that aren't tourist traps, including the old Joyce & Joyce law firm office at Park and Beacon Streets. But the montage in which Lake and Fraser stroll past the Paul Revere House and through the Common and the Public Garden show that the movie is just really interested in blending its greeting-card emotions with post-card views. There's really nothing in the story that depends on the Boston setting and couldn't have been transplanted anywhere else with minimal change in the script.

All in all, this is one of those if-you're-not-totally-sure-they're-filming-in-Boston-then-they're-in-Canada movies. Notice how they dragged a Boston cop car up to Ontario for the climax, yet that street with trolley tracks running down the middle sure isn't in Boston. In other words, it's the kind of movie that Chambers of Commerce love, but that ordinary moviegoers barely consider a Boston movie. Oddly enough, the same story had also been twisted into romantic-comedy territory in the more plausible *While You Were Sleeping* only a year before this.

▶**Locations:** Beacon Hill, North End, Back Bay, Boston; Beverly.

▶**Accents:** Aside from the female detective seen at the beginning and end, what we get are rich Bostonians—or at least someone's idea of rich Bostonians. They don't *have* accents. Ricki Lake's and Loren Dean's characters aren't locals, and they sport a generic New York-New Jersey blue-collar accent.

▶**Local color:** Despite Brendan Fraser and Lake's stroll on the Freedom Trail, not much. One character refers to "the Commons." Lose the s, sport.

Mission Hill

1982. Directed by Robert Jones. Written by Anne Jones and Robert Jones. With Brian Burke, Alice Barrett, Steve Kerman and Barbara Orson. Cinematography by John Hoover.

THE "BEANSTREETS" MOVIES OF the late 1970s through the mid-1980s fight similar struggles. They all toil to balance realistic backdrops

Mission Hill: Daniel Miller and Brian Burke in the South End.

with fictional foregrounds and the hard knocks depicted with the need to engage their audience. Too much levity and you trivialize the dilemmas onscreen; not enough story hooks and you risk turning out a joyless pity party for your characters.

Like Jan Egleson's Boston trilogy and Christine Dall and Randall Conrad's *The Dozens*, Robert Jones' kitchen-sink drama searches for the middle ground between social commentary and engaging entertainment. Of the lot, *Mission Hill* struggles most for that sweet spot; although its social concern is deep, its drama falters. But it's not for lack of trying.

Mission Hill isn't just about young adults and the legal system, the central combatants in the other homegrown Boston features of its time. We get that battle here in Danny Doyle (Brian Burke), the underachieving high-schooler who seemingly doesn't know how to avoid trouble. But the movie also focuses on his world-weary single mom (Barbara Orson), who waits tables; his older sister Laura (Alice Barrett), an aspiring singer whose life is full of crucial choices; and even his pre-teen brother Michael (John Mahoney), who already may be destined for a life of escalating crimes.

Economic and social circumstances trap the Doyle kids, a condition each deals with in different ways: Danny by thievery, Laura through her dream of singing and Michael, sorely in need of role models, by petty shoplifting. Their mother, meanwhile, has resigned herself to her put-upon lot in life.

The emphasis in *Mission Hill* is on Danny and Laura, and there are problems with each. Danny and his illegal endeavors come off like a less energized version of Henry Tomaszewski's title character in Egleson's previous *Billy in the Lowlands* (coincidentally, Burke appears in "one of the gang" bit parts in the subsequent two films in Egleson's Boston trilogy). Danny and Billy are both knuckleheads, but Danny isn't as *watchable* a knucklehead, and his path to tragedy feels pat and formulaic.

Laura's musical pursuits are more imaginative, as is her itch to break free of her social status ("Let's do something different. Let's go to a play or a museum or something like that," she says to a dumbfounded friend at one point). But Laura's actual music is a buzzkill. It's 1970s-style slick adult/contemporary music that has no passion. It wasn't very catchy in 1983, when the movie had its world premiere run at the Sack Beacon Hill, and it still isn't (Nancy Garrick performs the vocals, not lip-synching Barrett). Why isn't Laura down at the Rat or Cantone's trying to form a punk band? That might have given some charge to her quest and given the music relevance.

There's conflict between Laura and Danny, who doesn't approve of his sister's musical ambition. But this feels forced, especially Danny's hysterical line: "I don't want my sista hangin' around in Freddie's Bah!" The action with their mother and little brother, delivered in smaller doses, is more successful—the mother's weariness captured matter-of-factly in Orson's performance and the boy's relationship with the frustrated owner (Fred P. Steinharter) of the mom-and-pop store from which he steals comics convincing in its every moment.

Like *The Dozens'* Christine Dall and Randall Conrad (the latter is *Mission Hill's* sound editor), director Robert Jones came to feature films from a background of socially conscious documentaries. He'd co-directed a short about drug addicts called *No Expectations* and the feature-length documentary *Carry it On*, a look at Joan Baez and activist husband David Harris that's very revealing of its times. But, coming towards the end of the cycle of Boston blue-collar movies (Egleson's *The Little Sister* was still to come), *Mission Hill* is not as fresh a jolt of grassroots moviemaking as its "Beanstreets" predecessors.

> I always wanted to do a narrative feature about growing up in and around Boston. When I saw *Billy in the Lowlands*, I knew I had to get off my butt and do it.
> –Robert Jones

Typically for these movies, though, *Mission Hill* takes viewers to gritty locales. Jones actually didn't shoot anything in the real Mission Hill as it had changed so much since he had grown up there. The Doyles' triple-decker is in Allston. That's also where Laura often auditions for vocalist gigs and sings at clubs. Somerville's old Southern Junior High (torn down in 1991) and the Charlestown Housing Project are Danny's hangouts; the train yard where he hides out is also in Somerville. There is also the old Northampton Orange Line El station, while Charlestown Navy Yard is in the scenes with water backdrops and a North End location serves as the exterior of the bookie's bar.

▶**Locations:** Allston, Charlestown, South Boston, North End, Boston; Somerville; Cambridge.

▶**Accents:** There's a mix here. While Burke is local and talks in an authentic accent, Barrett and Steve Kerman—who plays Steve, the older boyfriend everyone but her realizes will turn out to be bad news—have light New York accents.

▶**Local color:** The Doyles only occasionally brush up against the pretty things in the city. Laura's boss' office has a nice view overlooking the Charles River and Longfellow Bridge, but neither she nor anyone else in her family is hobnobbing with the beautiful people. The color is strictly blue-collar grunge, as it should be. No Freedom Trail here.

Monument Ave.: Colm Meaney and Denis Leary in Charlestown.

Monument Ave.

1998. Directed by Ted Demme. Written by Mike Armstrong. With Denis Leary, Colm Meaney, Ian Hart, Jason Barry, Famke Janssen, Martin Sheen, John Diehl, Noah Emmerich and Billy Crudup. Cinematography by Adam Kimmel.

TED DEMME'S CHARLESTOWN CRIME thriller isn't the glittering showpiece local officials hope for when a movie comes to Boston to film. It's just better than almost every one of those movies. This bracing immersion into the often hateful tribalism that has long plagued the city is a gutsy piece of *Mean Streets*-style moviemaking.

Monument Ave. finds its tribalism in the Charlestown "code of silence" that corrosively eats away at the souls of its cast of characters and their beloved neighborhood. Car theft, petty thievery, sports betting and substance abuse are the main pastimes of those characters—30-ish, single, testosterone-fueled Irish-Americans who still live at home with their old-country moms.

Bobby O'Grady (Denis Leary) is our main focus. He's a townie who spends most of his time stealing cars *for*, losing sports bets *to* and sneaking around with the girlfriend (Famke Janssen) *of* local crime boss Jackie O'Hara (Colm Meaney). He and such buddies as Mouse (Ian Hart), Seamus (Jason Barry), Teddy (Billy Crudup), Red (Noah Emmerich) and Digger (John Diehl) have no plans of ever taking a good look at what the world beyond Charlestown has to offer.

Mike Armstrong's script and Demme's direction do a nifty job of letting you see the background details that make up Bobby and his pals' claustrophobic world. The outdoor scenes often find the background of the Tobin Bridge or the Southeast Expressway's upper and lower decks fencing in the characters, while the streets they walk and drive down are usually narrow, and the bars they frequent are dingy and full of drab paneling. So it's easy to feel Bobby's growing discontent with the insular ways that give Jackie license to run wild and fill the neighborhood with a fear of outsiders, a fear that all too easily gets expressed in racism—especially in a brave sequence in which Bobby calls the bluff of his big-talking buddies who want to harass a lost black man.

When the Charlestown code of silence causes one of Bobby's cousins to be murdered, then another, disgust begins to show on his face. But *Monument Ave.* doesn't stoop to putting big speeches in his mouth. Instead, the resentment comes out in such scenes as a street hockey game in which Bobby and Jackie continually jockey for position. Although Leary had made a name for himself as a comedian—collaborating with Demme on his MTV spots, *No Cure for Cancer* cable special and the very funny *The Ref*—he'd been acting for a long time, and this was a dramatic breakthrough for him. But everyone here is good (yes, Janssen is too good-looking for her role, as many have commented, but she does fine with it). Crudup is especially good at carving out a character during the early sequence in which he figures prominently.

> The Italian-American experience has been documented on film in this country from every particular angle. And the Irish, we still have this sort of underbelly of 'Well, let's not really tell the truth about that. Keep that to yourself.' Except for *Friends of Eddie Coyle*, which was a touchstone film for us, it hasn't been portrayed here.
> –Denis Leary

Most of the movie was indeed filmed in Charlestown, where Worcester native Leary lived during the 1980s. Such familiar movie sights as the Charlestown steps (also seen in *Blown Away* and *Celtic Pride*) and the Bunker Hill Monument are here, as are off-the-beaten-path locations such as the park off of Terminal Street where the street hockey game occurs. Leary's knowledge of the real events behind the movie led to him being almost a historical advisor to the film; he directed fellow cast members to J. Anthony Lukas' non-fiction book *Common Ground* and shared old newspaper clippings he'd saved about neighborhood crime.

Monument Ave. also ventures outside of Charlestown for several scenes at Malden's Ancient Order of Hibernians hall and Wellesley's Lee Imported Motors. Chelsea and East Boston locations also appear, as does Commonwealth Avenue in the Back Bay during the opening car-stealing sequence.

Although the movie went through a number of tentative titles, including *The Noose, Talk of the Town* and *Snitch*, before settling on one, there's nothing uncertain about the actual film. It hits with a more assured punch than any other 1990s Boston independent movie.

▶**Locations:** Charlestown, East Boston, Back Bay, Boston; Malden; Wellesley; Chelsea.

▶**Accents:** With Leary, Lenny Clarke (as a guy named Skunk, complete with fake grey patch of hair) and Don Gavin around, you get plenty of the real thing. And although the fake accents of the out-of-town actors are erratic, the cast as a whole does a very good job. No one's less-than-perfect accent taints his or her character.

▶**Local color:** "What ah ya, fuckin' re*tah*ded?" Leary's character barks at one point, like a true Bostonian. But this is not really a movie with a lot of conventional local color; these guys aren't taking the Duck Tour, after all. The Charlestown code of silence is all the color the movie needs, and it's all dark. Frighteningly dark.

▶**Local celeb alert!:** Bruins hero Cam Neely, who's collaborated with Leary on many charity events, has a cameo as the unsuspecting guy who comes home from work to find inept robber Mouse (Ian Hart) asleep in his bed.

Moonlight Mile

2002. Directed and written by Brad Silberling. With Jake Gyllenhaal, Dustin Hoffman, Susan Sarandon, Ellen Pompeo and Holly Hunter. Cinematography by Phedon Papamichael.

THE INDECISION OVER THE title of writer-director Brad Silberling's movie is perhaps indicative of the way nothing goes quite as smoothly in it as it might have. Shot mostly on the North Shore as *Baby's in Black*, then changing names to a twisting of another Beatles song title,

Goodbye Hello, it eventually came out with the name of a *Rolling Stones* song, *Moonlight Mile*.

Similarly, the actual movie strains to find the right tone. It's a very ambitious 1970s-set mix of big emotions and comedy, about a young man (Jake Gyllenhaal) and a middle-aged couple (Dustin Hoffman, Susan Sarandon) who suddenly find themselves thrown together after the murder of their daughter, his fiancée. The movie looks at grief, healing, parenting, love and loss, sometimes through a comic filter and sometimes dead-on. At its worst, it huffs and puffs like Fat Albert trying to pull off Jackie Chan moves. Other times, the goodwill of its effort is enough to offset clumsiness. Still other times, its mix of emotions really does have an amazing agility.

The main relationships here are between confused Joe (Gyllenhaal) and his fiancée's folks, fastidious nebbish Ben (Hoffman) and straight-talking JoJo (Sarandon). Joe can't think of anything better to do, so he moves into his fiancée's old bedroom and, just as had been planned, takes his place in Ben's commercial real estate office (the house filmed is in Swampscott, the office in Marblehead). But Joe's desire to help the couple heal from their loss runs up against two things: a secret about the fiancée he can't bring himself to tell them, and a new relationship with Bertie (pre-*Grey's Anatomy* Ellen Pompeo), the tomboy beauty who works at the local post office.

Moonlight Mile handles the internal pushes and pulls that motivate its three lead characters very inconsistently. Gyllenhaal, coming off of the amazing *Donnie Darko*, embodies Joe's ambivalence without shouting about it. But writer-director Silberling relies too often on big speeches or strained "big moments" whenever he wants to crank up the emotions.

Silberling was the boyfriend of actress Rebecca Schaeffer when she was slain in 1989, and here and there he incorporates his experiences into the movie (he talks about such moments on the movie's DVD commentaries). But the story is an odd hodgepodge also involving Joe's dreams about his dead fiancée and a murder trial with a prosecutor played by Holly Hunter (ironically, in her natural Georgia accent, instead of the suburban-Boston one she used in 1991's *Once Around*). Although Silberling's experiences inspire such tangents, the recurrent dreams don't serve much of a purpose and all the steps leading up to the trial are irrelevant to what ultimately happens in the courtroom.

Oddly enough, the movie's best-written and best-played moment comes in a scene shot in Gloucester, when Joe reluctantly enters a neighborhood bar that he's supposed to try to buy out for a redevelopment Ben is pulling together. He starts asking the bartender

(Richard T. Jones) nosy questions that the barkeep dodges. When Joe walks over to the jukebox and asks the bartender to pick a number on the machine, the song that comes up is Dave Edmunds' old hit with the "get lost" sentiment, "I Hear You Knocking." Joe gets the hint and quietly leaves.

There's not enough of that slyness, of the relationship between what's said and what isn't, in the rest of the movie. That's why that scene towers over big speeches like Sarandon's about "finding home," the overwrought sex scene between Joe and Bertie and the forced, cringe-inducing working-class slang of Bertie's initial scenes.

▶**Locations:** Marblehead; Gloucester; Swampscott; Cohasset; Plum Island; Martha's Vineyard.

▶**Accents:** There isn't much of an attempt to inject accents into the mix. Though from Everett, Pompeo doesn't have an accent and her character has a more universal blue-collar way of talking, but which comes off as caricature ("I sling stamps over at the post office," she actually says at one point, in a line that sounds as if it comes from a really bad movie from 1938). Lenny Clarke might have added his heavy accent, but he had what was presumably a speaking role cut down to what is now a glorified extra role as a barfly.

▶**Local color:** Like *Mermaids*, which was also shot on the North Shore a decade before, the movie goes for an almost generic coastal-New-England, Main Street U.S.A. hominess, and similarly uses a fictional town name for its setting (this time, it's the town of Cape Ann). So there's more regional color than specific local color. It's pretty similar to the 1970s detail, which never becomes downright central to the events. One little detail really did take me back, though, and that's something stuck on the wall at the bar named Cal's Place: one of the cardboard cones in which the Red Sox used to sell popcorn at Fenway Park back in the early 1970s.

My Father, The Genius

2002. Directed by Lucia Small. Cinematography by Laurel Greenberg and Lucia Small.

THE TITLE OF LUCIA Small's fascinating documentary is half-serious, half-kidding. But that's apt. Her movie is all about mixed emotions.

Glen Small, the father referred to in the title, was once a rising star in architecture. In the 1970s, he co-founded the iconoclastic Southern California Institute of Architecture (SCI-arc) and had grand, eco-friendly designs to take advantage of technology and still move us closer to nature. He wasn't just trying to build buildings, like his colleagues, he was trying to create utopia. His grandest idea was the Biomorphic Biosphere, a sort of vertical city shaped like a giant tree and organized to promote community and conservation. But the Biomorphic Biosphere and the Green Machine, a more practical version of the same concept, literally and figuratively never got off the ground. And, despite being an inspirational mentor to many students, outspoken Small later found himself elbowed off SCI-arc's faculty, after its 1960s-era idealistic camaraderie had faded. As we see in the movie, he's been struggling ever since.

The elder Small originally asked Lucia to write a biography of him, miffed at how undocumented his work was. Instead, local filmmaking vet Lucia (who'd worked on *The Blinking Madonna and Other Miracles*) made this movie, which touches as much on family history as it does on architecture. Before Glen Small's career started its slide, the architect had left Lucia, her two sisters and their mother, embarking on a series of relationships with other women and becoming an absent dad. The three girls (Lucia is the middle child) struggled to connect with their dad as they grew into women.

The separation between Lucia and her dad is the filter through which *My Father, The Genius* flows. It might not include a single frame of film shot in Boston, yet it is *such* a Boston-style documentary, with the filmmaker skillfully injecting her perspective into the "storytelling" and enriching it in the process.

The central question the movie raises is "So *is* Glen Small a genius?" While every viewer has his or her opinion, Lucia Small offers no simple answers and serves up her dad, warts and all. He turns out to be a very interesting mix of professional integrity and personal selfishness. The most amazing glimpse of him comes in a video clip moderating a 1976 architectural panel discussion, as he verbally tears down all the participants as he introduces them. You shake your head at the lack of diplomacy, but are amazed by its boldness. That many of Small's panelists were rising stars like Frank Gehry, whom he calls an "opportunist... usually with a gimmick," didn't help his career.

You'd have to sit through many a fiction film to find a character as watchable as Glen Small. And through her movie, Lucia Small lets us share her own ambiguous feelings towards him. *My Father, The Genius* didn't make as much of a national splash as 2003's *My Architect*, Nathaniel Kahn's somewhat similar movie in which a grown child explores an architect father's life and tries to reconcile professional passion and parental problems. But it's every bit as good.

Mystery Street

1950. Directed by John Sturges. Written by Sydney Boehm and Richard Brooks. Based on Leonard Spigelgass' story. With Ricardo Montalban, Sally Forrest, Bruce Bennett, Elsa Lanchester, Marshall Thompson, Edmon Ryan, Betsy Blair and Jan Sterling. Cinematography by John Alton.

HOLLYWOOD FINALLY CAME TO Boston for this 1950 thriller, the first commercial feature to be predominantly shot in the area. Like the later (and lesser) *Walk East on Beacon!*, *Mystery Street* (also known as *Murder at Harvard*) rides the post-war wave of realistic crime dramas, pioneered by low-budget films like Anthony Mann's *T-Men*, many of which were shot on location. Director John Sturges' movie doesn't quite use the semi-documentary approach that *Walk East* and other similar movies did. In this case, that's all for the better. *T-Men* director of photography John Alton, one of the essential film noir cinematographers, is behind the camera here, bringing a sense of shadowy dread to the Boston locations in this pre-*CSI* police procedural in which a human skeleton is the only evidence with which an investigation starts.

Mystery Street: Jan Sterling (right) in a studio backlot Scollay Square.

Alton's work is most evident in the set-up for the detective work that will follow. The movie opens in a Beacon Hill rooming house where darkness dominates, except for the light that shines on desperate Vivian Helding (Jan Sterling), the house phone she's using and the ajar door of eavesdropping landlady Mrs. Smerrling (Elsa Lanchester). It turns out Vivian, a B-girl at a Scollay Square dive called The Grass Skirt, is pregnant, and the married Hyannis man who fathered the child is giving her the brush-off.

At The Grass Skirt, where Vivian's boyfriend has stood her up, she gloms onto drunk Henry (Marshall Thompson), "helps" him move his car and keeps driving it to the Cape, where she eventually ditches Henry and meets with the boyfriend, whose face isn't shown. He shoots her, dumps her body in the ocean and pushes the stolen car into a lake.

It's only months later, when a birdwatcher finds Vivian's skeleton sticking out of a sandy beach, that the investigation begins. Barnstable County investigator Pete Moralas (Ricardo Montalban) is on the case, which eventually leads him to Beacon Hill, Cambridge and Harvard Medical School's Department of Legal Medicine in Roxbury. That's where Dr. McAdoo (Bruce Bennett) helps Moralas identify the body and build a case against unwitting Henry, who initially denies he met Vivian because he's married and wasn't supposed to be in The Grass Skirt (he was supposed to be at the Boston Lying-In Hospital with his pregnant wife). But that changes when McAdoo discovers the cause of death was a gunshot, putting Moralas on a collision course with the well-to-do Hyannis boyfriend (Edmon Ryan). He is finally shown to the audience halfway through the movie, when snooping Mrs. Smerrling tries to blackmail him.

As crime thrillers circa 1950 are wont to do, *Mystery Street* climaxes in a public place, Trinity Station. This long-gone train station adjacent to Back Bay Station is a suitably bustling, urban backdrop for the end chase (its train yard is apparently now part of the Mass. Pike). Although the rooming house is on fictional "Bunker Street," the building used appears to be on Pinckney Street near Anderson Street (you can see the old New England College of Pharmacy there at one point). Suspect Henry lives in Charlestown (in a forward-looking movie connection, just a half-block from Monument Avenue), while The Grass Skirt exterior is on a studio backlot. Aside from the dunes footage (presumably) it's unclear if any of the Cape Cod action was done there; the gas station with the greasy spoon attached looks to be in California (its signs for Caloco Oil sure sound West Coast). There's also a Harvard Yard sequence that turns out to be rather inconsequential (since the cop finds out he has to go over to the Med School), but it adds to the movie's local color. Amusingly, co-star Thompson (later of TV's *Daktari*) appears on the movie's trailer to offer special thanks to Harvard for its cooperation, something the school generally doesn't offer anymore.

Like Alton's artful Hollywood cinematography, non-local flavor comes from the cast, with Lanchester, the bride of Frankenstein herself, practically stealing the show with her proper yet hypocritically opportunistic landlady. Years before he became kitsch, Montalban is a sturdy presence in this brisk B-thriller.

►**Locations:** Beacon Hill, Roxbury, Back Bay, Charlestown, Boston; Cambridge; Cape Cod.

►**Accents:** Back in a time when there probably were a greater percentage of area residents with Boston accents than there are now, *Mystery Street* generally refrains from including them. But there are generic New England accents from Cape Cod characters talking about the found skeleton. And we do get what might be Hollywood's first overdone Boston accent from Wally Maher, who plays the Boston detective Moralas teams with in the city. Maher, who also voiced the title character in Tex Avery's Screwy Squirrel cartoons, couldn't quite get the Boston accent.

►**Local color:** Over 50 years later, many of the shooting locations will have you wondering their exact whereabouts, especially Trinity Station. But the movie's issues also hit close to home at times, specifically the hypocrisy of the landlady, a self-righteous moral guardian who no doubt supported many a Boston book banning, and the elitism of Vivian's blue-blooded killer, who not only victimizes her, but also feels superior to first-generation American Moralas, and lets him know it.

Mystic River

2003. Directed by Clint Eastwood. Written by Brian Helgeland. Based on Dennis Lehane's novel. With Sean Penn, Tim Robbins, Kevin Bacon, Laurence Fishburne, Laura Linney and Marcia Gay Harden. Cinematography by Tom Stern.

MYSTIC RIVER'S ACCLAIM AND boatload of local locations make it an important Boston movie. But, onscreen, it's a disappointment. Novelist Dennis Lehane has likened its plot to an opera, and it could have used a stylish visionary like the late Italian master Sergio Leone (*Once Upon a Time in America*) as a storyteller; coincidentally,

Mystic River: Sean Penn and Kevin Bacon in East Boston.

director Clint Eastwood starred in Leone's classic Man with No Name spaghetti-western trilogy, but his storytelling style is very different.

Lehane's operatic plot has a slow build that's tricky for a mainstream movie to pull off (especially in these days of instant cinematic gratification). But its drama about the murder of one man's (Sean Penn) 19-year-old daughter—with the case being investigated by one of his childhood friends (Kevin Bacon) and the main suspect being another (Tim Robbins)—deals with crime and male bonding, familiar territory for Eastwood. The movie he'd made just before this, *Blood Work*, had been a solid meat-and-potatoes thriller. But there's the rub. *Mystic River* isn't meat and potatoes, and its story of lingering emotional scars, bitter resentments and everyday drudgery does *not* play to Eastwood's strengths.

The typically murky Eastwood visuals are not such a bad thing for *Mystic River*'s far-from-the-Freedom-Trail, Dorchester-meets-Charlestown-meets-Southie setting. The movie is heavy on drab vinyl siding, asphalt and the back porches and front stoops of triple-deckers—especially the creepy 1970s prologue, when child molesters abduct one of the friends. The murkiness is less helpful to the cast, and emblematic of how the movie pales the book's characters, now grown into their late thirties and estranged enough to be just acquaintances.

Jimmy (Penn), whose daughter (Emmy Rossum) dies, is an ex-con who owns a convenience store; Sean (Bacon) is a detective just separated from his wife; and Dave (Robbins), the molesters' victim, with a perpetually hurt look on his face, happens to come home covered in blood on the night Jimmy's daughter dies in a nearby park.

New Bedford native Brian Helgeland's *Mystic River* screenplay retains nearly all the plot of the novel, but jettisons much of the detail that enriches it. The movie primarily follows the investigation into the murder. But the murderer was fairly easy to pick out in Lehane's book, and the case was just an excuse to explore the emotional wounds ailing Jimmy, Sean and Dave. Jimmy, the most volatile of the trio, is the most reduced onscreen. He doesn't feel like the big man in the neighborhood he's meant to be, and all the concentration on the investigation means that the detective's pragmatic partner (Laurence Fishburne) is onscreen as much as Jimmy. Lack of screen time also diminishes Jimmy's wife (Laura Linney), whose big Lady Macbeth power grab, which gives the novel a chilling resolution, comes out of nowhere in the movie.

Despite its all-around strong performances—Marcia Gay Harden's performance as Dave's conflicted wife is the best thing here—*Mystic River* rarely finds cinematic ways to replace the lost emotional details. But that's not Eastwood's way. He offers a few stylistic flourishes, like overhead shots of Jimmy bursting with rage upon discovering his missing daughter is dead, or interspersing two separate violent confrontations. But *Mystic River* is mainly a workmanlike Eastwood production, short on mood and with a strained orchestral score written by Clint himself.

Although Lehane uses fictional names for neighborhoods and the like (and although Eastwood strongly considered shooting the movie in Pittsburgh), there are recognizable locations in *Mystic River*: police find the murdered daughter's body in Franklin Park, she's seen before her death in Doyle's in Jamaica Plain and, of course, there's the Tobin Bridge. Miller's Market in Southie doubles for Jimmy's fictional Cottage Market, the flashback abduction occurs on East Boston's Border Street, while the liquor store is E.J. Costello's on Boylston Street (an exterior was shot at Loonie's in Dorchester, which explains why Eli Wallach's character is named Loonie, but it was not used). Production designers built The Black Emerald, the tucked-away bar where much dirty business takes place, and then demolished it. Sets were also built in Canton.

►**Locations:** Dorchester, Jamaica Plain, East Boston, South Boston, Charlestown, Back Bay, Boston; Canton (sets).

►**Accents:** Not so good, but not so bad. Much of the cast uses light accents that probably aren't as thick as these characters would have, but it works because the accents aren't distracting. Case in point: Laura Linney's is the thickest, and the most potentially distracting. Fortunately, Kevin Bacon does a better accent than he did years before in *The Little Sister*.

►**Local color:** With all of the local shooting, the flavor of Boston blue-collar neighborhoods comes through. But, just as importantly, so do the hard times in those neighborhoods. So many of the characters here have chips on their shoulders, and their environment is a big reason why. As in the later Lehane adaptation, *Gone Baby Gone*, you feel the hard times in the way the characters walk and talk.

Never Too Late

1965. Directed by Bud Yorkin. Written by Sumner Arthur Long. Based on his play. With Paul Ford, Maureen O'Sullivan, Connie Stevens, Jim Hutton and Lloyd Nolan. Cinematography by Philip H. Lathrop.

IF YOU THOUGHT EVERY Broadway play that's adapted into a movie is witty and sophisticated, think again. This 1965 comedy, shot partially in Concord (doubling for fictional Calvertown, Mass.), is so backwards it might as well have been set in 1955. This is a movie in which people are actually afraid to call a toilet, one that isn't even installed yet, by its name. Massachusetts native Sumner Arthur Long's screenplay, based on his hit Broadway play, is simply too childish to be amusing.

Long's characters—especially middle-aged Harry Lambert (Paul Ford), a frugal lumber yard owner whose wife Edith (Maureen O'Sullivan) becomes pregnant—just need to grow up. Sure, it's a little bit of a shock to the system for a guy who's hoping his daughter (Connie Stevens) and her husband (Jim Hutton) will provide him with a grandchild to learn he's going to be a father again. But small-town Harry, who thinks his and his wife's late-stage fertility means people will gossip about them, just won't deal with it, making *Never Too Late* a ridiculously contrived comedy. "Oh my God," immature Harry apparently thinks, "if my wife is pregnant then people will know we've had sex." Didn't he get over this when his wife was pregnant the *first* time? And while the movie often dotes on daughter Kate and husband Charlie's own attempts to get pregnant, the movie acts as if it's being naughty by doing so. As if.

Even in a context in which the quaint, small-town feel of the Concord locations suggests that Calvertown is a place where everyone knows everyone else's business, this is just stupid. Did Broadway audiences really go for this stuff for 1,000 performances, or was the play dumbed down for the movie? Ford is a likable actor—he's priceless as overmatched Col. Hall opposite Phil Silvers on *Sergeant Bilko*. But doltish Harry is symptomatic of the script's phony conflicts and gags. Another example comes when ill-equipped daughter Kate has to take over all the cooking and housekeeping after overworked Edith gets pregnant. Instead of sitting down and figuring out the situation like adults, the men just sit there and wait for their chow, with no thought of helping, meal after meal. Ironically, director Bud Yorkin and producer Norman Lear would soon mock this sort of arrogance on TV's *All in the Family*; here, they present it at face value.

Concord provides the sort of small-town Americana in *Never Too Late* that it would later bring to *Housesitter*. Although it seems as if all the interiors were filmed on Hollywood soundstages, there is occasional action outside the house the two married couples share and in the town center. According to a 1999 article in *Concord Magazine*, the house is on Nashawtuc Road, while Wilson's Lumber Yard (which later became the site of a Chinese restaurant) plays the movie's Lambert's Lumber Yard. The town's police chief at the time, Ned Finnan, Jr., is the traffic cop who stops cars to escort pregnant Edith across Main Street. Two generic shots accompany a trip into Boston—one, from Memorial Drive in Cambridge, shows the then-new Prudential Center, while the other is the exterior of the Statler Hilton, now the Park Plaza.

▶ **Locations:** Concord.

▶ **Accents:** There's no attempt to get too specific with voices here. For better or worse, having Irish-born, English-educated O'Sullivan use her natural British accent is deemed appropriate for New England, as is so often the case.

▶ **Local color:** Concord is very scenic, but any movie set in Massachusetts in 1965 in which one character insults another for being a Democrat simply isn't concerned with local color. This might have worked if the movie were set in Connecticut, but Massachusetts? I half-expected JFK's ghost to emerge and throttle the offender.

▶ **Local celeb alert!:** Boston Patriots receiver and kicker extraordinaire Gino Cappelletti is reportedly among the lumber yard workers. But since the widescreen movie is never revived theatrically and has never been released letterboxed on video, it's hard to pick the longtime Pats radio commentator out. That may be him in the back of a pickup truck, mocking Paul Ford's character. Or he might even be in a portion of the picture that simply isn't visible on the video.

The Next Karate Kid

1994. Directed by Christopher Cain. Written by Mark Lee. With Hilary Swank, Noriyuki "Pat" Morita, Michael Ironside, Chris Conrad, Michael Cavalieri and Constance Towers. Cinematography by Laszlo Kovacs.

IT'S NOT EXACTLY THE stuff from which double Oscar winners usually spring. But long before she boxed, Hilary Swank kicked. The athletic actress stars in the last of the *Karate Kid* series, which, unlike its predecessors, was shot in Greater Boston. While it's always refreshing when a teenaged girl headlines a movie with action in it, *The Next Karate Kid* is a cartoonish coming-of-age drama in which there's little action until the last 10 minutes.

Swank plays Julie, the sullen granddaughter of an Anglo officer with whom Noriyuki "Pat" Morita's Mr. Miyagi served during World War II. He is invited by his late comrade's wife (Constance Towers) to stay at her home in suburban Boston while she's away, and to watch over quick-tempered Julie—with designs of channeling the girl's emotions into something more productive.

Of course, Julie wants no part of Miyagi's quaint sermonizing at first—and who can blame her? The guy has been in the country over 50 years—he was on *our* side in WWII—so why does he speak like a Japanese Charlie Chan and talk in fortune-cookie messages like "Ambition without knowledge is like boat on dry land"? What an embarrassing, minstrel-show character.

But Miyagi's cartoonishness is par for this course. If Miyagi is a font of wisdom here, the appropriately named Colonel Dugan (Michael Ironside) spews evil. Even a great scenery-chomper like Ironside (*Scanners*) can't overcome the silliness of his character, a sort of security officer at Julie's high school who mentors a squad of campus jock-vigilante goons called Alpha Elite (adding even more silliness is the fact that the school scenes were shot at Brookline High School, which, at least when I attended it, was among the most permissive high schools anywhere). The Colonel's prized pupil is a bully named

Ned (Michael Cavalieri) who seems like a Ben Stiller parody of a goofy, eager Tom Cruise character.

In fact, nothing really clicks here. We're told Julie learned karate from her late father when she was little, and the story makes it seem as if all she needs is an attitude-tweaking from Miyagi—who takes her to a Buddhist monastery for a dose of humility—and she'll be the female Bruce Lee. But the movie never really convinces you she's any good at karate, despite the obligatory sports training montage. And sometimes *The Next Karate Kid* is more disturbing than unconvincing, as when it surprisingly offers two threats of sexual assault on Julie to build sympathy for her. This is very misguided for a movie designed to appeal to teen and pre-teen girls.

As a way of setting the movie apart from the previous *Karate Kid* films, the Greater Boston locations are great. From the cafeteria to the quadrangle and the rooftop to the field in front of it, director Christopher Cain fully exploits Brookline High (despite the Brookline exterior, the prom interiors were shot at Tufts University). Hollywood-friendly Cape Ann appears, with Ipswich's Crane Estate housing the monastery and Rockport's Halibut Point quarry being the coastal spot where Julie frees the wounded hawk she's nursed. And it all climaxes in a rumble of sorts on the East Boston docks. Too little, too late.

▶**Locations:** Brookline; Dorchester, East Boston, Boston; Ipswich; Rockport; Medford; Newton.

▶**Accents:** None. The knucklehead who harasses the Buddhist monks at Boston Bowl just has a generic blue-collar voice, while Michael Ironside, who used a light accent a few years later as the boat owner in *The Perfect Storm*, refrains from doing so here.

▶**Local color:** Be grateful this Hollywood production came to town, dropped some money and gave a few local technicians work. That is always welcome. And though the movie offers many locations that are pleasing to the eye, don't expect any area flavor. It's not that kind of movie. It's setting is merely Suburbia, not necessarily Suburban Boston. Just look at the bowling scene: if local color were a consideration, the monks would have been rolling candlepin, not ten pin.

Next Stop Wonderland

1997. Directed by Brad Anderson. Written by Lyn Vaus and Brad Anderson. With Hope Davis, Alan Gelfant, Sam Seder, Holland Taylor, Callie Thorne, Victor Argo, Robert Klein, Jose Zuniga, Lyn Vaus and H. Jon Benjamin. Cinematography by Uta Briesewitz.

THE BAR HAD BEEN raised quite a bit in the time between Connecticut native Brad Anderson's scruffy but charming *The Darien Gap* (1994), which partially filmed locally, and this, his more professional follow-up, filmed entirely in Greater Boston. Indie and homegrown movies such as *Home Before Dark, Squeeze, Good Will Hunting, The North End* and *Urban Relics* had raised expectations about what a "Boston movie" could do, both creatively and financially.

Next Stop Wonderland broke some ground itself. It secured a big distribution deal from Miramax Films at the 1998 Sundance Film Festival—though much media coverage at the time and certainly legend since then has overlooked the fact that the $6 million deal also figured in future work for Anderson at Miramax (none of which, including a proposed remake of the French import *When the Cat's Away*, ever went before the camera).

Distribution deal aside, Anderson's romantic comedy is less of a breakthrough onscreen. It certainly holds its own against other independent films of its time, or against glossier Hollywood romances, and it did well nationally on the arthouse circuit. But it feels like half of an outstanding movie. With its distinctive structure in which two potential lovers don't meet until the final sequence, despite often crossing paths, it feels as if just about all the cleverness has been packed into just one half of the story. That's the part about Erin (Hope Davis), a nurse who comes home to her South End apartment as the

Next Stop Wonderland: Alan Gelfant and Hope Davis at the New England Aquarium.

movie opens, only to discover that her lefty activist boyfriend (Philip Seymour Hoffman) is moving out.

Although we're supposed to think the boyfriend is a schmuck (and we do), Erin is still broken up by being suddenly single. She struggles to find a purpose in the loneliness she feels, rejects the pity of her co-workers and puts up with advice from her more carefree mother (Holland Taylor). Erin's mother puts an ad in the *Herald*'s personals section without consulting her, and Erin is so forlorn that she starts meeting up with men who respond—resulting in two energetic montages, one in which pathetic men leave phone replies to her ad and another in which she goes on dates and listens as would-be suitors try to win her over.

Erin is very engaging. She's smart, skeptical and very sympathetic (Anderson and co-writer Lyn Vaus actually drew inspiration for Erin from a Grimm Brothers tale about a princess who never smiles). Her fellow protagonist is Alan (Alan Gelfant), an East Boston plumber and New England Aquarium volunteer who's trying to be a marine biologist. He's the man fated to meet her. He's endearing, too, but his scenes pale next to Erin's. For instance, his brother (Worcester's Sam Seder) and their friends (Vaus, H. Jon Benjamin) make a bet to answer the same personal ad and see who can score first—and the scenes these guys share with Erin have much more pop than those they have

> I like the idea of films that capture other landscapes, other locales. There's a lot of indie film that comes out of New York, L.A., Austin. Boston seems to be getting put on the map. Which is fine. Audiences for these sorts of movies want to see other places.
> –Brad Anderson

with Alan. Alan's scenes, many of which involve a thug (Victor Argo) to whom he owes money and a shady developer (comic Robert Klein), are more cartoonish and less entertaining than Erin's scenes.

This imbalance keeps *Next Stop Wonderland* patchy, and it's not as effective an unconventional romance as Anderson's later *Happy Accidents*. But it's still a minor success. Slightly higher in budget than other homegrown movies of its day (Newton real estate developer Mitchell Robbins ended up bankrolling it), Anderson's movie dared to dream a little higher than most and to attract up-and-coming national talent like Davis, Seder, Callie Thorne and Hoffman. In addition to the Blue Line, the Aquarium and the South End, where Erin lives and characters sometimes eat (at On the Park and The Purple Cactus Café), the movie also uses Mass. General and St. Elizabeth's Hospitals (for Erin's workplace), Bunker Hill Community College (where Alan studies), the Barking Crab Restaurant (where Erin and Brazilian hunk

Andre dine), the Public Garden and, aptly, Wonderland Dog Track. The exterior of Davis Square's The Burren is seen, though interiors were not filmed in the Irish bar, but in Chelsea.

In the original version of *NSW* that showed at the Sundance Film Festival, Erin and Alan never actually meet. But Miramax Films honcho Harvey Weinstein insisted Brad Anderson shoot a new Revere Beach ending in which the two lead characters connect. Anderson later described having to reshoot his ending as "being strong-armed by Harvey."

►**Locations:** South End, East Boston, Boston; Revere; Chelsea; Cambridge; Somerville.

►**Accents:** There's every reason why Erin and Alan don't have accents. She's an out-of-towner who came here to study, while he's trying to escape the family business and overcome his townie background. *NSW* is not a neighborhood movie, it has more of a mix of characters. But the presence of such locals as comics Jimmy Tingle (the bartender at Erin's preferred tavern) and Steve Sweeney (her gabby cabbie) keep the accent in play.

►**Local color:** It's not every movie that uses the Blue Line as a source of romance and even poetry. But any movie in which Waltham is pronounced "Walthum," with a big emphasis on the first syllable, automatically rates low. The casting of local character actors such as Charley Broderick (one of Erin's personal-ad dates) and Ken Cheeseman (her gay co-worker) helps, though.

►**Local celeb alert!:** One-time radio fixture Charles Laquidara plays one of the unimpressive men who respond to Erin's personal ad, while TV reporter Paula Lyons plays a news anchor.

The North End

1997. Directed by Frank Ciota. Written by Joseph Ciota. With Frank Vincent, Tony Darrow, Matthew Del Negro, Lina Sivio and Mark Hartmann. Cinematography by Jon Bekemeier.

AS ITALIAN-AMERICANS WHO moved from their native Lynn to the North End after college, brothers Frank and Joseph Ciota understand both the old-timers and the new arrivals in Boston's Italian-American enclave. That's what makes their *The North End*, which places a love triangle against the backdrop of the neighborhood, work.

Frank directs Joseph's script about Freddie (Matthew Del Negro) and Mac (Mark Hartmann), Harvard grads who move into a North

End apartment and both fall for waitress Danielle (Lina Sivio). As the love triangle plays out, the pals learn about their new neighborhood from their everyday life, as well as from the documentary that aspiring filmmaker Freddie is shooting about the clash between old and new in the community.

It's the backdrop that adds most of the spice to *The North End*. For the more prominent old-timers, the Ciotas recruited two character actors with familiar faces, Martin Scorsese regular Frank Vincent and Tony Darrow, Woody Allen's favorite 1990s wiseguy character actor. These two know how to tread the line between reassuring protector and menacing mobster with style. *The North End* is not shy about undercutting the "old values" that fellows like Vincent's Dom Di Bella (a mobster/character actor) espouse during their interviews with Freddie—most obviously when Dom's boast that "We protect our women" follows the scene where Danielle's brother Gio (Peter Marciano) slaps his sister around for going out with Mac, who's asked Danielle out before Freddie can.

In the North Ender vs. newcomer battle, *The North End* takes a balanced perspective, but its ambivalence towards the yuppie invasion of the neighborhood is pretty simplistic. With Freddie and Mac as the only newcomer characters—we see others only briefly in the documentary interviews—Joseph Ciota's script merely paints one (Mac) as bad and the other (Freddie) as good. Mac, after catching his girlfriend with another man at the start of the movie, is then a violent tyrant with Danielle, bristling at any casual affection she shows towards any other man, while Freddie silently suffers, nursing his own feelings and his desire not to confront his college buddy. This black-and-white situation contrasts with the more interesting grey area in which characters such as Dom exist.

Another simplistic touch comes when Freddie likens the North End to a beauty everyone wants to possess, and the image cuts to Danielle, who's across town at the time—a too-literal edit that detracts from the metaphor. I think the Ciotas respect her too much to turn her into just a symbol for her neighborhood, but sometimes awkward storytelling smothers the brothers' sincerity. Like Michael Corrente's Providence Italian-American drama, *Federal Hill*, *The North End* draws from the same love-hate relationship with its neighborhood as the movie that inspired both of them to some degree, Scorsese's *Mean Streets*. *The North End* is not the most slick or stylish movie, but that wouldn't be the North End, would it? The movie's sense of humor also must be mentioned, and the Ciotas' tale exits on an amusing note with a bonus Dom scene after the end credits.

Filmed under the working title *The Handsome Thing*—an oft-used term that takes on ironic meaning here—the movie is a cornucopia of North End hangouts, including The European, Dolce Vita, Spagnuolo's, Il Bacio, Rabia's and Caffe Roma—some no longer around (the first is now a CVS). The sidewalks of Hanover Street are all over the action, too, and the apartment Freddie and Mac share was actually Joseph's condo at the time.

Like a lot of Boston indie films, *The North End* struggled to be seen, despite warm receptions at the Montreal and Boston film festivals. Lacking formal distribution, the

> We shot all over the place, and no one asked for location fees. You can't put a dollar value on it. We didn't have to change anything. The biggest art-department expense was Frank Vincent's cigars.
> –Joseph Ciota

producers opened the movie at theaters in Revere, Seekonk and Providence, where engagements were often held over due to its popularity. But it had little exposure beyond this, and as of this writing the movie still has never been released on home video. Frank—like Mac, a one-time Harvard football player—next made *Ciao America*, from Joe's script based on his experiences coaching American football in Italy. The two more recently made *Stiffs* locally.

▶ **Locations:** North End, Back Bay, Allston, Boston.

▶ **Accents:** "So he's from Haaavahd. So this makes him, like, wicked smaht?" says a friend of Danielle's in one of the movie's funniest lines, while Peter (nephew to the late Rocky) Marciano, the Ciotas' third cousin, provides the most sustained local accent. Frank Vincent and Tony Darrow are New York-New Jersey guys, so their accents are a stretch for their Boston characters. But their contributions here, especially Vincent's, outweigh the discrepancy in their voices.

▶ **Local color:** You can't shoot a movie about Boston's North End in New York's Little Italy, Philadelphia or Toronto. The locations are totally authentic in *The North End*, as are such customs as "saved" parking spaces. To add North End film lineage, some of the interviews for the documentary-within-the-movie were done by *The Blinking Madonna and Other Miracles* director Beth Harrington.

▶ **Aftermath:** Several cast members from *The North End* went on to play roles in *The Sopranos*. Not surprisingly, Frank Vincent had the most significant, as hotheaded Phil Leotardo, while Matthew Del Negro played Carmela Soprano's cousin and financial advisor, Brian Cammarata, and Tony Darrow is one of the show's many "friends of ours," Lorenzo "Larry Boy" Barese.

▶ **Local celeb alert!:** Via Providence... boxing's Vinny Pazienza.

Once Around

1991. Directed by Lasse Hallström. Written by Malia Scotch Marmo. With Holly Hunter, Richard Dreyfuss, Danny Aiello, Laura San Giacomo and Gena Rowlands. Cinematography by Theo Van de Sande.

YOU GOTTA LOVE A Boston movie in which a rotary figures prominently. But there's much more to like in Lasse Hallström's comedy than the traffic circle at Mystic Valley Parkway and Route 60 in Arlington. The Swedish director who made an international name for himself with *My Life as a Dog* had been set to make his American debut with another Bay State movie, *Mermaids*, but he and Cher clashed over the mixture of comedy and drama in that story and, in the end, it was Cher's wish to keep things light that won out and Richard Benjamin who directed the movie.

Hallström got his chance to juggle emotions this time, and he does a great job of it. So, too, do stars Holly Hunter, Richard Dreyfuss and Danny Aiello. One of the reasons we stick with *Once Around* when it veers from romantic comedy to domestic drama is because of the characters, and the life the cast breathes into them. One-time Winchester resident Malia Scotch Marmo's script centers on Renata (Hunter), the unlucky-in-love member of Wakefield's tightly knit Bella family. After being dumped by her longtime boyfriend (Griffin Dunne) on the day her sister Jan (Laura San Giacomo) gets married, she heads to St. Maarten and a condo-selling seminar that she hopes will pull her out of waitressing. Instead of a new career, though, she finds a new man—Sam Sharpe (Dreyfuss), a rich, sometimes annoyingly self-confident supersalesman.

Renata's whirlwind romance with Sam is heavenly for the 30-ish late bloomer, whose sense of life's possibilities expands after she meets him. When she refuses to move to New York, where he lives, he packs up himself and his business and moves to Boston, showing up with her in his limo at the house of her parents (Aiello, Gena Rowlands). Her folks are pleased to see their oldest daughter happy, but it doesn't take long for Sam's non-stop zeal to wear them down, especially patriarch Joe. While steering clear of any "losing my little girl" clichés, *Once Around* lets us feel Joe's bittersweetness at being elbowed aside by Sam, who means well but always has to be the center of attention. (Sam, to borrow another movie's line, goes to 11. Always.)

Dreyfuss was at a creative peak in 1991—*Once Around* followed *Tin Men*, *Stakeout* and *Let it Ride*—and he's one of the few actors who could successfully pull off this headstrong dynamo who turns people off, only to win them back and then turn them away again. Sam Sharpe is one of his trademark manic characters from this period. This is also one of many standout roles for Hunter. She makes Renata lonely and a little immature at the story's start, but not pathetic. The two stars work wonderfully together, and what starts out in tried-and-true romantic-comedy territory turns very unpredictable.

Once Around is a movie that doesn't need to be set locally. It's not a Boston neighborhood movie adapting an existing novel; it's not based on real events. But it simply works that way. The rotary its characters frequently ride around is the perfect visual symbol for the family unit from which those characters may temporarily stray, but around which they will always revolve. In addition to the Arlington rotary, there's also a scene on the Longfellow Bridge featuring Hunter and Dreyfuss, and action at a familiar movie sight, Charlestown's Flagship Wharf condos, later featured in *The Departed* and *What's the Worst That Could Happen?* But the complex wasn't even inhabited when *Once Around* used it. Much of the movie was also filmed in North Carolina (where the family house is, among other things), while the skating scenes were done in New Hampshire.

> The accent was a wonderful challenge. It's a wonderful sound. It's an accent where you can really sound over the top, even though you're not. But there's only 10,000,000 different ones in Boston alone—everybody has a slightly different Boston sound.
> –Holly Hunter

▶**Locations:** Arlington; Charlestown, Boston.

▶**Accents:** Critics creamed Holly Hunter's and Laura San Giacomo's accents, but I think they're very good nasal, suburban Boston accents. They're not the most flattering voices in the world, and I think that's why they bothered some people. But I have a cousin who sounds just like Renata. Sure, sometimes a tone or inflection is wrong and the idea of parents without accents having children *with* accents is unrealistic. But the actresses definitely nail lines such as "Yo-wa suit is gawjus" (as Renata says to Sam) and "Ma, cahm yahself" (as Jan says). This isn't Ally-Sheedy-in-*Autumn-Heart* nails-on-a-blackboard time. They're in control of their accents and they're consistent and convincing. And the accent is very important for conveying the fact that Renata would feel out of place anywhere else, which is why she turns down Sam's offer to move to New York.

▶**Local color:** A rotary, convincing accents, Mike's Pastry. It's not hardcore local color, but it's enough to impart the local idiosyncrasies that make Renata feel at home.

The Perfect Storm

2000. Directed by Wolfgang Petersen. Written by Bill Wittliff. Based on Sebastian Junger's book. With George Clooney, Mark Wahlberg, Diane Lane, John C. Reilly, William Fichtner, Karen Allen, Cherry Jones, Bob Gunton, Michael Ironside, Allen Payne, John Hawkes, Dash Mihok and Josh Hopkins. Cinematography by John Seale.

LIKE *A CIVIL ACTION*, which had come out 18 months earlier, this is another big studio movie based on a real local incident and partially filmed in Greater Boston. But it's hard to think of a movie that takes a more different approach to its source material than *The Perfect Storm* does. Sebastian Junger's non-fiction book about the tragedy that took the Gloucester swordfish boat *Andrea Gail* and its six-man crew during October 1991's megastorm achieves tragedy through a very detached perspective. The author painstakingly looks at the storm and its victims from many angles, and he also refrains from speculating on the actual sinking of the boat, since there were no survivors from the *Andrea Gail* to relate exactly what happened.

But big-budget movies aren't in the detached-perspective and subtle-climax business. They're in the business of trying to grab audiences by the collective throat and figuratively pull them into the screen. So instead of understatement that accumulates into tragedy, the movie offers overkill: the lush orchestral music intrudes at nearly every turn, the script ludicrously gilds the proverbial lily by injecting a life-threatening situation every 10 minutes (I guess the storm of the century just isn't enough) and, of course, the movie goes ahead and speculates away by dramatizing the sinking of the *Andrea Gail*.

The Perfect Storm actually does a decent job of both developing its setting and characters and of staging the windswept, wave-tossed action at sea once the storm hits. But the whole movie is so at odds with itself that it only gets mixed marks. The subplots aren't very strong, since Diane Lane's off performance hurts the doted-upon romance between Christina (her character) and Mark Wahlberg's Bobby, while the conflict between two crew members (John C. Reilly and William Fichtner) comes off like a grand contrivance. Meanwhile, scenes devoted to the trio of characters in a sailboat also caught in the storm and rescue workers poorly fit in with the action about the Gloucester characters, despite being integral parts of the book. The friendship between Bobby and *Andrea Gail* captain Billy Tyne, one of George Clooney's more subdued movie characters, plays better, as Wahlberg and Clooney, already colleagues from *Three Kings*, are very comfortable with each other. (At one point, Mel Gibson and Nicolas Cage had been eyed for their roles.)

Shooting in Gloucester for three weeks (out of three months of filming), Petersen and crew used local churches like St. Anne's. They also built a replica of the Crow's Nest bar on the pier (the real thing is a longer walk from the dock), turning it into the social center of town. Of course, little of the fishing action was done locally; that was done in California—some of it asea and most of it in a soundstage tank with the boat and the actors superimposed in front of a special-effects "ocean." That's how the storm action blends the cast and the life-threatening waves. In its last third, *The Perfect Storm* essentially becomes a special-effects horror movie, with human characters fighting off a relentless force of nature. Despite the reverence the movie shows for Gloucester's seafaring tradition and the town's regular loss of life, it's a little disconcerting to see such tragedy poured into the Hollywood entertainment grinder. But it's not as if that doesn't happen at the multiplex nearly every Friday. As with *A Civil Action*, that just makes it hard at times to connect the movie to the real-life tragedy it depicts.

▶ **Locations:** Gloucester.

▶ **Accents:** Mark Wahlberg is here, so there's a certain level of authenticity to this movie about a *big stawm* right there. John Hawkes, later of TV's *Deadwood*, adds a good accent to his portrayal of the loneliest member of the crew, and his bantering with Rusty Schwimmer's Irene is the comic highlight of the movie. Like Hawkes, Schwimmer is a non-local who nails the accent. William Fichtner, Mary Elizabeth Mastrantonio (as the captain of the *Andrea Gail*'s sister ship) and Michael Ironside (as the boat's owner) also get by. But Diane Lane, a damn fine actress, spits out one of the worst Boston accents in movie history. That her character is so high-strung doesn't help the accent get over.

▶ **Local color:** After one character's apt reference to shopping at Ames, there's a clumsy mention of JC Penney. Not only are there no JC Penneys within 15 miles of Gloucester, but it's not a very Massachusetts store. I'm a lifelong resident; I've never even been *in* a JC Penney. Bradlee's would have worked much better.

▶ **Local celeb alert!:** In an odd bit of scripting and casting, instead of getting a real TV weatherman to play himself and read lines, we get Chris McDonald *playing* Channel 7's weatherman at the time, Todd Gross. Yet there appears to be nothing specific about Gross' experiences during the storm, and the movie's scenes are at a fictitious Channel 9, so it's all very puzzling. They could just as well have called the TV meteorologist Gern Blandsten.

The Proposition

1998. Directed by Lesli Linka Glatter. Written by Rick Ramage. With Kenneth Branagh, Madeleine Stowe, William Hurt, Neil Patrick Harris and Blythe Danner. Cinematography by Peter Sova.

DIRECTOR LESLI LINKA GLATTER'S 1930s drama was shot entirely within Massachusetts under the title *Shakespeare's Sister,* and its dialogue periodically trots out Virginia Woolf's reference to the Bard's non-existent sibling. Had Shakespeare had a sister, Woolf surmised, she would have been less privileged than her brother and suffered in his shadow. But whenever that sentiment is conveyed here, it clouds an already elaborate plot involving sex, money, family and religion.

By ditching the film's working title, it's as if the moviemakers realized its central metaphor doesn't come across very well. But that's *The Proposition.* It has a burnished look fitting its old-time setting and it uses locations such as Ipswich's Crane Estate and Newbury Street's Emmanuel Church well. But it just sits there.

Part of the problem is that everyone acts as if they're making great art, while the story of sin and salvation is as trashy as a mini-series like *The Thorn Birds.* It's told in flashback by Father Michael McKinnon (Kenneth Branagh), a Catholic priest who relates his experiences with powerful banker Arthur Barrett (William Hurt) and Barrett's novelist wife Eleanor (Madeleine Stowe). The 1930s equivalent of a power couple, the Barretts have wealth and influence, but no male heir, since Arthur is sterile.

An offer is made to a Harvard grad (Neil Patrick Harris) applying for a job at Barrett's firm—to impregnate Eleanor for a large sum of money and a vow of secrecy. But the boyish Ivy Leaguer falls for Eleanor and won't go quietly into the night. She soon finds his dead body, collapses and loses the child. And that's only the half of it. There's still much more about the English priest's kinship to Arthur, the murder and Eleanor getting pregnant a second time—thanks to the clergyman.

Now maybe you see how a delicate metaphor about Shakespeare's sister might get lost in *this* shuffle, with Eleanor fretting about how, whomever she gets pregnant with, her child will always "belong" to her husband. What wouldn't get lost? The characters certainly do. I don't know if Rick Ramage's script was written with Boston in mind or not, but it's particularly odd that a presumably old-money, power-broking WASP like Barrett is Catholic. But, of course, the story does that so it can have Father McKinnon break his vow of celibacy. The priest is a very fuzzy character, the son of a rich man who entered the priesthood because, as he says, "my father couldn't buy the company." But *The Proposition* devotes *no* time to developing any actual interest in religion in the guy. He's the head of the church's charity work, he's never shown preaching and he has about as much willpower as a 14-year-old when it comes to getting hot and bothered by Eleanor. She remains the most interesting character, with Stowe embodying her allure, idealism and insecurities.

While Emmanuel Church is the front and interior of the Catholic church here, the movie's cathedral backs into Copp's Hill Burying Ground in the North End. The outside of the soup kitchen the church runs also appears to be in the same neighborhood. The Barretts' mansion is the Great House at Ipswich's Crane Estate, with Paxton's Moore State Park also used for some of its grounds. Barrett's swankily-appointed office is Boston University's Castle on Bay State Road.

By the time the movie's title changed to *The Proposition*, it was a real non-event. Polygram Films was financially struggling at the time (and rightly devoted more marketing money to *The Big Lebowski*), barely releasing the movie in theaters. In the time since, a better movie with the same title has emerged (the Australian western), while this *Proposition* has yet to be released on DVD.

▶**Locations:** North End, Back Bay, Boston; Ipswich; Paxton.

▶**Accents:** Not on your life. This is not a tale of workingmen and kindly parish priests.

▶**Local color:** With most any period piece set as far back as *The Proposition*, color will be minimal, since only the most lavish productions can afford to recreate the past for large public scenes. That's true here. But the Boston locations conjure the intersection of power, money and religion very well. It's an intersection that continues to exist, here and elsewhere.

Ruby

1971. Directed by Dick Bartlett. Written by Ray Loring and Dick Bartlett. With Ruth Hurd, George Bartlett, Joanie Andrews, Philip Webben, Susan Peters and Danny Kosow. Cinematography by Dick Bartlett.

THE FILM-SCHOOL GENERATION that stormed Hollywood's gates during the 1970s was responsible for one of the earliest homegrown fiction features in Greater Boston. Long before he won an Emmy for editing one of the many PBS science documentaries on which he's worked, Dick Bartlett had been runner-up to George Lucas in a national student short film contest. He then directed and co-wrote this deadpan comedy feature filmed in the Georgetown area, cast with non-professionals and only loosely scripted. His co-producer, co-writer and B.U. classmate, Ray Loring, also became a regular *Nova* contributor years later, writing musical scores, a function he also fulfills here.

Like most any DIY film made before the 1980s, *Ruby* shows little inclination to be like a Hollywood film. Although Hollywood might occasionally release an off-kilter movie—and *Ruby* could easily fit in a double feature with *the* alternative hit from its time, *Harold and Maude*—the movie studios weren't exactly churning out unpredictable stories named for crabby fifty-something school-bus drivers. That's Ruby (Ruth Hurd), who's fed up with her husband Clifford (Philip Webben), who sells homemade fudge door-to-door from his wheelchair, and fed up with her bus, which keeps breaking down.

The first half of the movie focuses on her, as she goes out looking for fun one night (cruising in the bus, of course) and finds it in the form of toupee-wearing lounge singer Earl Tibbitts (Danny Kosow). Earl is consistent—he has a tacky toupee and a tacky act—but Ruby connects with him and suddenly finds a reason to dress up and buy a wig of her own to cover her grey hair (TV-addicted Clifford barely notices her nights out).

The title character's escape from drudgery shares the screen with generation-gap comedy as *Ruby* progresses. This involves Ruby's brother George (George Bartlett, the director's dad), his wife Joan (Joanie Andrews) and their 18-year-old daughter Vivian (Susan Peters). After the teen starts seeing a horseback-riding beau (Jay Rubero), her parents outfit her with a jerry-built chastity belt so she won't go bad like her older sister. "We gave them everything—the best of meats, the choicest cuts of beef," the mother laments in one of the movie's funniest lines.

> When we showed the movie at Yale, a woman got up and said I was taking advantage of these people and making fun of them. But I love these people. They're my people.
> –Dick Bartlett

The absurdity of bad wigs and chastity belts balances Bartlett's eye for everyday detail. He can turn ordinary events, like the scene in which Vivian's parents and another couple eat steamers and drink beer, into daffy little moments (eating is apparently a staple of Bartlett's short films, too). There's the sense that most of the middle-aged adults here are as self-involved as any child would be, what with Clifford's rampant fudge-making and TV-watching, lounge lizard Earl Tibbitts' girl-in-every-port life and, especially, a scene in which George plays with his new lawn tractor and Joan entertains a cosmetics saleswoman while their daughter, unbeknownst to them, flees her locked bedroom.

The absurdity makes *Ruby* a little like a milder version of John (*Pink Flamingos*) Waters' early movies. Aside from the generation-gap laughs, Bartlett doesn't really mock his characters, though. In her quest to find meaningful relationships, Ruby is a melancholy heroine, and she brings a sad shading to some of the action. *Ruby* is only mildly successful, meandering along as the title character's old bus might, but it creates its own little world—a lot like ours, but sometimes funnier and a little more grotesque (not surprisingly, Bartlett cites Fellini as an influence). A July 1975 *Real Paper* feature implies the movie attracted more attention in Europe than it did in the U.S., though it did play briefly at the Orson Welles Cinema in Cambridge and at New York's Whitney Museum, exposure that got Bartlett a New York agent. Unfortunately, though, she was not able to sell Hollywood on his script about a small-town New England police chief, with Bartlett attached to direct. At one point, Robert Altman wanted to buy it to direct himself, but Bartlett said no. The film never got made.

▶**Locations:** Georgetown.

▶**Accents:** The wonderful accents of the middle-aged cast of *Ruby* are the sort you just don't hear much anymore. There's something generational going on here, I think. Those accents have a raspiness gained perhaps from a life of smoking cigarettes, yet it's different from the Boston accents of today's smokers; it's the same sort of accent you find in *Titicut Follies*, made five years before and also populated with the middle-aged (just listen to the way the bus drivers' boss says "bee-ah joint" or Ruby's brother George talking about his "*gaw*-dam *daugh*tahs"). Maybe unfiltered cigarettes give you such an accent.

▶**Local color:** Beyond those accents and the general New England crustiness on display, there's not a whole lot beyond some shots along Route 97. But the accents and the crustiness are both very thick and very important to the story.

School Ties

1992. Directed by Robert Mandel. Written by Dick Wolf and Darryl Ponicsan. With Brendan Fraser, Matt Damon, Randall Batinkoff, Chris O'Donnell, Amy Locane and Ben Affleck. Cinematography by Freddie Francis.

BEFORE *GOOD WILL HUNTING*, Cambridge buddies Matt Damon and Ben Affleck appeared together in this effective, if rather toothless, anti-prejudice message movie starring Brendan Fraser. Shot in a variety of Massachusetts locations (save for the Pennsylvania mining country of the prologue), director Robert Mandel's drama casts Fraser as a star Jewish quarterback at an exclusive WASP prep school who hides his religion from his schoolmates, only to incur their anti-Semitism when the truth comes out.

School Ties pulls its punches by safely setting its story in 1954, lifting some burden of responsibility from today's viewers, and by making Fraser's David Greene such a perfect character. David comes to the prep school—with action shot at Concord's Middlesex School, Southborough's Saint Mark's School and Worcester Academy—from working-class coal-mining country, and the movie opens with him getting into a scrape back home with an anti-Semitic greaser. Because of the threat David's hot temper poses to success at the school and to his Ivy League future, his father advises him to tell people only as much about himself as he must. Upon arrival in Massachusetts, his coach (Kevin Tighe) advises him similarly.

David keeps things on a "don't ask, don't tell" basis with his teammates, and he ignores the casual anti-Semitism he hears around the school. That situation, of course, all changes when the truth eventually slips out, even though David has helped the school beat their big football rival. Casual anti-Semitism now turns pointed, especially by Damon's character, Dillon, from whom David has taken the quarterback spot and the affection of dreamy Sally (Amy Locane). The *Protestant Like Me* tale ultimately turns into a sort of *Twelve Angry Boys* when a teacher discovers someone has cheated on a final exam and, because of the school's internal policing policy, the class must decide whether David or Dillon did the deed.

The climactic dilemma becomes long-winded and a little self-important, but that's a fair enough trade-off for the complexities *School Ties* brings to its story. There are no winners, ultimately, and the movie succeeds as an indictment of the old-boy networks that groom the future power-mongers of the world (it actually makes a nice companion piece to a more substantial and unjustly overlooked Damon picture to come years later, *The Good Shepherd*).

It might be hard to believe now, but when this came out in 1992, there was little local publicity push devoted to Damon and Affleck. There was more general hype about *School Ties* using an assortment of area locations (it's great to see Skip's Blue Moon Diner in Gardner in a movie). Brookline's Coolidge Corner Moviehouse even assembled a retrospective of veteran cinematographer Freddie Francis' movies, with the English film icon appearing there in late 1991 while in the area shooting the movie.

But it's indicative of how new to the scene Damon and Affleck were that the former gets much lower billing in the opening titles than he should (to show how important his character is, he's listed second in the cast when the end credits roll). Affleck has a much smaller role and doesn't get much dialogue until the climax. Fraser, who'd made a good impression in the otherwise bad *Encino Man*, and Boston College's Chris O'Donnell, who made this just before *Scent of a Woman*, were on a fast track much more than Damon and Affleck were. Interestingly, both friends ending up in the movie was coincidental—Damon, then at Harvard, got cast through East Coast auditions, while Affleck, then going to Occidental College, auditioned on the West Coast. The boys from Cambridge, Damon especially, showed that they fit in next to guys being groomed to be stars. Of course, their time would come.

▶ **Locations:** Acton; Concord; Southborough; Worcester; Gardner; Lowell; Andover.

▶ **Accents:** This is *prep* school, not public school.

▶ **Local color:** Little in the conventional sense. But prep schools are a kind of hidden local color. They're all over the place, and *School Ties* shot at several, so I guess that has to count for local flavor.

▶ **Aftermath:** The bond Cole Hauser forged with Matt Damon and Ben Affleck on the *School Ties* set is the reason he was later cast in *Good Will Hunting*, in addition to his talent. Hauser, who plays academically challenged Connors, also appeared with Affleck again in *Dazed and Confused*, shortly after *School Ties*.

Session 9

2001. Directed by Brad Anderson. Written by Brad Anderson and Stephen Gevedon. With David Caruso, Peter Mullan, Josh Lucas, Stephen Gevedon, Brandon Sexton III and Paul Guilfoyle. Cinematography by Uta Briesewitz.

NEXT STOP WONDERLAND WRITER-director Brad Anderson made this very creepy American Gothic chiller after parting ways with Miramax Films, the distributor of his breakthrough romantic comedy, for whom he was to have written and directed a remake of the French comedy-drama *When the Cat's Away* (he was also slated for a remake of producer Val Lewton's 1940s suspense classic *The Seventh Victim* for reborn RKO). *Session 9* is not only a cool, *Shining*-style story of madness festering in a confined setting, it's also an outstanding updating of the sort of low-budget, unseen-menace picture mastered by Lewton (who also made the original *Cat People*).

The setting that is the undeniable star of *Session 9* is the long-closed (and now condo-converted) Danvers State Hospital. Since the Massachusetts Film Office had long given visiting film productions free office space in the former "lunatics asylum," which closed in 1982, perhaps it was inevitable the photogenic, bat-shaped Victorian complex would become the setting of its own movie. Anderson gets the most out of the ornate but crumbling complex's dread-filled atmosphere.

It is there that the movie's five main characters, the men of Hazmat Elimination Co., are hired to remove asbestos, so the building can be turned into municipal offices. The Scottish-immigrant boss (Peter Mullan) has promised the town they can get the big job done in a week; the crew chief (David Caruso) has a chip on his shoulder; the jerk of the bunch (Josh Lucas) has stolen the chief's girlfriend and won't let him forget it; the smartest (co-writer Stephen Gevedon) is more interested in sifting through old patient files than working; and the new guy (Brandon Sexton III), the boss' teen nephew, is clueless.

> Danvers State Hospital was the entire reason to do *Session 9*. Steve, the co-writer, and I patterned the script and many scenes based on the location.
> –Brad Anderson

Take these guys' egos and personality clashes, add in spooky recordings of therapy sessions involving a woman with multiple personalities and drizzle lingering spirits of psychotic patients over the situation, and you've got yourself a movie. From the time Mullan's and Caruso's characters do a walkthrough of the decrepit main building before making a bid on the job, things start to get weird for them and their co-workers.

In one thread of intrigue, an incident between the boss and his wife repeatedly replays in recurring flashbacks that take on more and more meaning each time. In another, the behavior of the crew chief seems more and more mysterious: Is he plotting against the guy who stole his girlfriend? Is he selling drugs on the side?

Bolstered by the strong, no-nonsense performances of Mullan and Caruso, the story generates sufficient non-horror drama in its early going to hook you, with the location a backdrop no production designer could recreate and cinematographer Uta Briesewitz's digital-video images giving the action an intimacy that, in the best sense, recalls *The Blair Witch Project*. It's like a home movie gone awry.

Eventually, the unseen horror kicks in, and *Session 9* brings a refreshingly ungimmicky, character-based treatment to the genre that, at the time of its theatrical release, was dominated by groups of teens and quick, empty scares. Right down to its disturbing, ambiguous ending, this is a nifty little creepshow.

▶**Locations:** Danvers.

▶**Accents:** Not really a factor here, although Southie native Paul Guilfoyle revives his lapsed Boston accent as the town official who hires the crew.

▶**Local color:** The old asylum could be anywhere, but then again it's not. Is it just coincidence that Bridgewater State Hospital of *Titicut Follies* and Danvers State Hospital of *Session 9* tap into the cruel intolerance of local mental health outposts? Or is there something about our area that gave birth to such hellholes?

Sherman's March

1985. Directed by Ross McElwee. Cinematography by Ross McElwee.

BY MOST OF THE usual criteria, Ross McElwee's breakthrough documentary doesn't qualify as a Boston movie. Little of *Sherman's March* takes place here and its laconic mood is certainly truer to the moviemaker's birthplace, North Carolina, where much of it unfurls, than to his adopted home of Boston.

Yet the movie is a significant touchstone in Boston documentary filmmaking, carrying on the tradition of Ed Pincus' earlier *Diaries (1971-1976)* and similarly challenging fellow and future filmmakers to look within their own lives for inspiration. Just check out the names in the end credits: Richard Leacock, the documentary innovator who ran M.I.T.'s film program (with Pincus) and taught McElwee, does the opening narration; Alyson Denny and Kate Davis (*Girltalk*) are among the editors; and there are acknowledgements in the credits of, among others, Cambridge documentarians Robb Moss (*The Tourist*) and the husband-and-wife team of Steve Ascher and Jeanne Jordan (*Troublesome Creek: A Midwestern*).

McElwee began his movie—subtitled *A Meditation on the Possibility of Love in the South During an Era of Nuclear Weapons Proliferation*—with the intention of making a documentary on the lingering effects of General William T. Sherman's destructive Civil War offensive. But the Charlotte native was so devastated by a breakup that he lost most of his interest in that idea. Instead, he filmed his *own* Southern journey, and what might have seemed self-indulgent is instead distinctive. It's equal parts "direct cinema" documentary, film essay, visual memoir, romantic comedy and road movie.

With his now-trademark lightweight camera perched on his shoulder, then-single McElwee crosses a minefield of women once he arrives down South and, for lack of better motivation, retraces some of Sherman's path whenever the search for love dead-ends. He emerges as a romantic anti-hero, prevented by circumstance from attaining the women he desires and unimpressed by those who become most available to him. The desired include aspiring actress Pat and old friend Karen, each tangled in a troubled relationship McElwee wishes they'd let go of (the latter with a guy who collects life-sized plastic animals). Meanwhile, some of the women he's fixed up with (one by his amusingly flibbertigibbet former teacher Charleen Swansea, a fixture in his films) are poor fits for McElwee. These would-be love connections are often amusing in their emotional snafus, but just as often they're melancholy.

> I didn't get the idea of addressing the camera until I had been filming for a while. Later, I realized if I didn't do something like that, the film probably wouldn't cohere. It needed a persona.
> –Ross McElwee

The result is a pleasantly meandering movie full of detours, irony and bittersweet humor (I love the pursuit of Burt Reynolds, whom Pat pursues professionally and with whom McElwee unexpectedly, and unsuccessfully, crosses paths). Some of the Cold War rhetoric—like the group of gun-toting survivalists who talk of the threat of "commies"—dates the action a tad, as do the big 1980s eyeglasses on display, but only a surprisingly small fraction of the movie shows its age. Otherwise, it's as emotionally fresh as ever. As it did in 1985, *Sherman's March* comes off like a thoughtful, life-sized alternative to the contrivances of Hollywood "relationship movies."

Sherman's March became a textbook example of a grassroots alternative hit, originally opening at the Institute of Contemporary Art Cinema, moving over to commercial Copley Place Cinema and then getting national distribution and replicating its Boston success. By finding an audience, eventually grabbing the attention of *People* magazine and providing the foundation upon which Harvard film professor McElwee could subsequently build a niche career (with such follow-ups as *Time Indefinite* and *Six O'Clock News*), *Sherman's March* isn't just a significant independent movie. It's also a role model for Boston moviemakers.

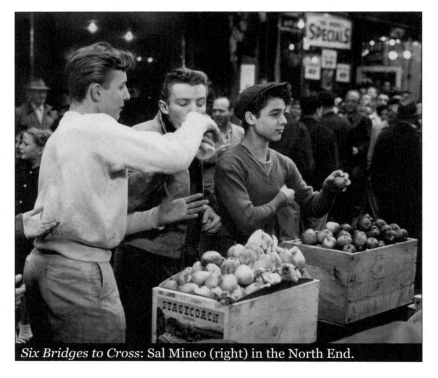

Six Bridges to Cross: Sal Mineo (right) in the North End.

Six Bridges to Cross

1955. Directed by Joseph Pevney. Written by Sydney Boehm. Based on Joseph F. Dinneen's magazine article, *They Stole $2,500,000—And Got Away With It*. With Tony Curtis, George Nader, Julie Adams, Jay C. Flippen and Sal Mineo. Cinematography by William Daniels.

IN 1978, THE BRINK'S robbery of 1950 became the basis for William Friedkin's Boston-shot comedy, *The Brink's Job*. But it had already been the subject of this 1955 drama. Of course, at that time no one had been arrested for the robbery. That wouldn't happen until early 1956. Legend has it many cops and North Enders long knew who did it, but there wasn't yet sufficient evidence for anyone to be arrested. The fact that technically innocent men couldn't be accused in print provided a small obstacle for *Globe* reporter Joseph Dinneen. He fictionalized the events and the character of Tony Pino (who was eventually convicted of the crime and is the protagonist of *The Brink's Job*) in a *Collier's* article that became the source material for *Six Bridges to Cross* (scripted by *Mystery Street*'s Sydney Boehm). Dinneen later expanded the article into the 1954 novel *Anatomy of a Crime*.

Aside from the armored car heist that it eventually works towards, *Six Bridges* has little to do with real events. Instead, it's a rather clumsy movie that tries to balance light drama, suspense, a crime-doesn't-pay ending and a social conscience (somehow, there's an improbable Sammy Davis, Jr. theme song to start the show, too). The social conscience comes through in the first half-hour, in which Sal Mineo (in his movie debut) plays Jerry Florea, a North End street urchin who's first seen leading a group of kids in swiping fruit from Haymarket vendors. During a nighttime robbery of a mom-and-pop store, he's shot and wounded by beat cop Ed Gallagher (George Nader) who, regretful for his actions, takes an interest in the kid, who in return feeds the cop tips about crimes in other neighborhoods.

With Curtis taking over the role as an older teen, *Six Bridges* follows the crook and the cop over the years. The basic pattern is that Gallagher tries to help Jerry reform, but then Jerry backslides, again and again. Coincidentally, Jerry's crimes get more serious and Gallagher climbs in the police ranks. It's a little hard to believe Gallagher wouldn't get totally fed up with Jerry, but that's why handsome Curtis, with his winning smile, is here. Jerry's periodic steps towards decency always win Gallagher and his wife (Julie Adams) back to his side.

One of the ways the movie tries to keep Jerry likable is by not delving too deeply into his crimes. Still, Jerry never turns into a Runyonesque rogue like the characters in *The Brink's Job*. The actual armored car robbery (of a company *not* named Brink's) is a small part of the story, and *Six Bridges* culminates in a sequence in which the guilty do not get away with the money or their freedom—contradicting the title of Dinneen's magazine article.

The movie may not mix its moods well, but it at least offers glimpses of a pre-urban renewal Boston, in which the Custom House Tower and the McCormack Post Office and Courthouse dominate the skyline. Although there are many exteriors seen, especially in the early North End action, my guess is that few interiors were shot locally. So although we see Charles Street Jail, Concord's Massachusetts Reformatory and the old Boston Police Department HQ on Berkeley Street, I'd be surprised if anything was shot inside of them. It's also very hard to tell if the scene taking place in a neighborhood overlooking Suffolk Downs is shot where it's set (I know it was over 50 years ago, but it looks so small-town). Many office scenes obviously filmed in a studio, with photos and murals as outside backdrops (one in an immigration office even has mountains in the background). Similarly, the neighborhood where the movie climaxes is clearly a studio backlot, as it has unusually high curbstones often seen there, but not in a city like Boston.

▶**Locations:** North End, Back Bay, Boston; Concord.

▶**Accents:** Sal Mineo and Tony "Yawnda lies da castle of my fodda" Curtis share the same Bronx accent. So Jerry at least sounds *consistently* wrong. There's not much accent to hear in this one, aside from a neighbor of the Gallaghers saying "Good mahnin'" and the police dispatcher. He is reportedly Edward R. Skrickus, the real dispatcher the night of the robbery.

▶**Local color:** The shots of the old city are cool, but any movie in which the narrator (Jay C. Flippen's police supervisor) pronounces Worcester as if it rhymes with rooster can't rate that highly. And what's the deal with the six bridges that we're led to believe were criminals' *only* routes out of the city? The movie never gets very specific about its title "characters," which is puzzling. Such possible exits as the North Washington Street Bridge, Charles River Dam Bridge, Mass. Ave. Bridge (Harvard Bridge), Anderson Bridge (between Allston and Harvard Square), Longfellow Bridge, B.U. Bridge and the Tobin aren't mentioned by name at all, and you never get a sense of a city in lockdown mode because of the robbery. Maybe the whole concept is just Hollywood hooey. Hey, couldn't the criminals just escape by boat from any one of 1,000 places?

A Small Circle of Friends

1980. Directed by Rob Cohen. Written by Ezra Sacks. With Brad Davis, Karen Allen, Jameson Parker and Shelley Long. Cinematography by Michael Butler.

HAS ANY MOVIE GOTTEN the political passion of the 1960s counterculture right, both as pop history and as entertainment? Not really, and Rob Cohen's 1980 drama is an ambitious and admirable attempt to do so that doesn't quite succeed. I'll give *A Small Circle of Friends* credit for one big thing. Although it starts with a reunion of college pals, as the later hit *The Big Chill* would, *A Small Circle* has the nerve to set most of its action between 1967 and 1971.

The extended flashbacks begin after ex-lovers Nick (Jameson Parker) and Jessica (Karen Allen) bump into each other in the present-day opening. In a rare bit of urban geographical authenticity, he sees her coming out of the old Ritz (now The Taj) as he bikes out of the Public Garden (authenticity quickly takes a back seat to visuals, though; when he chases after the cab she gets into, the shot is on Charles Street, not Newbury, where she enters the cab).

Cut to 1967, when Nick, Jessica and their mercurial friend Leo (Brad Davis) are all Harvard freshmen. As it seeks to transpose the love triangle of François Truffaut's French New Wave classic *Jules and Jim* to the U.S. counterculture, the movie also charts the political metamorphosis of them and their classmates over their four undergraduate years. The fact that two friends could both fall for a character played by Allen is convincing enough (the eternally pretty actress made this between *Animal House* and *Raiders of the Lost Ark*). But the characters are the real stumbling block to the movie's success. Maybe it's the fact that Allen and Davis were in their late 20s and Parker in his early 30s. In no way do they seem like 18-21-year-olds. Maybe it's the ever-changing hairstyles (hair seems to especially dominate Parker's Nick). I just never got into these people.

But *A Small Circle* does better with the historical and political. Even if it does sometimes come off like a Cliff Notes version of the late 1960s, the transformations the students undergo—the most extreme being Haddox (John Friedrich), who goes from Texas rube to radical rabble-rouser—is indicative of the journey many baby boomers took. Director Cohen attended Harvard during the same period in which his movie is set, and Ezra Sacks' script stirred up old campus wounds there. After faculty members protested the huge anti-war mural Jessica hangs from Memorial Hall, Harvard ejected the production after just one week. Cohen and his crew then scrambled to find stand-ins for Harvard, shooting its big anti-war protest at Bridgewater State and using Tufts and Wellesley, too (the dorm interior is a studio set, while many other interiors are in Los Angeles). *Small Circle* is still the last film granted extensive access to the Harvard campus, though, more recently, Denzel Washington's *The Great Debaters* shot on-campus at Sanders Theater.

Despite the change in locations imposed upon it, *Small Circle* includes a taste of the Boston-Cambridge experience. Leo, Jessica and Nick's house is in Somerville, the real Boston military induction center

> I had a small role, so I had a lot of time to wander around. The luck of Boston, for me, is that I did my first movie here, then came back when we were doing reshoots for *Night Shift* in New York. I had agreed to do *Cheers*, and I thought, 'I'll be a good actress and prepare for my role and make a stop in Boston.' It really paid off.
> –Shelley Long

was used (it looks to be in South Boston) and the present-day action includes the Common as well as the Public Garden. Leo and Jessica go see *The Graduate* at the Orson Welles Cinema, which actually hadn't opened at the time this scene occurs in the film (the Arthur Penn Film

Festival teased on the marquee is a nod to Penn, who served as back-up director for first-timer Cohen, a stipulation of the latter's contract with United Artists). Similarly, there's action taking place at John Hancock Tower, which also wasn't around in 1967.

▶**Locations:** Cambridge; South Boston, Back Bay, Beacon Hill, Boston; Somerville; Worcester; Bridgewater; Medford; Wellesley.

▶**Accents:** Most of the characters aren't from the area, so there's no need for accents. In a fitting change that enhances Leo's vulnerability in the "outer world" beyond Harvard, there are accents from the locals playing bit parts at the military induction center, including Wilmington's Big Joe La Creta, a sometime wrestler, sometime actor, sometime sandwich maker.

▶**Local color:** The movie is more concerned with *temporal* color than local color. That's why the inclusion of the Orson Welles Cinema before it was open works, because the moviehouse was born out of counterculture idealism of the flashback's time range. You also get a taste of the back-to-nature movement of the day, in the farmhouses in which the three lovers weekend and the extreme radicals hole up (the latter was in Worcester, and was really blown up by the production).

Southie

1998. Directed by John Shea. Written by James Cummings, Dave McLaughlin and John Shea. With Donnie Wahlberg, Anne Meara, Rose McGowan, James Cummings, Lawrence Tierney and John Shea. Cinematography by Allen Baker.

SHOT ON LOCATION BEFORE *Good Will Hunting* and *Monument Ave.* took to the streets of Boston's Irish-American neighborhoods—but released later—*Southie* ultimately couldn't compete with its better-written competition.

The famous old saying says you can't go back home again—but in this drama, who'd want to? Springfield-born actor turned director John Shea's film tells of Danny Quinn (Donnie Wahlberg), a South Boston native who left town when he realized his crime-ridden surroundings were making him, as he says, "an animal." When he returns home for a friend's wedding, he decides to stick around to help his ailing mom (Anne Meara) deal with his rowdy brothers (Steve Koslowski, Robert Wahlberg) and alcoholic little sister (Rose McGowan).

But almost as soon as he steps off the Amtrak from New York, the same problems he fled swallow him up. His brothers, like so many other locals, are in debt to bookies. His widowed mother, stressed-out from her kids' self-destruction, has a bad heart, no insurance and a $25,000 hospital bill. His sister is on a full-time bender. His old friends Whitey (Will Arnett, later of TV's *Arrested Development*) and Will (Josh Marchette of *Floating*) want him to invest in their scheme to open an after-hours gambling club. And everyone—from the characters played by Boston comedy perennials Lenny Clarke and Steve Sweeney to the mob boss played by tough-guy icon Lawrence Tierney—has a chip on his shoulder the size of a Zamboni.

Desperate situations call for desperate measures, but not the stupidity with which Danny behaves. What does he do? He piles on in a fight his brothers are in at the wedding, pissing off the guy at the laborers' union who was going to give him work. Frozen out of union work, he then puts all his money in his buddies' dubious club venture. It turns out that his friends didn't tell him they're involved with a local gangster's

> I don't think (the extras at the wedding) realized how tedious moviemaking is. The only reason a lot of people showed up is because half of them were taught by nuns. They're *real* obedient.
> –Anne Meara

son (co-writer James Cummings), the hothead on whom Danny pulled a gun before he left town three years earlier.

Danny's entanglements thicken, but it's hard to feel much sympathy, because he really should know better. He should have enough perspective on his native neighborhood to avoid his troubles. This sort of story, in which a young man has hopes that stretch beyond his violent surroundings, can work—and work well, in the cases of *Mean Streets* and *Monument Ave.*—when the hero is still trying to figure out how to escape his confining neighborhood. But when that character, like Danny, has already freed himself and then backslides, it's very hard to make it work. Did Danny suddenly forget that Amtrak takes passengers back to New York?

Southie's wholesale use of Boston locations—many more than *Good Will Hunting*—offers a good sense of the characters' tightly knit world. South Boston Candlepin Bowling, The Quencher Tavern, The L St. Gym, St. Augustine's Cemetery and South Boston Yacht Club, where the wedding occurs, are just some of the places they go.

▶ **Locations:** South Boston, South End, Jamaica Plain, South Station, Boston.

▶ **Accents:** The cast includes many locals, from Donnie Wahlberg and James Cummings to Josh Marchette and Steve Sweeney. Anne Meara and Rose McGowan do an especially good job for non-locals.

▶ **Local color:** Candlepins! 'Nuff said.

Squeeze

1997. Written and directed by Robert Patton-Spruill. Based on stories by Emmett Folgert. With Tyrone Burton, Eddie Cutanda, Phuong Duong, Geoffrey Rhue and Beresford Bennett. Cinematography by Richard Moos.

WRITER-DIRECTOR ROBERT PATTON-Spruill's homegrown movie has aged well. When it came out in the late 1990s, the Dorchester-set drama seemed to me like an overmatched entry in the 1990s 'hood-films genre. Made by an inexperienced moviemaker with an inexperienced cast, it lacked the oomph of such better-marketed, similar movies as *Juice, Fresh* and *Boyz N The Hood*, all of which had preceded it. A rather chest-thumping Patton-Spruill interview in *The Boston Phoenix* and the fact that Miramax Films bought *Squeeze* for national distribution—generating a good deal of local hype for it—and then opened it in only three cities (Boston among them) added a sour taste to the movie's reputation.

All these years later, it's easier to appreciate *Squeeze* for the ways in which it's different from the other 'hood films than to be unimpressed by the ways in which it's similar. Stories about young men trapped by their neighborhoods and tempted by lives of crime are hardly the province of just that mini-genre; they have been made at least since the days of Jimmy Cagney's searing 1930s Warner Bros. pictures.

So if the tale of three 14-year-old Dorchester pals—Ty (Tyrone Burton), Hector (Eddie Cutanda) and Bao (Phuong Duong)—torn between the temptation of crime and the more sober rewards of the local youth center is not the most original—so be it. Neither are many of those Cagney movies. Most of the appeal in *Squeeze* lays in its down-to-earth sensibility. Inspired by Jan Egleson turning Group School students' anecdotes into *Billy in the Lowlands* and *The Dark End of the Street* 15 years earlier, *Squeeze* sprang from Patton-Spruill's work at the Dorchester Youth Collaborative and grew out of the stories told to him by DYC's Emmett Folgert.

> I made a movie heavily influenced by François Truffaut's *The 400 Blows* and Jan Egleson's Boston movies. It was sort of like history repeating itself.
> –Robert Patton-Spruill

So, in keeping with those earthy films, Burton—whose Ty gets the most focus—might be charismatic, but he's not slick. In some ways, he's the conscience of the movie, yet he's no angel. Ty and his buddies' lives change when an SUV full of older gang-bangers threatens the trio as they're pumping gas at a self-serve in exchange for tips. Scared

Squeeze: Phuong Duong, Eddie Cutanda and Tyrone Burton in Mattapan.

away from the gas station and now without a source of spending money, they gravitate to two diametrically opposed protectors: J.J. (Geoffrey Rhue), the calming, sensible big brother figure from the youth center, and Derick (Beresford Bennett), a drug dealer friend of Hector's incarcerated brother, who offers protection at the end of a gun, so long as the buddies deal on the corner for him.

And although *Squeeze* is indeed about survival on mean streets, it's not all fury. There's a yin to its yang, particularly in Bruce Flowers' score. With its moody cello and jazzy bass lines, the music is a subdued counterpart to the more boisterous hip-hop songs that also fuel the action. Some of that action is still clunky. Derick's "lair" feels like something out of a cheesier movie or music video and sometimes the staging is awkward, especially during one adult's suicide attempt. That's one of the scenes in which Patton-Spruill distorts visuals seen from Ty's perspective, and it doesn't really come across with the intended intimacy or emotional power.

Squeeze does, however, use its locations well, and its cinematography is much crisper than that of most low-budget movies. Many of the locations are on Dorchester Avenue (including the gas station), Dudley Street in Roxbury (the barber shop and the little park where Hector visits J.J. towards the end) and in Mattapan (the old Boston State Hospital grounds and the Boston Specialty and Rehabilitation Hospital).

▶**Locations:** Dorchester, Roxbury, Mattapan, Boston.

▶**Accents:** No one would know this is Boston from the accents; but everyone talks in his or her natural voice and most are from Boston, so no complaints here.

▶**Local color:** Inner-city murals are definitely the motif of the movie, from the Dudley Square Neighborhood Initiative mural to one for Puerto Rican Power and, in the distance in two scenes, the Corita Kent-designed oil tank between Dorchester Bay and Route 93. These splashes of color, history and pride are symbols of hope in the world of Ty, Hector and Bao.

Starting Over

1979. Directed by Alan J. Pakula. Written by James L. Brooks. Based on Dan Wakefield's novel. With Burt Reynolds, Jill Clayburgh, Candice Bergen, Charles Durning and Frances Sternhagen. Cinematography by Sven Nykvist.

THERE'S LITTLE REASON WHY director Alan J. Pakula's amiable Burt Reynolds comedy *had* to be shot in Boston. But novelist Dan Wakefield, on whose book the movie is based, was a Boston resident at the time and, perhaps because his work was also the source for the late-1970s Boston-set TV series *James at 15*, the city lucked out in that someone thought it best to keep *Starting Over* here.

A few years after he filmed *Fuzz* in Boston, when he was one of the movies' biggest masculine icons, Reynolds sheds the machismo cool (and the trademark moustache) of his more physical movies. He's very endearing as Phil Potter, a magazine writer adjusting to life in the movie's post-women's-lib era. His wife (Candice Bergen), an aspiring singer-songwriter whose anthemic, female-empowerment song becomes a hit, splits up with him, so he moves from New York to Boston, where new love interest Marilyn (Jill Clayburgh) is a different sort of empowered female. She's an unattached woman who's gotten comfortable with the idea that no man is going to come along and change her life. Then Phil shows up.

Phil is an uncharacteristically insecure Reynolds character. He's unnerved by his split with his wife, for whom he still has feelings, and flustered by Marilyn, who amusingly mistakes him for an attacker when they first meet (after both get off the #57 bus). She then refuses to go out with him for three months. Phil is trying hard to be respectful of these women's wishes, and there are even scenes in *Starting Over* where his character declines to have sex. The slow pan around the room at the divorced men's support group Phil joins says it all: like the other men, Phil is simply stunned by the end of his marriage and the upheaval of the society he thought he knew.

James L. Brooks' screenplay, though only occasionally laugh-out-loud funny, yields smiles from this battle of the sexes, circa 1979, when many of the old rules had been discarded and the new rules were still unclear. (One of Brooks' big gags suffers from poor direction by Pakula, though. When Phil's ex-wife travels to Boston unannounced in hopes of seducing him, she arrives at his apartment on the same day Marilyn is moving in, part of the joke being the open blouse that conspicuously announces why she wants to see Phil. But continuity is non-existent in the sequence, as her blouse is open only about a quarter of the time, killing the references to her revealing clothes.)

Clayburgh and Reynolds appeared together previously in *Semi-Tough*, but that was before *An Unmarried Woman* made her a huge star. Her starring roles and time on the A-list are largely forgotten, perhaps because she epitomized the late-1970s, post-women's-lib woman so well. She does it again here, making her character conflicted, difficult, frustrating, yet still somehow likable. So the teaming of Reynolds and Clayburgh was a big deal in 1979, especially because *Starting Over* addresses many of the same themes as *An Unmarried Woman*, but from the male perspective. And despite being from the male perspective, it never belittles its women (though it surely belittles the wife's atrocious songs).

Pakula picked his cinematographer well for the wintry Boston of the movie (few interiors were shot here). Sven Nykvist was Ingmar Bergman's favorite cinematographer, and the Swedish film icon rarely did commercial comedies like this in his Hollywood work. I'm sure the fact that it's directed by *Klute* and *All the President's Men* director Pakula helped to entice him to Boston. Although *Starting Over* is hardly an insider's "Boston movie," setting a romantic comedy in the area in 1979, after the anti-busing violence had made the city seem a less welcome place, was pretty significant. The movie shows off then-young Quincy Market, while another scene plays out on Boylston Street and Boston Garden plays its part, too. There's a stop outside the Chestnut Hill Mall, and Phil stocks up for his bachelor pad at Building 19 in Lynn, though it's almost impossible to recognize unless you know the location beforehand.

▶**Locations:** Beacon Hill, Back Bay, Boston; Chestnut Hill; Lynn.

▶**Accents:** No attempt at all is made to localize the story through accents. One guy in Phil's support group sounds like a local, but he has only a few lines. Yet it's not as if Burt Reynolds trying to do a Boston accent would have been a good thing. He's a *star*, not a character actor, and though Phil's brother (Charles Durning) already lives here, it's unclear whether the siblings grew up in Boston.

▶ **Local color:** For a movie that climaxes at the Boston Garden, there are surprisingly few specific local touches. Of course, it's an empty Boston Garden, but everywhere else the movie shoots (like Quincy Market and the streets of Beacon Hill) is pretty empty, too. The Celtics were in a real funk in 1978-79, the year between the John Havlicek and Larry Bird eras, but a cameo by *someone* in the Garden would have added some color. Where's Cedric Maxwell when you need him?

▶ **Don't blink!:** Three years before they appeared together in the ensemble of Barry Levinson's brilliant *Diner*, Daniel Stern and Kevin Bacon can each be spotted separately in small parts.

State and Main

2000. Written and directed by David Mamet. With William H. Macy, Philip Seymour Hoffman, Rebecca Pidgeon, Alec Baldwin, Sarah Jessica Parker, Clark Gregg, David Paymer, Julia Stiles, Patti LuPone and Charles Durning. Cinematography by Oliver Stapleton.

HERE'S SOMETHING DIFFERENT. INSTEAD of Toronto or New York or New Brunswick pinch-hitting for Massachusetts, the Bay State substitutes for elsewhere in David Mamet's comedy. Several movies have shot in the Cape Ann area in recent decades, but in *State and Main*—the best of the bunch—the movie actually takes place in Waterford, Vermont. Oddly enough, despite filming in Massachusetts, Mamet uses the name of a real Vermont town here.

Although lighter in tone than most Mamet—which includes *Glengarry Glen Ross*, *The Spanish Prisoner* and *Spartan*—his screenplay is no less shrewd than his more intense material, and no less focused on sins of the heart, mind and wallet. Egotism, insensitivity, opportunism, extortion and statutory rape all figure in this story of a movie production that, after being cast out of a New Hampshire town for one indiscretion too many, descends upon the quaint Vermont town with the eponymous central intersection to make its 1895-set film. The director (William H. Macy) wants everything done his way, the producer (David Paymer) wants it all done cheaply, the naïve writer (Philip Seymour Hoffman) wants to survive with a shred of artistic integrity, the male lead (Alec Baldwin) wants an underage girl and the leading lady (Sarah Jessica Parker) suddenly wants $800,000 more to do the nude scene she'd already agreed to perform.

Those are just the Hollywood visitors. The locals include a high-schooler (Julia Stiles) eager to tempt the easily seduced actor, an aspiring politician (Clark Gregg) hoping to make a name for himself at any cost and the mayor's wife (Patti LuPone). After the film folk no-show for her dinner party, the mayor's fussy wife convinces her husband (Charles Durning) to let the ambitious pol expose the jailbait-chasing star.

Next to the maneuvering and malfeasance, there's a gentler side to *State and Main*. The movie shows a real affection for its small-town setting, in such unpretentious, perceptive characters as the town doctor (Michael Higgins), two smart-asses (Morris Lamore and Allen Soule) who sit in the local coffee shop and crack wise, à la *The Muppets Show*'s Statler and Waldorf, and especially Annie (Rebecca Pidgeon). The owner of the local bookstore, Annie not only turns out to be a resource for the overmatched young screenwriter, selling him a typewriter and advising him on revisions. She also discovers in him an alternative to a life with the cold politician, to whom she's engaged. Similarly, she provides the writer with an alternative to a life in Hollywood, for which he's clearly not cut out. *State and Main* is as much a warm romance as it is a from-the-hip satire of location moviemaking or a playful tweak of old-fashioned small-town stereotypes.

One-time Greater Boston resident Mamet found the quaint setting for his unquaint tale close to home, using Manchester-by-the-Sea for many of the exteriors, including turning an old grocery store into the coffee shop and a bridal shop into a sporting goods store. Dedham's Endicott Estate is the location for the Tavern Inn, where the movie company establishes its production offices, a home in Beverly for the mayor's house and Malden's then-closed and since-condo-converted Belmont School for the fake courtroom and Waterford's high school. Mamet returned to the Belmont for *Spartan*.

▶ **Locations:** Manchester-by-the-Sea; Dedham; Beverly; Malden.

▶ **Accents:** Many of the locals have generically crusty New England accents, which provide exactly the sort of archetypal small-town feeling the movie seeks.

▶ **Local color:** Since the story is not set in the places where it was shot, it's going for more of a regional flavor, which the main street, old houses and town square capture. The unusual thing here is that *State and Main* is a movie shot on the coast yet not *set* on the coast. So you get none of the coastal shots that are the trademark of Cape Ann films.

▶**Don't blink!:** Alexandra Kerry, one of Senator John Kerry's daughters, plays the director of opportunistic politician Doug's TV broadcast (she's in Mamet's *Spartan*, too), while Newton native John Krasinski, later of TV's *The Office*, has a non-speaking role as the judge's golf-bag-toting assistant.

▶**Aftermath:** Considering that Mamet was inspired to write and direct *State and Main* because of the insensitive-film-productions-on-location tales movie folk regularly trade, it's a cruel irony that Floyd's, a longtime Manchester-by-the-Sea five-and-dime the movie paid to shut down for two months so it could "play" the bookstore, closed for good three years later, and the film was part of the reason why. "It broke [the customers'] routine," owner Alice Rice told the *Globe* of the time she let the production take over the shop. "If a person came in for the paper, now they went somewhere else, and never came back."

Still, We Believe

2004. Directed by Paul Doyle, Jr. Cinematography by Tony Flanagan.

OH, THE PAIN. OH, the suffering. Although many Red Sox fans are now spoiled by the team having won *two* titles in just four years, the winless streak was up to 85 years—and counting—since the Sox had last won a World Series when Paul Doyle made his well-assembled documentary about the team's 2003 season. By that time, the Sox's penchant for snatching defeat from the jaws of victory (the 1978 playoff game, the 1986 World Series, etc.) was etched on every New Englander's brain. The team's also-ran status to the Yankees had brought their divisional rivalry to an intensity matching the Celtics-Lakers feud of the 1980s.

Of course, 2003's dramatic playoff victory over the Athletics and an even more dramatic playoff loss to the Yankees focused increased attention to the Red Sox' failed championship quest (and made the happy ending to the 2004 season that much sweeter). You would think the saturated media coverage the Sox receive left no potential perspective on their exploits uncovered. But Doyle found it. He and his crew received unprecedented access to the Sox clubhouse, dugout and offices over the '03 season. But *Still, We Believe* focuses instead on eight fans that we see figuratively live and die with the Sox, from spring training to the wee hours of the night when Aaron Boone's home run sent the Sox on winter vacation.

So there's relatively little reference to such regular 2003 newspaper and talk-radio topics as curses, cowboying up and shaving heads. *Still, We Believe* touches on more eternal issues, like having your guts twisted into a half-hitch when the Sox are holding on to a slim lead and going for the wild card spot.

The eight fans include Steve Craven, a Boston firefighter, and Jim Conners, a transplanted Foxboro native who owns a Boston-themed sports bar in Santa Monica. But four of the eight definitely stand out. There's Brockton's Jermaine Evans, who is definitely the fan most aware of the folly of being a die-hard Sox rooter. When mayhem breaks out during Game 3 in the American League Championship Series against the Yankees (remember Pedro Martinez diverting the charging Don Zimmer like a matador eluding a bull?), he's immediately on the phone to a friend, faulting Manny Ramirez and Martinez. Despite this semi-detached perspective, when he goes to a game, he can't help being disappointed and disgusted.

> I don't want to hear clichés, like you can in the locker room. I want to hear 'It ripped my heart out.' Because that's real. That's why I liked the fans.
> –Paul Doyle, Jr.

There are also East Boston's Erin Nanstad and Jessamy Finet, two superstitious best friends who, with their matching blond hair and Red Sox gear, are like a two-headed BoSox Club (the second was later tapped for a speaking role in *Fever Pitch*). They make no attempt to get out of the rain during the downpour that eventually postpones the home opener; they clearly realize suffering is a necessary part of the Red Sox equation. And when starting pitcher Derek Lowe is brought in to relieve late in the deciding playoff game against Oakland, they superstitiously rush to put on their Lowe gear.

Best of all is undoubtedly Watertown's Paul "Angry Bill" Costine, who proclaims, "It's more fun to be pessimistic." But his Sox-doubting is really camouflage for the fan within, and his mood swings during Game 7 against the Yanks are amusingly bipolar. Having missed work all week because of sickness from the emotional turmoil of the series, he says "My whole life turned around in about half an hour" when the Sox take an early lead. But he slumps in his chair and moans "I'm gonna be sick" when the lead evaporates. After the Sox lose, he makes a plea to viewers: "Don't have your kids watch sports."

Still, We Believe captures the state of mind of hard-luck Red Sox fans with more humor and less self-pity than the raft of other documentaries that came out following 2003's heartbreaking defeat. Oh, the pain. Oh, the suffering. Make your kids watch it to feel the angst. Leave the room first.

The Strangler's Wife

2002. Directed by Michael Allosso. Written by Jay Laird. With Sarah Huling, Ciaran Crawford, Christy Scott Cashman and Nivya Frabetti. Cinematography by Patrick Ruth.

BOSTON MOVIEMAKING GOES EXPLOITATION in this low-budget thriller about a meek young woman (Sarah Huling) who realizes her husband (Ciaran Crawford) might be a serial rapist-murderer. It's the result of an unusual collaboration between legendary producer Roger Corman (*Little Shop of Horrors, Hollywood Boulevard*) and Jamaica Plain's Cityscape Motion Pictures.

Corman's video company bankrolled the production, and Cityscape made director Michael Allosso's and producer Laura Wilson's movie with a local cast and crew augmented by film students who were able to gain hands-on experience as the movie took shape. A local screenplay contest had yielded Charlestown lawyer Mark Dickison's 1960s-set story, a fictionalized drama about the Boston Strangler's wife becoming aware of her powerlessness and taking control of her life in the process.

Budget concerns shifted the story to the present-day, and rewrites and screenplay credit went to Jay Laird. But the central dilemmas of Dickison's story apparently remain (as a nod to the original's setting, the media refers to the perpetrator in the present-day story as the "Son of Strangler"). Mae (Huling) is the sheltered housewife whose suspicions about husband Kevin (Crawford) coincide with the sense of self-confidence and empowerment she gets from an art class and a new, less inhibited best friend, Elana (Nivya Frabetti). The new friend encourages Mae to get out of her house and climb out of the emotional shell in which she's lived her life.

> It wasn't a quota, but they made it clear we had to have the requisite nudity and violence. We knew we were going to have to do that.
>
> –Laura Wilson

Perhaps the most interesting aspect of *The Strangler's Wife* is that it couches Mae's female-empowerment story within the skin-and-violence confines of an R-rated movie full of sexual assaults, killings, shower scenes and voyeurism. Kevin—who rescued Mae from a sexually abusive father, only to try to control her himself—is clearly threatened by her signs of independence. He sometimes targets fellow women from his wife's art class, including the teacher (Linda Carmichael). The drama builds to his inevitable conflicts with Elana and, once her suspicions about Kevin are confirmed, Mae.

Although the storytelling never musters much style and the whole production is rather rudimentary, the tale manages to hold together both its feminism and sexploitation. For a cash-strapped production in which getting it "in the can" cheaply is sometimes the most important consideration, *The Strangler's Wife* does an admirable job. A good yardstick to judge it against is *Stolen Summer*, the low-budget movie whose production was chronicled on the first season HBO's *Project Greenlight* series. *The Strangler's Wife*, released at about the same time, has much more going on than that higher-profile movie made under similar circumstances.

Among the interesting ingredients here are a very effective score by Boston avant-rockers Cul de Sac, as well as some little-seen locations. Most of the houses seen are in Jamaica Plain, as is that favorite movie hot spot, Doyle's. A few of the houses are in Roxbury, as well. East Cambridge also appears frequently (Kevin works at Cambridgeside Galleria mall), while such touristy spots as the Public Garden and the Comm. Ave. Mall show up in montages. A Quincy skating rink was also used to build interior sets in, and to house production offices.

►**Locations:** Jamaica Plain, Roxbury, Boston; Cambridge; Quincy (interior sets).

►**Accents:** There's hardly a Boston accent to be heard, but everyone seems to be talking in his or her natural voice.

►**Local color:** *The Strangler's Wife* isn't a very public movie. Its crimes take place mainly indoors, and its dilemmas are intimate ones. The montages and the trips to Doyle's and the Cambridgeside Galleria add a little spice, though.

►**Don't blink!:** Future *American Idol* contestant Constantine Maroulis plays "Detective's Assistant."

Tell Me That You Love Me, Junie Moon

1970. Directed by Otto Preminger. Written by Marjorie Kellogg. Based on her novel. With Liza Minnelli, Ken Howard, Robert Moore and James Coco. Cinematography by Boris Kaufman.

OTTO PREMINGER IS AN unlikely source of humanism. The veteran director, who'd shot brief bits of 1963's *The Cardinal* locally and returned for a longer visit in 1969, delighted at being domineering. He cultivated an imperious image on talk shows, played the most chilling version of *Batman* nemesis Mr. Freeze and ran notoriously strict sets on his movies.

Maybe that's why 1970's *Tell Me That You Love Me, Junie Moon* feels a little odd. Although Preminger's storytelling exudes sympathy for his scarred characters, the movie is an uneasy blend of comedy and drama that often glosses over its characters' problems. Although not as bizarre as Preminger's freaky 1968 comedy *Skidoo*, it's another unusual effort from an "old Hollywood" director (*Laura, The Man with the Golden Arm*) trying to adapt to changing times.

Junie Moon, played by pre-*Cabaret* Liza Minnelli, bears the scars of a date with a creepy fetishist (Ben Piazza) seen in a prologue. He takes her to a cemetery and asks her to disrobe; when she later laughs at how he gets his jollies, he takes her to a junkyard, beats her and pours battery acid on her. Overlooked objects like Junie and two other misfits she meets in the hospital, seizure-prone Arthur (Ken Howard) and paraplegic Warren (Robert Moore), are all over *Tell Me That You Love Me, Junie Moon.* There's the boarded-up house they share upon their release, the abandoned dog that takes to Arthur and the blacks that gay Warren befriends when the trio goes on vacation.

The nonconformist late-1960s mood that the movie tries to tap into says that we're *all* misfits, not just Junie, Arthur and Warren. So their landlady (Kay Thompson) lives in a castle and is out of touch with reality, à la *Sunset Boulevard*'s Norma Desmond, their neighbor (James Beard) is a bigoted snoop and even the fishmonger (James Coco) in their Cape Ann town is more complicated than he appears.

But *Tell Me That You Love Me, Junie Moon* offers only a sketchy picture of the world around its characters, and doesn't dig beyond the quips that help Junie cope with her disfigurement and the stereotypical gay sass, circa 1970, of Warren. Arthur's mental scars cut deeper, thanks to the eerie childhood flashbacks in which he appears fully grown and in color, while everything else is black and white. It's Arthur's epilepsy-like condition that's problematically vague, especially since it figures heavily in the late action.

The performances of the three leads and especially Coco are amiable enough, but the movie really stumbles once the misfits go on a vacation to the beach. Not only is there a jarring transition to non-local locations—even though they're supposed to be vacationing somewhere along Route 128, scenes were shot at a palm-tree-filled San Diego resort—but the drama is iffy, particularly gay Warren's one-night stand with a woman (Emily Yancy) and his friendship with the resort's hunky social director (Fred Williamson), who improbably bonds with him.

After the vacation, there's a brief return to the Massachusetts coastal locations along Route 127. Preminger filmed parts of *Tell Me You Love Me, Junie Moon* in Manchester-by-the-Sea, Beverly and Salem (the location of the house the lead trio rents). But apart from a shot of Salem Hospital and another of Manchester Public Library, the movie doesn't reference town names. Braintree's Blue Hill Cemetery is the location of Junie's disrobing, which caused a big stink, even though Minnelli wore a body stocking during the scene and there's no nudity in the movie.

▶**Locations:** Manchester-by-the-Sea; Salem; Rockport; Braintree; Beverly.

▶**Accents:** A secretary in the Salem Hospital, who's presumably a non-professional, is definitely local, as is whoever makes the P.A. announcements there (could be the same woman). But that's it.

▶**Local color:** The Cape Ann locations offer a regional, New England coastal feel here, as they are so often called upon to do. Boston is mentioned once or twice, so that's a geographical frame of reference, but the movie could have easily been shot in a Long Island fishing village or in a small California coastal town.

▶**Off the set:** An outraged Braintree resident lodged a complaint after the filming of the cemetery striptease, but Preminger successfully fended off desecration charges in Quincy District Court. According to *Time*, though, the incident provoked the Massachusetts legislature to ban the filming of nude scenes in cemeteries. Of course, Liza Minnelli wasn't nude in the scene, but state legislators don't miss a grandstanding trick.

Theme: Murder

1998. Directed by Martha Swetzoff. Cinematography by Jane Gillooly and Martha Swetzoff.

MARTHA SWETZOFF'S HOUR-LONG film is one of the more mesmerizing documentaries to come out of Boston. It's about the effect of the unsolved 1968 murder of her father—Newbury Street art gallery owner Hyman Swetzoff—on her life. The murder, committed when she was nine, not only put an inescapable before-and-after point in her childhood. It also haunted her as she grew older, something she documents so stirringly in *Theme: Murder*.

Swetzoff's struggle to put her perspective of the murder on film reflects her struggle with the actual event. *The Garden*, a short film she made while attending Harvard (excerpted here), had been an unsatisfying attempt to find a catharsis by addressing the murder. Instead, this initial attempt at investigating the incident had only exposed troubling facts previously kept from her: that Hyman Swetzoff, who had divorced Martha's mom when she was two, had been living a secret life as a gay man, and that, after being beaten in his apartment, he had stumbled, bleeding, through Bay Village, but no one aided him.

> By the time I had the resources to finish the film I had more understanding of how, in fact, my experience was kind of common, in terms of families and murder victims: seemingly obsessive questioning, the fact that everyone wants you to get over it and you just can't.
> –Martha Swetzoff

Such disturbing revelations caused Swetzoff to leave college for four years, playing in the fearsome all-female Boston punk band Bound & Gagged and living in New York for a spell. While residing in Los Angeles in the early 1990s, she began to revisit the topic. Eventually, in 1997, she moved back to Boston to complete filming and edit *Theme: Murder*, which takes its name from a line in one of her dad's many journals.

The movie weaves several strands together into a satisfying whole. There's a very involving look at her father's life in the local art world and in the pre-Stonewall closet, replete with peeks at many old snapshots and interviews with those who were in the 1960s Boston gay subculture. There's the true horror of his death, illustrated by shots of newspaper headlines of the day (and eerily amplified by the fact that Martha's mother, who was about to remarry, moved Martha and her brother David to their new relatives' house immediately and they *never* returned to their Beacon Hill apartment). There are soulful descriptions—sometimes delivered directly to the camera—of how the murder shook survivor Martha. And there's the more universal story of a child trying to understand his or her relationship with parents.

It's hard not to be seriously pulled into this easy-flowing mix of the personal and universal. That's part of what makes it a quintessential, first-person Boston documentary. Swetzoff's first film teacher was Harvard's influential Alfred Guzzetti (also an influence on Kate Davis' *Girltalk*), and she made *Theme: Murder* in collaboration with local film stalwarts Jane Gillooly and Karen Schmeer, counting Robb Moss (*The Tourist*) and Jeanne Jordan and Steven Ascher (*Troublesome Creek*) as informal advisors on her project. Swetzoff is similar to many others in the Boston-Cambridge documentary community who edit, film or record sound on others' films and perhaps teach; they all seem to have personal stories to tell and, when the time is right, they do.

Theme: Murder: Martha and Hyman Swetzoff on Boston Common.

The Thomas Crown Affair

1968. Directed by Norman Jewison. Written by Alan Trustman. With Steve McQueen, Faye Dunaway, Paul Burke and Jack Weston. Cinematography by Haskell Wexler.

I HAVE VERY VAGUE recollection of the media coverage of the glittery Boston premiere that greeted Norman Jewison's movie. Such events were (and still are) a very rare occurrence down around here, but for some reason Hollywood really, *really* liked Boston in 1968. Along with *Charly* and *The Boston Strangler*, the original version of *The Thomas Crown Affair* gave the city a Hollywood hat trick that year. For better or worse, none of them is as "Hollywood" as this glossy romantic drama.

It's a state-of-the-art confection set in an impossibly urbane Boston concocted by Alan Trustman, a local lawyer who went on to pen more movies. Director Jewison and composer Michel Legrand then buffed it to a spiffy sheen. Steve McQueen plays the title character,

The Thomas Crown Affair: Faye Dunaway and Steve McQueen in Copp's Hill Burying Ground.

a blue-blooded investment wiz who, between buying low and selling high at his Post Office Square headquarters, masterminds crimes and seeks thrills wherever he can find them, whether it's from golf-course betting or piloting gliders. He's a sort of American James Bond in a three-piece suit, but he serves only his own interests.

As with *The Boston Strangler*, this exercise in style shows the influence of the split-screen films screened at Expo '67—Christopher Chapman's *A Place to Stand* in this case. Jewison uses multiple imagery often in the story's first third, when a Crown-hired crew descends on a bank and robs it of $2.6 million (in scenes shot at the old Shawmut Bank on Congress Street). The build-up and execution of the heist are thrilling and offer glimpses of a wide variety of sights, from Washington Street and Stuart Street to the corner of Cambridge and Linden Streets, with the Allston train yard behind it.

The little celebratory dance and chuckle in which Crown privately indulges once the job is done, and he can kick back in his Mt. Vernon Street townhouse, tells you all you need to know about why he takes risks that jeopardize his cushy life. He gets a life-affirming kick out of it. Posh insurance investigator Vicky Anderson (Dunaway) recognizes Crown's need to push himself because she has the same sort of driven personality. When she's called in to crack the case, *The Thomas Crown Affair* ignites its romantic sparks and turns into the tale of two alpha dogs in heat. Canine personalities aside, their affair is pure cat-and-mouse stuff, with Vicky telling him why she's in town and why she's keeping an eye on him, and Crown similarly finding her to be both a kindred spirit and an enemy.

But sometimes the movie overdoes it. It's one thing for the romance to be a metaphorical chess game, it's another for it to have Crown and Vicky sit down and *play* chess, especially with the overripe chess-as-sex images that accompany the game. It's enough to make you think the moviemakers *aren't* in on the fact that the movie is a fluffy, silly diversion, nothing more. Then again, any movie containing the hats Dunaway wears would have to be partially silly.

Jewison estimates on the movie's DVD that he shot "70%" of *The Thomas Crown Affair* on location. Hamilton's Myopia Hunt Club (the polo sequence) and Crane Beach's dunes provide outside-the-city scenery, Cambridge Cemetery figures heavily in the plot and the Haymarket and Copp's Hill Burying Ground add urban atmosphere. Of course, the 1999 remake decided Boston just wasn't upscale enough and moved the story to New York.

▶**Locations:** Beacon Hill, Financial District, Allston, North End, Back Bay, Boston; Cambridge; Ipswich; Hamilton; Beverly; Belmont.

▶**Accents:** McQueen attempted a Boston accent in rehearsals, but it was decided against. Hopefully, someone told him a character like Crown most likely wouldn't even have a Boston accent. Locals in supporting roles provide the accents here, including Worcester-born Nina Marlowe as cop Paul Burke's secretary and the two real Boston Police patrolmen who rouse the detective that Crown KO's, douses in booze and then puts in a car.

▶**Local color:** While there are plenty of familiar and not-so-familiar sights on display, the movie takes place in a rarefied, upper-class Boston. For those of us who don't drive a Rolls, stable a polo mount at the Myopia and bed down in a Beacon Hill townhouse (complete with butler), this is a Bizarro Boston we don't generally experience. But it is true to Crown's world. The color is more class-specific than location-specific, since Crown has more in common with other rich people, regardless of where they're from, than he does with other Bostonians. It's not as if he's hanging out with bookies from Jamaica Plain or cheering on Ken Harrelson from the bleachers at Fenway.

Titicut Follies

1967. Directed by Frederick Wiseman. Cinematography by John Marshall.

FREDERICK WISEMAN'S FIRST DOCUMENTARY is still shocking today. Just imagine what *Titicut Follies* was like in 1967, when it was first shown. The Commonwealth of Massachusetts banned his peek behind the walls at Bridgewater State Hospital, claiming the movie invaded the privacy of patients there, who are often shown nude and in various states of helplessness. Of course, the ban—finally lifted in 1991—couldn't have had anything to do with the cruelty with which the institution often treats those patients, right?

Although Wiseman (*High School, Domestic Violence*) has long been a pillar of the documentary, he came to filmmaking in a roundabout way in the 1960s. He was already a lawyer when he made *Titicut Follies*, having lectured in law at Boston University from 1958 to 1961 and taken his students to Bridgewater State Hospital during that time. After working on Shirley Clarke's minor independent classic *Cool World*, he decided to make a movie about the hospital. He asked for permission in 1964, and ultimately was allowed to film there in 1966.

From the moment the movie begins, we enter a sort of absurd hellhole. The absurdity comes through mainly in the talent show that gives the movie its name (and bookends it). First, we see a group of uncomfortable men sing "Strike Up the Band"; then an eager emcee tells a corny joke about two beetles and a priest. But, wait, in the next sequence, in which guards search the belongings of stripped patients, we see that this emcee is not a patient, but a guard. One thing is sure: there is no scorecard to tell us who's sane and who's insane, who's dangerous and who's not dangerous.

What follows—as is so often the case in Wiseman's films about various institutions—is an impressionistic portrait of the hospital. Sometimes Wiseman focuses on specific threads, like a psychiatrist's therapy session with a man sent to Bridgewater for molesting an underage girl, while other times there's a more random series of sights and sounds, as when we follow the goings-on in the courtyard outlined by the hospital's buildings. The treatment is never sensational.

These glimpses of daily life can be amusing. One incessant ranter lets loose a stream-of-consciousness barrage of gibberish, real words and famous names that's a cross between a jazz solo, a sermon and a stand-up routine. A later shot of the guy spewing verbiage in the courtyard while, behind him, another fellow stands on his head and sings a hymn may be *the* emblematic image of the collision of individual realities in the movie.

But, mostly, *Titicut Follies* is grim and disturbing. Clearly Bridgewater, an exile for the maladjusted, presents a tough situation for staff there to handle. It is practically a no-win situation. But the

Titicut Follies: "The ranter" in Bridgewater.

casual cruelty dished out by the same staff can be striking, particularly in two instances. The first comes when one guard repeatedly questions a patient named Jim about his cell's cleanliness. "How's that room gonna be?" he asks over and over. And after nearly every reply from Jim, he says "What'd you say?" Treat the most normal person like this, and he or she will get agitated; try it on someone who's locked up and vulnerable, and the effect is tragic. Later, a force-feeding of a patient who won't eat—the movie's most squirm-inducing sequence— is performed so casually that the psychiatrist doesn't even put down his cigarette as he shoves inch after inch of tubing up the patient's nose and funnels soup into the guy's stomach. To make the action even more unsettling, Wiseman inserts shots of the patient's corpse— presumably, taken not long after—into the sequence.

Rejecting the *cinema vérité* label and the objectivity it implies, Wiseman has regularly examined the relationship between individuals and society's institutions in his movies (including *Near Death*, filmed at Beth Israel Hospital). *Titicut Follies* remains one of his most potent looks at this difficult relationship.

Troublesome Creek: A Midwestern

1995. Written and directed by Jeanne Jordan and Steven Ascher. Cinematography by Steven Ascher.

HERE'S ANOTHER LITTLE BOSTON documentary that could. The story of co-director Jeanne Jordan's parents' attempt to hang on to their Iowa family farm might not reflect Boston onscreen, but offscreen it surely does: Robb Moss (*The Tourist*) and John Osborne (a vet of many PBS productions) lent sound equipment to Jordan and co-director Steven Ascher; Ross McElwee (*Sherman's March*) contributed one of the lenses they shot with; and Frederick Wiseman (*Titicut Follies*) let them use his editing equipment.

The Cambridge-based husband-and-wife team's *Troublesome Creek: A Midwestern* is Iowa filtered through Boston. It engages its audience with a distinctively low-key personal perspective so often found in Boston documentaries. As in Beth Harrington's *The Blinking Madonna* and Moss' and McElwee's films, it has a first-person perspective that's intimate, but leaves room for a little detachment.

But chronicling challenging times in your family's life is naturally a cause for reflection and—much like the body of water on the farm that gives the movie its name—Jordan's narration snakes its way from one part of the movie to the next. Calling parents Russ and Mary Jane's situation "a *Reader's Digest* condensed version of the farm crisis," she leads us through the circumstances we find them in: how the farm had long operated on yearly loans from local banks that they had dutifully paid back after harvests for 40 years; how the low food prices of the 1980s had caused them to steadily get behind in payments; and how, once the local bank was bought out, they found themselves dealing with a numbers-crunching loan officer instead of an understanding neighbor with whom they'd built up years of goodwill.

> We worked on this film in total isolation for four and a half years. We had no idea whether people were going to see it as a 'nice little farm film' or something more.
> –Steven Ascher

Jeanne, her two brothers and three sisters help their parents scrape together enough funds so at least one of the farming brothers can keep working their land. But *Troublesome Creek* isn't just about money. It's also about a way of life. Thrust back into the rural life she'd left behind, Jordan is saddened to find the country life she once thought "mundane" is now "downright exotic." A visit to the farm her parents rented when she was a kid reveals it to be abandoned; similarly, the nearby high school she attended has closed down due to a lack of students.

But if ex-schoolteacher Mary Jane and strong-but-silent Russ struggle to find the honor codes of their beloved western movies in real life, the documentary is not as grim as it might sound. Along with the drama, there is also a lot of humor in the face of adversity and a bittersweet mourning of the passing of time. The two-pronged plan—to auction their livestock, machinery and household belongings to pay off the bank debt and then allow son Jim to work the land with his equipment—works, and as we leave them, Russ and Mary Jane actually enjoy their cozy new rental house "in town."

Troublesome Creek, which won two prizes at Sundance and was a Best Documentary Oscar nominee, led in a roundabout way to Jordan and Ascher's subsequent film as directors, *So Much, So Fast*. Shortly before the first film's release, Mary Jane Jordan died of Lou Gehrig's Disease. *So Much, So Fast* details the battles of Newton's Stephen Heywood against the disease, and his brother Jamie's obsessive attempt to jump-start research to cure it. Like its predecessor, it's another documentary about a family pulling together.

Unfinished Symphony

2001. Directed by Bestor Cram and Mike Majoros.

NO FILM MADE IN Boston is as profoundly moving as Bestor Cram and Mike Majoros' hour-long documentary. For a movie made over 25 years after the Vietnam War ended, *Unfinished Symphony: Democracy and Dissent* takes an unusually immediate look back. That's because it's built around remarkable vintage footage of the Memorial Day 1971 march from Concord to Bunker Hill Monument by Vietnam Veterans Against the War. VVAW arranged to have a film crew, led by Hart Perry, shoot the march, but aside from brief use on a 1970s PBS show, the raw footage lay unseen for decades.

Retracing Paul Revere's ride in reverse, the outraged vets took their eyewitness accounts of what was really going on in Vietnam directly to the American public, in hopes of getting citizens to force the federal government to end the war. They called it Operation POW.

Footage of the march plus other archival clips of the war and of VVAW activity (some of which is also in *Winter Soldier*, an amazing 1972 documentary that has resurfaced on DVD) make the movie an uninterrupted highlight film. The mix includes soldiers, fresh from Vietnam, bravely bearing witness to atrocities they committed or saw being committed; effectively graphic combat footage; John Kerry's eloquent testimony before a congressional committee on the immorality of the war; the vets' guerrilla theater of rounding up "villagers" in Concord; and the powerful Washington demonstration at which they tossed the medals they'd been awarded onto the Capitol steps.

> We said, "We know this is a Vietnam film. Let's not make another *Vietnam film*."
> –Bestor Cram

The movie finds unspeakable tragedy in what the United States did to Vietnam—and to itself—by decimating the rural country with more bombs than were used in all of World War II, by sending a generation of unprivileged young men to do its dirty work there and by lying to the people back home about the scope of the war and the American military's success overseas.

But *Unfinished Symphony* also finds an instructive lesson in democracy in the discourse the Vietnam War opened up in this country in the late 1960s and early 1970s, and in the dissent that emerged. As we see happen, authorities in Lexington decide to not let the marching vets, who consider themselves dissenters in the tradition of the

Revolutionary War Minutemen, camp overnight on Lexington Green. Some townspeople urge the authorities to reconsider, a town meeting convenes and the cameras capture a bracing exercise of democracy in action. When the dust clears, permission is not granted. But the vets and many supporters stand up for their rights in what is still the largest arrest in Massachusetts history.

The strength of the movie isn't just in its ingredients. It's also in how Mike Majoros and longtime local filmmaker Bestor Cram—an ex-Marine and VVAW member seen in the vintage footage (he's the guy talking on the megaphone)—assemble them. There's no overt narration or busy editing. Instead, there's a refreshing restraint, and almost all of the film is somberly accompanied by Polish composer Henryk Gorecki's 3rd Symphony.

Interspersed interview clips with Boston University professor emeritus Howard Zinn also provide historical perspective, while *Unfinished Symphony* closes dramatically with Ho Chi Minh's 1946 letter of friendship to President Truman, which humbly asks for support of Vietnam's recent declaration of independence. Truman never responded.

Urban Relics

1998. Written and directed by Roger Saquet. With Richard Romanus, Frank Sivero, Richard Donnelly, Terry Donohoe, Tony V. and Sheila Stasack. Cinematography by Jeri Sopanen.

BELMONT PAINTING CONTRACTOR TURNED writer-director Roger Saquet's gangster comedy is *the* Boston shaggy dog movie. Its production values are low, its performances uneven and its pacing slack at times. But there's a real comic spark to South End native Saquet's writing, and it lets you savor the good things about *Urban Relics* and generally forgive the bad.

As in the Coen brothers' *The Big Lebowski*, also from 1998, a rug is the comic instigator. And, as in *The Big Lebowski*, it triggers absurdity. This time, bookie Charlie Shivers (Richard Romanus of *Mean Streets* and *The Sopranos*) is the poor sap at the middle of the comic intrigue. Because Charlie's painter cousin Louis (Richard Donnelly) stains Charlie and his wife Nikki's (Terry Donohoe) Oriental, she wants something new to replace it. But going to a store and buying a rug isn't Charlie's style. Instead, he offers pal Tommy Two-Lips (Frank Sivero of *New York, New York* and *GoodFellas*) money to steal one for him.

Urban Relics: Frank Sivero and Richard Romanus in the Back Bay.

The scene sealing this deal offers the first hints of Saquet's comic knack, as Charlie gets in an argument with Tommy because he wants his friend to steal the rug he likes from the "fancy store" that sells it for $3500, not from the "cheap store" that sells the same rug for $2700. In the best Chico Marx absurd-math tradition, Tommy naturally wants more money to steal a $3500 rug than he'd ask for to steal a $2700 rug. (How much to *not* steal the rug? You can't afford that.)

Saquet throws in more complications to floor covering satisfaction, like Tommy's asthma causing him to get caught mid-robbery, Charlie hiring inept Louie to whack Tommy (knowing he'll botch the job) and Charlie himself ending up in jail for a spell. Even the purchase of a replacement rug doesn't settle the matter (but can paying retail ever bring happiness?).

If *Urban Relics* sounds thick on subplots, it is. Too thick. Some of them go nowhere and could have been trimmed from the script before shooting even began (what's all the talk about Nikki's "Fashion Channel notebook"?). Others are headscratchers, especially the mannequin that's supposed to be Al Capone or the spirit of Tommy or *something*. Similarly, there are too many characters, with comedian Tony V.'s Willy and some of the girlfriends failing to develop very much. And even in the movie's Runyonesque, heightened reality, the action involving Louis' nephew Mikey (Tom DeLuca) is a dead spot, as the guy is just too cartoonish a palooka.

But lack of polish is part of the charm in *Urban Relics*. So, too, are the 1950s-style songs; characters that, to quote an old teacher of mine, are forever running between the raindrops; and unglamourous locations such as Woburn's Boston Sports Boxing Club, Dedham's old Norfolk County Jail and Saquet's own Belmont neighborhood. The writer-director even makes a funny cameo as the local godfather, mediating a dispute as he fills his face at a Vinny Testa's. Throughout, Romanus makes an engaging straight man to the lunacy around him, while Sivero is a great foil for him. The movie sags in the second half, when Sivero is less prominent.

But, despite its problems, *Urban Relics* has more laughs than many more consistent comedies. It's not comedy by committee, as so many commercial movies are. It has personality. Even though it was well-received critically when Saquet premiered the movie at Belmont's Studio Cinema, its exposure never went much further than that. It's no classic, but it's definitely one of the more memorable homegrown comedies.

►**Locations:** Belmont; South End, Theater District, Dorchester, Boston; Woburn; Dedham; Watertown.

►**Accents:** There's a mix of local accents and New York accents. Generally speaking, we're talking East Coast working-class lingo.

►**Local color:** As with the accents, the sensibility isn't specifically Boston, but more big-city blue collar. *Urban Relics* could easily have been set in Philadelphia or, for that matter, Chicago. Anywhere where there are Oriental rug stores and overly "creative" guys who don't want to pay the asking price. Boston certainly qualifies.

The Verdict

1982. Directed by Sidney Lumet. Written by David Mamet. Based on Barry Reed's novel. With Paul Newman, James Mason, Jack Warden, Charlotte Rampling, Milo O'Shea, Edward Binns and Lindsay Crouse. Cinematography by Andrzej Bartowiak.

IF YOU WANT TO make a film in which the power and influence wielded by the Catholic Church and crusty law firms are a factor, Boston is obviously a natural setting. So local lawyer-novelist Barry Reed didn't need to look very far when he wrote his novel of *The Verdict*, and director Sidney Lumet kept the book's setting, though the quintessential New York moviemaker (*Dog Day Afternoon*, *Prince of the City*) shot only bits and pieces of the story here.

The role of Frank Galvin, the on-the-skids, alcoholic lawyer seeking professional and personal redemption, is Paul Newman's best role of the 1980s. Oddly enough, the part was originally to be played by his *Butch Cassidy and the Sundance Kid* and *The Sting* pal Robert Redford, with James Bridges directing. The Redford version had been planned for a late-1981 Boston shoot but, as Lumet says on the movie's DVD commentary, Redford pulled out, unsatisfied after having commissioned several different scripts. Bridges had already exited, due to creative differences with Redford. After being hired, Lumet returned to the David Mamet script Redford had rejected, and shot his Boston segments in February 1982.

The Verdict weaves together its character study of guilt-ridden Galvin with a courtroom drama concerning the personal-injury case that's either going to pull the dissipated attorney out of the gutter (if he wins) or keep him there forever (if he doesn't). Because of Newman's performance—in which his famous blue eyes show only a glint of whatever fire might be left in Frank—and Lumet's quiet storytelling (just check out the effectively somber opening-titles sequence), the character drama hits harder than the courtroom tension.

It's a grey movie, filmed primarily on wintry, cloudy days, and greyest of all is Galvin. The guy is awash in grey hair, pale skin and

The Verdict: Paul Newman in South Boston.

the occasional redness from the brisk weather and the Bushmills he downs. There's something very pathetic about Galvin getting tossed out of Southie's Spencer Funeral Home for handing out his business card, pretending to be an acquaintance of the deceased. The case eventually thrown his way by an old colleague (Jack Warden) out of pity is his only lifeline to a better future.

Newman's performance benefits from Lumet's penchant for long takes. You feel the completeness of this performance much more than you would in a movie with quick editing, particularly in the sequence in Galvin's office in which he desperately tries to find a doctor to be his expert witness, and the trial-closing scene in which he addresses the jury. The way the script supplies a triumph for Frank—with a surprise witness (Lindsay Crouse) who practically springs out of nowhere, and a cash award for the plaintiff that's more than was ever asked for—is a little hard to take. Fortunately, the subdued last scene, involving Frank's former love interest (Charlotte Rampling), shows that, to a certain extent, he's still wounded and vulnerable. Not everything is wrapped up neatly.

Although the movie takes no cheap shots at the Catholic Church, and the bishop played by Edward Binns shows sympathy for Gavin's client, who came to the Church-run hospital to deliver a baby and ended up in a coma, time has only added resonance to *The Verdict*'s presentation of the Church as a power structure that, like most any other, will go to great lengths to defend itself. Because of the 1990s revelation of priests' sexual misconduct within the same archdiocese, an eerie tragedy has attached itself to the story.

The movie also features the oddity of the State House serving as two buildings, neither a seat of government. The front steps, shot from an angle in which the actual building can't be seen, "play" the front of the movie's courthouse, while its grand stairways, back exit and parking lot are used as part of the hospital. On his DVD commentary, Lumet says the courtroom set built in New York is a replica of the courtroom where the trial would have taken place in Boston.

▶**Locations:** South Boston, Beacon Hill, South Station, Boston.

▶**Accents:** There's not much of an attempt to include Boston accents. As the plaintiff's sister and brother-in-law, Roxanne Hart and James Handy, neither of whom is Bostonian, do a good job. But both Paul Newman and Jack Warden are supposed to be playing Boston Irish-Americans, and they just talk in their normal voices. Like Warden, Julie Bovasso, as the elusive obstetrics nurse, just uses her New York blue-collar voice. And the movie has more foreign accents than Boston accents: James Mason's and Charlotte Rampling's real English accents, Milo O'Shea's real Irish brogue (as the judge) and Lindsay Crouse's pretend Irish accent.

▶ **Local color:** With more of its action shot in New York than in Boston, *The Verdict* gets by with just a taste. Having a Sarni Dry Cleaners bag in Frank Galvin's apartment (which is probably a set in New York) is a nice touch, while it's great to see the old Essex Hotel in the background of the scene outside South Station. And is that the #11 bus whizzing by in the background when Galvin heads to the obstetrics nurse's home on G Street in Southie?

The spotty local elements may suffice for those of us who can pick them out, but rather than being a full-fledged Boston movie, *The Verdict* seems more like a *less* New York Lumet movie. A telling moment comes in Galvin's big speech, when he tells off the judge by calling him "a bag man for the boys downtown." Well, "downtown" is, strictly speaking, a Manhattan notion, not a Boston one; a middle-aged guy from Boston would more likely say "*in* town" (for example: My mother took me in town to shop for clothes). As in another Boston personal-injury courtroom drama and character study, *A Civil Action*, when the time comes to film the trial back in New York or Los Angeles, as both movies did, it wouldn't hurt to fly in a few Irish-American Bostonians to play bailiffs and court clerks. As in the later legal drama, these ubiquitous Irish-American figures in Greater Boston courts are conspicuously absent here. Dude, this is Boston. Where's the patronage!?

▶ **Don't blink!:** Bruce Willis is an extra during the courtroom scenes. If you have the DVD, you can get the best look at him by pausing the picture at 1:53:57. He's just above Roxanne Hart, a veteran of Jan Egleson's *The Little Sister*.

Walk East on Beacon!

1952. Directed by Alfred Werker. Written by Leo Rosten and Emmett Murphy. Based on *Crime of the Century* by J. Edgar Hoover. With George Murphy, Finlay Currie, Virginia Gilmore and Karel Stepanek. Cinematography by Joseph C. Brun.

CHELSEA NATIVE LOUIS DE Rochemont was one of the producers behind the post-World War II wave of docudrama thrillers that includes *Mystery Street* and this 1952 Boston movie. Some of these movies take creative inspiration from Italian neorealism, Jules Dassin's *The Naked City* or Anthony Mann's *T-Men*. But de Rochemont's inspiration wasn't

Walk East on Beacon!: Virginia Gilmore in the Back Bay.

fictional entertainment, it was his own career producing the *March of Time* newsreels. At the tail end of WWII, he wed the heavy narration and real locations of newsreels with a ripped-from-the-headlines plot in the Manhattan-set *The House on 92nd Street*, in which an FBI agent infiltrates a Nazi spy ring.

Seven years later, he came home for *Walk East on Beacon!* There's no infiltration in this overheated Cold War drama, but there is a spy ring and the FBI to crack it, led by the agent played by future politician George Murphy. The movie adapts an article written by FBI director J. Edgar Hoover (or by whoever ghostwrote it for him), and it starts and ends with much flag-waving on behalf of the Bureau and the fine, upstanding men who keep America safe from its "hidden enemies."

Although *Walk East* is painless enough to sit through, a more expressive story might have better paid tribute to law enforcement than the anti-Communist message movie we get. Whatever legitimate threat there was from Soviet espionage after WWII was clearly exploited by Hoover into a menace that allowed him to position himself as America's watch dog, and the movie eagerly plays Hoover's enabler. After all, what can you say when a character who lost two children in a concentration camp tells an FBI agent, "I survived Buchenwald, Inspector. I know many Communists and how they work." That, of all people, this survivor should know better than to shift Nazi blame? That the screenwriters ought to be ashamed of themselves?

But that's the kind of hysteria *Walk East* seeks to inspire. The story itself is a rather routine investigative thriller lacking much emotion and mood. If it has any style, it's an *anti*-style. But since this was made at a time when shadowy, visually expressive film noir was in full swing, such anti-style seems flat by comparison. When there actually is a scene of human emotion—when the Commie-aiding cab driver (Jack Manning) confesses to his wife about being trapped into helping them—you momentarily see what the movie is missing. But that's the only taste you get of such human drama.

The value of the movie's real Boston footage in the early 1950s is much greater than that of its FBI cheerleading, stock characters (like pipe-smoking intellectuals) and forensic gadgetry (*Mystery Street* integrated the last into a thriller much better). Action takes place in the Public Garden, Louisburg Square, South Station, Longfellow Bridge, Storrow Drive and the Robert Gould Shaw Memorial across from the State House, among other places, while there are incidental shots of Harvard Square, Memorial Drive, the Mystic River (Tobin) Bridge, the old Ritz (now the Taj), pre-makeover Faneuil Hall and the corner of Park and Tremont streets, with a nice shot of a Dorothy Muriel's bakery. And that's legendary Scollay Square where we see the amazing sign for Jack's Lighthouse, as well as a tattoo parlor and The Tasty (any relation to the one in Harvard Square seen in *Love Story* and *Good Will Hunting*?).

►**Locations:** Charlestown, Back Bay, South Station, East Boston, Scollay Square, Beacon Hill, West End, Boston.

►**Accents:** Full of FBI agents from all over the country, spies who've come to Boston to hide their real identities and immigrants, the story doesn't have much call for local accents. But it seems that many of the bit parts—lower-lever agents, dispatchers, etc.—were cast with local non-professionals (probably guys who did those real jobs everyday). So every so often you'll get a real Bostonian talking.

▶**Local color:** Although some of the movie was shot in New Hampshire and beyond—the *huuuge* mainframe computer seen was the Selective Service Electronic Calculator at IBM in New York—this is the one category where *Walk East* outdoes *Mystery Street*. The latter is a much better movie, because its dark mood summons the danger *Walk East* does not, but that darkness obscures the shooting locations. *Walk East* isn't a quarter as creative, but its preponderance of broad daylight shots in public places is just great for playing "Where's *that?*" and seeing how certain spots have changed in 50-plus years.

What's the Worst That Could Happen?

2001. Directed by Sam Weisman. Written by Matthew Chapman. Based on Donald E. Westlake's novel. With Martin Lawrence, Danny DeVito, John Leguizamo, Glenne Headly, Carmen Ejogo and Bernie Mac. Cinematography by Anastas Michos.

IF ONLY THE MOVIE could live up to its opening title sequence. *What's the Worst That Could Happen?* starts with the sort of colorful montage and hip-hop beat that you don't often see in Hollywood's Boston movies. *That's* not what they come to Boston for. So the movie tries to put a much more cosmopolitan, multi-cultural twist on the usual Boston setting. It doesn't want the brick sidewalks and iron railings of the South End and Beacon Hill to be old-fashioned; it wants them to be contemporary. It doesn't want Boston to be a frigid outpost of cold tribalism; it wants the city to be inclusive and warm.

If any movie could have been an advertisement for the so-called New Boston, this is it. But the movie is lousy. And a lousy movie stands for only one thing: its own lousiness.

When I saw director Sam Weisman's movie upon its initial release, this comedy about a feud between a thief (Martin Lawrence) and an unethical tycoon (Danny DeVito) struck me as a bad version of *Dirty Rotten Scoundrels*. It has the tit-for-tat antics of the better Michael Caine-Steve Martin movie (and actress Glenne Headly from it, too), but it musters little of its predecessor's absurdity. When I rewatched it years later for this book, *What's the Worst That Can Happen?* also seemed like a bad Elmore Leonard wannabe, with lots of roguish characters à la Leonard (*Get Shorty, Maximum Bob*), but a sitcom tone that prevents them from being funny.

The feud begins when rich Max Fairbanks (DeVito) catches thief Kevin Caffrey (Lawrence) robbing his Marblehead beach house (in reality, the house seen is in Manchester). When the police arrive, Max says the ring Kevin is wearing is his, and the officers make Kevin hand it over to Max. But Max is lying. Not only is the ring Kevin's, but it's his lucky ring, given to him by posh girlfriend Amber (Carmen Ejogo). Thus begins Kevin's quest to get the ring back and Max's quest to thwart him at every turn. Wives, mistresses, girlfriends, partners in crime and in business and an effeminate detective are just some of the others drawn into the spiraling feud. But there's hardly a smile to be had, let alone a laugh, because Lawrence and especially DeVito play the sort of characters they've tackled before, and because Newton resident Weisman, a veteran of sitcoms, has all his characters act as if they're in a comedy. But characters who *think* they're funny rarely are, and this is no exception.

Weisman at least knows how to show off his adopted city well. *What's the Worst That Could Happen?* is very resourceful with its locations, setting scenes at the real Café Vanille (at Charles and Mt. Vernon Streets), turning Hamersley's Bistro (on Tremont Street) into Jack's, the restaurant where the characters gather, and using the old Beacon Hill firehouse, seen on MTV's *Real World: Boston*, as Kevin's apartment. The State House and Milton Academy also appear as, respectively, a courthouse and an auction house. The movie also uses car hawker Herb Chambers' Flagship Wharf (Charlestown) condo as Max's Washington, D.C. apartment and the Hunnewell Mansion on Dartmouth Street as his Beacon Hill digs. Builder Jay Cashman and wife Christy Scott Cashman, an actress (*The Strangler's Wife*), let Weisman use the last, while Christy nabbed a role in the movie. She plays the friend advising Max's put-upon wife (Nora Dunn) as the two sit outside at Jack's.

▶ **Locations:** South End, Beacon Hill, Back Bay, Charlestown, Boston; Manchester-by-the-Sea; Milton; Cambridge.

▶ **Accents:** Boisterous Lenny Clarke not only injects his accent, but the crooked pyro expert he plays and the wife he bickers with (Siobhan Fallon, who does a good put-on accent) offer most of the rare laughs here. They'd be together again in *Fever Pitch*.

▶ **Local color:** It's definitely wishful thinking, but the movie's optimistic portrayal of a bright, summery Boston less constricted by class and race is the only really appealing thing about it. Many of the best Boston movies heavily factor in class structure and tribalism, and dramatically exploit the bleak realities of such inequities. *What's the Worst That Could Happen?* goes so against that grain in that regard that it's actually bold. Not that it makes the movie's 99 minutes any more entertaining, though. It's worth noting that the script includes one of those lazy, New York-derived movie-dialogue clichés, when John Leguizamo's character mentions someone going away "upstate" to prison. Sing Sing is upstate, Walpole is just... Walpole. There *is* no upstate in Massachusetts, unless you mean New Hampshire.

▶**Local celeb alert!:** Take your pick: Former Bruins great Cam Neely as a police detective, longtime radio dude Matt Siegel as a charity dinner MC or Four Seasons Hotel general manager (at the time) Robin Brown as an auctioneer.

When Stand Up Stood Out

2003. Directed by Fran Solomita. With Lenny Clarke, Barry Crimmins, Steven Wright, Kenny Rogerson, Don Gavin, Kevin Meaney, Bob Goldthwait, Tony V., Janeane Garofalo, Denis Leary, Jimmy Tingle, Paula Poundstone and Colin Quinn.

IT SOUNDS A LITTLE like an old Hair Club for Men commercial: Newton native Fran Solomita isn't just the director of this sharp documentary about the Boston comedy boom of the late 1970s and 1980s; he's also one of the comics who played such clubs as the original Comedy Connection, Stitches, Nick's and the Ding Ho. In his opening voice-over to *When Stand Up Stood Out*, Solomita lays out his place in the story. "The good part [is] I've had an amazing journey," he says. "The bad part [is] you have no idea who I am."

Solomita may not have made the leap from working comic to comedy star, but his "journey" gives him a rare perspective on the events he chronicles. A self-proclaimed minor player in those events, he was closer than all but a few to the intense Boston comedy scene of the late 1970s and 1980s, the impact of which is still felt today. Homegrown comics such as Worcester's Denis Leary and Burlington's Steven Wright are still national stars, as are non-locals Janeane Garofalo and Bob Goldthwait, who moved here and nurtured their acts on local stages. And local stalwarts such as Lenny Clarke, Barry Crimmins (now semi-retired from stand-up), Jimmy Tingle, Don Gavin, Kenny Rogerson and Steve Sweeney still can fill clubs whenever they perform.

Now a Los Angeles resident who works in comedy promotion for NBC, Solomita looks back at Boston's competitive comedy breeding grounds with fondness and irreverence. The movie has two deserving guiding lights, Clarke and Crimmins. Clarke's rambunctious personality set the tone for much of the comedy being performed, and one of the movie's highlights comes when Clarke details the night he played nine different shows (keeping a cab driver on retainer for the evening to shuttle him back and forth). Meanwhile, Crimmins' uninhibited vision was responsible for the unlikely opening of a comedy club within The Ding Ho, a long-gone Inman Square Chinese restaurant, turning the kitchen into a comic incubator.

Like the stream of old performance clips, the friendly rivalry between the professional Connection and the freeform "The Ding" runs throughout the movie. So, too, does the in-fighting that struck the scene once local comics started breaking nationally and the lure of fame appeared, beginning with Steven Wright's triumphant *Tonight Show with Johnny Carson* performance in August 1982. *Carson* producer Peter Lassally is interviewed, talking about the local audition he set up while in town to check out colleges with his teenaged kids. Assessing all the coincidences that occurred to land him his big break, Wright, in his typical deadpan, calls it "a fluke festival."

> We ended up doing 85 hours' worth of interviews. We could have made an hour film of each interview we did.
> –Fran Solomita

After Wright broke nationally, other top local comedians thought their chance was next—Clarke admits he felt he had "seniority"—but that didn't always happen. And when Bob Goldthwait, then a 20-year-old who'd only recently moved to Boston from Syracuse, landed a *Late Night with David Letterman* appearance in 1983, desperation started to set in among the comics who felt they were being overlooked.

But it wouldn't be a Boston scene if it wasn't contentious, right? Just listen to the hilarious "turf war" mentality that permeated local comedy clubs, as New Yorker Colin Quinn recalls bombing at Nick's simply because he was from New York.

Some of the better old clips come from Clarke, Rogerson and Kevin Meaney (Meaney would wander out on Commonwealth Avenue during his Stitches shows, a cameraman beaming his comic encounters back into the club). A 1999 Ding Ho reunion concert at the Somerville Theater provides newer performances by Goldthwait, Gavin and many other comics whose worked sparked the 1980s comedy club boom here and across the country.

There's a ton of local color in every frame of *When Stand Up Stood Out*. But those who were lucky enough to see the movie when it played in film festivals got even more. The official DVD release of the movie unfortunately replaces the fest version's soundtrack of vintage Boston rock that included Nervous Eaters' "Loretta," Thrills' "Not Another Face in the Crowd," La Peste's "Better Off Dead," The Modern Lovers' "Roadrunner" and The Cars' "Good Times Roll." The "official version" has an instrumental score. There's nothing wrong with it, but those authentic songs made the movie even *more* evocative of Boston in the late 1970s and 1980s. Alas, the licensing fees to put them on the DVD were beyond the movie's limited budget.

The Witches of Eastwick

1987. Directed by George Miller. Written by Michael Cristofer. Based on John Updike's novel. With Jack Nicholson, Cher, Susan Sarandon, Michelle Pfeiffer, Veronica Cartwright and Richard Jenkins. Cinematography by Vilmos Zsigmond.

IF THIS IS A Cher movie, even a big-budget comedy, there has to be a little drama involved, right? *Mad Max* director George Miller wanted to film his adaptation of John Updike's randy battle-of-the-sexes tale in Little Compton, Rhode Island, but the town fathers there said no, apparently spooked by the script's frank language and devilish lead male character. Instead, Cohasset was all too pleased to step in. Its expansive town common with the steepled church at one end beautifully epitomizes small-town New England—the old church representing the Puritanical past that led to the infamous witch hunts.

The change of filming location was nothing compared to what happened when Susan Sarandon showed up, ready to play Alexandra. She was told that, no, she wasn't going to be the frisky sculptress anymore; she was now playing Jane, the prim musician who undergoes an emotional awakening over the course of the movie. Cher was playing Alexandra now. Then, as shooting progressed, Miller endured a tug-of-war for power with the studio making *The Witches of Eastwick*, clawing for the resources he needed and ultimately prevailing when he got a vote of confidence from star Jack Nicholson.

It seems like an awful lot of fuss for a movie that succeeds as a glossy 1980s comedy with several star turns, but which is nothing more. Maybe that's a small disappointment considering *Witches'* high-powered cast and literary pedigree. But, with so many movies failing on every level, it's hard to scoff at a colorful popcorn movie.

Michelle Pfeiffer's Sukie is the third of the title characters—like the others, an unattached woman in her thirties left wanting by their staid small town, Eastwick. The trio casually wishes for someone new and exciting to come along and, lo and behold, in rides mysterious Daryl Van Horne (Nicholson), buying a lush mansion and soon hitting on each woman as if he knows *exactly* what each yearns for. The women feel liberated from their blahs by Daryl, the town prude (Veronica Cartwright) raises a stink and everything seems fine—until Alexandra, Jane and Sukie realize they're now considered the town sluts, and they don't like it (they're also a little unnerved that they're all pregnant). But when they break off with Daryl, *he* doesn't like it, and starts placing curses on them, landing Sukie in the hospital. They return to him, but only long enough to put their own curse on *him*.

Witches works best as a broad take on both small-town social life and the perpetual tussle between men and women. Although Nicholson's eyebrow-wiggling leering has often been detrimental to his performances ever since *Terms of Endearment*, it's fitting here, and his rant about women and God, delivered to pews full of uninviting churchgoers ("Woman: A mistake, or did He do it to us on purpose!?") is the movie's funniest moment. The topics and perspectives here are nothing new, and the big special-effects climax could surely have been improved upon, but the characters and the cast are all very enjoyable to watch (after 20 years of additional special-effects gimmicks, the climax is not as hideous as it once seemed). Despite being elbowed aside by Cher, Sarandon actually gets to play the title character with the biggest emotional arc.

In addition to Cohasset (where the First Parish Meeting House and Mill River Boatyard are among the sights), a few other local landmarks come in handy in *Witches*. The lobby of the Wang Center (now Citi Performing Arts Center) becomes a portion of Daryl Van Horne's excessive mansion and a favorite movie location, Ipswich's Crane Estate, provides at least some of its exterior (including the vast back "yard"). Production designer Polly Platt realized that the grounds of Milton Academy would be perfect when the alumna attended her 30-year reunion there, shortly before shooting began (it's used as the fictional Lenox School's grounds in the early ceremony outside). The movie was so popular that over the years it's spawned a musical theater version and two different TV pilots, though neither of the pilots was picked up for a network series.

▶**Locations:** Cohasset; Boston; Ipswich; Milton; Marblehead.

▶**Accents:** A crusty New England accent pops out every so often, at one point from a nurse and at another from a deli counterman. One might have served Veronica Cartwright's town prude, but not the title characters, who are supposed to be alienated from the town, not entirely *of* it.

The Witches of Eastwick: Jack Nicholson, Susan Sarandon, Cher and Michelle Pfeiffer in Ipswich.

▶**Local color:** Steve's Ice Cream products appear onscreen twice, but that's really it. The local color here is an unspoken undercurrent meant to link Eastwick to reactionary Salem of old. You feel it, but don't always see it.

▶**Off the set:** It was a literally bumpy ride for Cher on the evening of August 2, 1986. While being driven from the set back to her Cambridge hotel, her vehicle was one of several hit by a drunk driver in Hingham, while waiting at a red light. She was mildly shaken up.

▶**Aftermath:** Why, 2005's soft-core comedy *The Witches of Breastwick*, of course.

With Honors

1994. Directed by Alek Keshishian. Written by William Mastrosimone. With Brendan Fraser, Joe Pesci, Moira Kelly, Patrick Dempsey and Josh Hamilton. Cinematography by Sven Nykvist.

SCHOOL TIES STAR BRENDAN Fraser returns to the area for another socially conscious campus drama. But Brookline native Alek Keshishian's movie owes less to Fraser's previous film than it does to 1992's *Scent of a Woman*. *With Honors*, an old script that was quickly dusted off after the success of the Al Pacino movie, takes the *Scent* premise of a bland preppie whose outlook on life is changed by a blind man, and alters it into the tale of a bland Ivy Leaguer whose outlook on life is changed by a homeless man.

Fraser is that Ivy Leaguer—Monty Kessler, a Harvard government student devoting every waking minute to his senior thesis so he can graduate with honors. But after his hard drive dies and he heads out to photocopy his only printout of his draft, he trips, sending the envelope containing the thesis through a Harvard Yard grate and, thanks to gravity, into the hands of Simon Wilder (Joe Pesci), the homeless man squatting in the university library. He'll only return the manuscript page-by-page, each in return for food or some other kind of favor.

So begins the real-world education of Monty. The driven student starts out treating Simon like a lesser being, and ends up respecting and liking him as a person with wisdom to impart. The relationship also gives Monty a broadened perspective that causes him to rip up his old thesis—which parroted the views of his imposing advisor (Gore Vidal)—and write something in which he genuinely believes.

With Honors manages a modicum of sincerity, while Fraser's earnestness works and Monty's roommates (Moira Kelly, Patrick Dempsey and Josh Hamilton) add comic relief and, in the case of Kelly's character, sexual tension. But it's very formulaic stuff, right down to Simon's favorite phrase, "Boy, oh boy," acting as the equivalent to Pacino's irritating "Hoo-haw!" in *Scent*. Although the message of the movie is to think beyond your preconceptions about people and ideas, the by-the-numbers movie doesn't dare practice what it preaches.

Even though set at Harvard—and very loosely based on a real 1970s incident there—*With Honors* shows how difficult it is for moviemakers to get on Harvard's campus, ever since university authorities booted 1981's *A Small Circle of Friends* midway through principal photography. Keshishian brought his lead actors to Cambridge to rehearse and soak up the atmosphere, yet only two weeks of filming was done locally, despite the fact that Keshishian was a hotshot young Crimson grad at the time, having directed Madonna's *Truth or Dare* documentary.

> It could have been set at any university. It's at Harvard because Harvard is an easy moniker to symbolize the ivory tower or privilege or whatever.
> –Alek Keshishian

Almost all of the Cambridge shooting was done on public streets running between Harvard property (such as Quincy Street), in Harvard Square or on Memorial Drive and the Weeks Footbridge. That's why the camera doesn't follow characters inside Harvard Yard's gates, though Keshishian was apparently allowed a few long shots of Widener Library. Most of the interiors that are supposed to be Widener take place inside the Boston Athenaeum. Chicago doubles for Cambridge in most of the neighborhood and city footage, with the campuses of the University of Illinois at Urbana and the University of Minnesota at Minneapolis also enlisted. I don't know if *With Honors* ever might have been special, but the budget concerns and logistics that limited its local filming rendered it rather generic.

►**Locations:** Cambridge; Beacon Hill, Boston.

►**Accents:** Nothing. The Simon-inspired opening of Monty's eyes to the world around him might have included being exposed to locals who've never had the pleasure of attending Harvard.

►**Local color:** Despite the limited access to Harvard, it's surprising that Harvard grad Keshishian didn't at least convey more of the flavor of Harvard Square as compensation. How about a scene at Bartley's Burger Cottage or Algiers Coffee House?

Brief
Visits,
Day
Trips &
the Rest

Ah, Wilderness! (1935)

The Hollywood film of playwright Eugene O'Neill's turn-of-the-20th-century comedy includes Worcester County exteriors.

Alex & Emma (2003)

Boston-set, but filmed mainly on Los Angeles sets and backlots (love the phony MBTA bus and subway exit). This contrived romantic comedy about a writer's-block-stricken novelist (Luke Wilson) and his stenographer (Kate Hudson) also includes a montage of the two leads doing the tourists' grand tour of the Public Garden, the Charles via Duck Tour and Washington Street.

Alice's Restaurant (1969)

Bonnie and Clyde director Arthur Penn's movie of Arlo Guthrie's song, starring the singer-songwriter, is an amiable counterculture comedy, much of it shot in such Berkshires communities as Great Barrington and Stockbridge. Guthrie now owns the converted Great Barrington church where some of the action takes place; it's the HQ of the non-denominational Guthrie Center.

All Kindsa Girls (2003)

Cheryl Eagan-Donovan's evocative documentary about Boston garage-rockers The Real Kids, named for one of their quintessential

All Kindsa Girls: John Felice in Kenmore Square.

1970s Boston rock songs, isn't just a portrait of John Felice's on-again, off-again band. It also delves into what might be called "Boston band syndrome" (great band that should've become big, but doesn't) and, to give the music context, dips into Boston rock history and the city's preference for guitar-driven garage rock, with both Barry Tashian of The Remains and Jonathan Richman (who started the Modern Lovers with Natick neighbor Felice when the latter was 15) appearing. Of course, there's onstage footage of The Real Kids, too, filmed at the Middle East, the Abbey and Avalon.

Altered States (1980)
Ken Russell's mindbending and often muddled tale of an obsessed scientist (William Hurt) exploring his inner being includes a brief scene in front of Harvard Medical School. But the rest of its Boston portion is in studios and on the backlot.

Amazing Grace and Chuck (1987)
There is footage in the North Station area in this jaw-dropper about a Celtics player (Denver Nuggets star Alex English) who joins the boycott begun by a Montana Little Leaguer (Joshua Zuehlke)—no more sports until the superpowers disarm their nukes! It's a latter-day Cold War camp classic.

American Buffalo (1996)
Pawtucket gives director Michael Corrente just the right rundown industrial vibe for his adaptation of David Mamet's three-character play. Although it doesn't have Al Pacino, who famously played hotheaded Teach onstage (Dustin Hoffman plays him here), this is a prime Mamet exposé of corrosive capitalism.

American Wake (2004)
The impact of the second movie by Maureen (*Home Before Dark*) Foley may depend on your fondness for Irish fiddle music. Her drama offers two separate Cambridge Irish-American characters at crossroads in life: Jack (co-writer Billy Smith), a hard-drinking firefighter on a prolonged leave of absence ever since a blaze claimed his best friend; and Niall (Sam Amidon), a young fiddler pushed to pursue his talent by his Irish dad (Brian Delate). Jack is more involving, as Smith (who later had a small role in *The Departed*) is a much more animated performer than musician Amidon is.

Amistad (1997)
Steven Spielberg's disappointing slave drama shot in the legislative chambers of the State House briefly, but long enough for some of the longwinded speeches of John Quincy Adams (Anthony Hopkins) that

American Wake: Billy Smith on the Charles.

mar this talky movie. The movie's Boston stop is, however, notable to local movie lore because Robin Williams, in town filming *Good Will Hunting*, visited the set with Matt Damon. The visit helped Damon land the title role in Spielberg's *Saving Private Ryan*.

Apocalypse Bop (1996)

No comedy should plod along as deliberately as former *Harvard Lampoon* writer Andrew Osborne's does. This homegrown tale of a hopeless college dropout (Scott Van Doviak) stuck in a menial job simply never develops any cinematic style or comic sensibility. A sequence shot in Middleboro conveys the weirdness of returning to your high school's Thanksgiving Day football game after graduating, but that's hardly enough to put Osborne's movie over.

The Art of Passion (1994)

This precious romantic drama about an up-and-coming painter (Pablo Bryant) who's unsure of where to dip his paint brush—so to speak— was shot mostly in Provincetown. It originally played in film festivals as *Unconditional Love*.

Author! Author! (1982)

An overbearing comedy about a neurotic Broadway playwright (Al Pacino) dealing with his new play, the break-up of his marriage and his brood of children, this includes a five-minute scene set and shot in Gloucester. Cape Ann playwright Israel Horovitz scripted.

The Autumn Heart (1999)

Unhappy with his Hollywood acting career, Saugus-born Davidlee Willson headed back East to star in his own screenplay. He plays the upwardly mobile son in a divorce-split family that is uneasily reunited when his mother (Tyne Daly) suffers a heart attack. But the culture clash between the Harvard student Willson plays and his townie sisters (including one played by Ally Sheedy, in the shrillest fake-Boston accent on record) is cartoonish, and the domestic melodrama is just as over the top. If the movie relaxed a little, its intended heartwarming elements might have worked more. In addition to Saugus, this Sundance Film Festival selection also shot in Cambridge, Winchester, Watertown, Needham and Waltham.

Beacon Hill (2000)

When filmed in 1999 as *The Gentleman from Boston*, this indie production grabbed a ton of publicity, since it's co-directed by former state rep and Massachusetts Secretary of State Michael Connolly. He shot it with co-director John Stimpson at such locations as The Lenox Hotel, Ernie Boch, Jr.'s Norwood mansion, West Roxbury's Carol's Batting Cages, Doyle's in Jamaica Plain and the State House. You'd think a politician might offer a knowing peek behind the curtain, but this political tale reminiscent of *Mr. Smith Goes to Washington* is, in its own way, guilty of the cynicism it detests. Its idealistic young rep (Michael Landes of *Getting Personal*) doesn't just run up against the usual hardball tactics; his opponents also try to frame him for rape and, it turns out, are guilty of attempted murder, too. We're supposed to feel good at the end of this, but you end up simply feeling dirty.

Beantown (2008)

In this corner, Irish-American gangsters from South Boston; and, in the other corner, Italian-American gangsters from the North End. Theoretically, they come out swinging in this digital thriller that was being completed in the summer of 2007.

Before and After (1996)

Lee and several other Berkshires towns serve as fictional Hyland in this disappointing domestic drama starring Meryl Streep, Liam Neeson and Edward Furlong. Local girl Alison Folland (*To Die For*, *Good Will Hunting*) co-stars.

Besotted (2001)

With indulgent writer-director Holly Angel Hardman playing a sorceress on vacation who starts manipulating the love lives of a handful of Cape Cod locals, this is magical realism—minus any of the emotional magic. Staggeringly tedious.

Black & White & Red All Over (1997)

The passion and social commentary running through *Lift* directors DeMane Davis and Khari Streeter's first film (co-directed with Harry McCoy) hints at the better things to come. But this drama about six friends pulled into a spiral of black-on-black violence, set within one Cambridge apartment "sometime in the near future," takes place almost entirely within a single room; that and the sometimes overstated dialogue make it feel more suited to the theater than film. Its problems deepen in the second half, as gimmickry—including a brief switch from black-and-white to color and a scene shot from a blunt's-eye view—intrudes.

Blue Hill Avenue (2001)

Local native Craig Ross, Jr.'s overly long gangster drama takes place in Roxbury, and a few supporting roles were cast with Boston actors. But it was shot in Saint John, New Brunswick (sometimes the cars even have N.B. license plates). Ross, whose tale is a mix of the clichéd and the ostentatiously artsy, inserts generic shots of Roxbury and Dorchester landmarks every so often (street signs, school signs, local institutions like Warren Street's A Nubian Notion) to try to create the illusion of Boston.

Bluff (2000)

Director Bill Miller shot this so-so comedy-drama about a card game in and around the Magoun Square, Somerville bar at the corner of Broadway and Medford Street that seems to change management and name about every four years (it's the On the Hill Tavern at the time of this writing). Local comics Lenny Clarke, Kenny Rogerson and George MacDonald are among the players whose long night of gambling dredges up much emotional history. Veteran Boston blues musician James Montgomery provides the musical accompaniment.

The Box (2008)

Donnie Darko writer-director Richard Kelly came to Boston in late 2007 to make another mindbender—though, like his earlier movie, it's set in his native Virginia (where parts of it were also filmed). Based on a Richard Matheson story, it stars Cameron Diaz, James Marsden and Frank Langella, who set up shop in Milton, Quincy, the Back Bay and a South Boston soundstage, among other places.

The Busker (2006)

Writer-director Stephen Croke's hometown of Lowell is the primary location for his tale of Irish music and puppy love. There, amid recent racial strife, pre-teens Seamus (Alex Alexander), a young Irish-American fiddler who plays on street corners for change, and Ruby

(Ayla Rose Barreau), a gregarious black girl, fall for each other. It's a bit like an after-school special, but it's also quite moving at times.

Camp Stories (1997)
This nostalgic Pennsylvania-set tale, which takes place during the 1950s, filmed in the Berkshires.

Captive Audience (1999)
Former WFNX DJs Mike Goscia and Kurt St. Thomas co-directed this indie comedy-drama set in the wee hours at a radio station. Filmed over three years, often when the two could find common vacation time from their jobs, it was shot partially in Lynn and Beverly, as well as in St. Thomas' New York apartment.

The Cardinal (1963)
Otto Preminger's *very* lengthy epic about a Boston priest (wooden Tom Tryon) who rises to a position of influence in the Vatican includes such local locations as the waterfront, Trinity Station and Boston Common. There is also at least one shot done near the old Orange Line El by Ruggles Street. Stamford and Bridgeport, Connecticut also doubled for much of the Boston action.

A Change of Seasons (1980)
What's good for the gander is good for the goose in this comedy about a college professor (Anthony Hopkins) who has a fling with a student (Bo Derek), only to lead his wife to dally with a hunky carpenter (Michael Brandon). Some shooting was done at and around Williams College, while there's also a scene at Mass. Ave. and Memorial Drive in Cambridge and at the exterior of 85 Mt. Vernon Street on Beacon Hill (the same mansion the title character of *The Thomas Crown Affair* calls home). As always, the casting of Bo Derek opposite Anthony Hopkins is a mind-blower.

The Charms: Easy Trouble (2006)
A documentary about the Boston garage/power-pop band should have been a lot of fun. Benjamin Oliver's meandering movie sometimes is, as The Charms have good songs and Ellie Vee is a killer frontwoman. But the sound on most of the performance footage is muddy and the way the movie just plows through the band's history lacks imagination. More rock and less talk would've really helped.

Chatham (2008)
Rip Torn, David Carradine and Bruce Dern play seafaring coots looking for love in this 1905-set tale from Cape Cod filmmaker Daniel Adams (*The Mouse*), who adapts a novel by local writer Joseph Lincoln. In

addition to the title town, the movie also filmed in other Cape locales, including Provincetown and Hyannis. It was in post-production as this book was being prepared.

The Cider House Rules (1999)
Perhaps no movie taps into a New England autumnal mood on as grand a scale as Lasse Hallström's adaptation of John Irving's novel. Sometimes the rich production design overshadows the characters and the intended emotion, but much of the Maine-set tale was filmed in Northampton and Lenox, as well as Great Barrington, Northfield and Egremont.

Coffee & Donuts (2000)
Adam Green's homegrown comedy, shot in his native Holliston and Malden, took a weird path. Instead of attracting Hollywood interest for distribution, his semi-autobiographical story of two buddies who DJ at their school was acquired by a studio and then developed into a sitcom pilot. But the pilot did not lead to a series. Green has continued making low-budget movies, though not locally.

Coma (1978)
The adaptation of Robin Cook's novel is a solid Hitchcockian thriller about a doctor (Genevieve Bujold) at fictional Boston Memorial Hospital who uncovers a shady plot by her craven bosses. Since the movie takes place mainly indoors, very little was filmed locally. But there is a smattering of area sights, including the exterior of Boston City Hospital and, best of all, a great, slow pan from the heroine's room at the Holiday Inn on Blossom Street across Beacon Hill to the Back Bay skyline.

Complex World (1990)
This grungy Providence rock 'n' roll comedy has a winning underdog charm. Set in Lupo's Heartbreak Hotel club, it suffers from subplot overload, though most of them work fine (look for Captain Lou Albano in a supporting role). The movie includes plenty of amusing musical interludes, especially from The Young Adults, the mock-rockers who reunited especially for the movie. But the goofily endearing heart of the movie beats in Stanley Matis, as the self-proclaimed "folksinger from Hell" who debuts at the club with songs such as "New Jersey," with the refrain "pave it over, pave it over."

Dad (1989)
The farm flashbacks in the shameless Jack Lemmon-Ted Danson melodrama—which feature Chris Lemmon as the younger version of his real-life dad's character—were done in Duxbury.

The Dance (2007)

Religious filmmaker McKay Daines shot at least some exteriors of his story, revolving around a dance on the Harvard campus, in the area.

The Darien Gap (1996)

Before Brad Anderson directed *Next Stop Wonderland*, he and co-writer Lyn Vaus made this scruffy, no-budget comedy-drama. It's about a dispirited Boston slacker (Vaus) who's dumped by his girlfriend (Sandi Carroll) and decides to pursue his dream of crossing the swampy Panamanian Darien Gap in order to get to South America. In addition to Boston locations, much of the oddball hero's ill-fated journey was shot in Anderson's home state, Connecticut. The first Boston independent movie to be accepted into competition at the Sundance Film Festival, Anderson's appealing feature debut has never resurfaced on any form of home video.

Dark Assassin (2006)

Boston-based martial-arts champ Jason Yee wrote, directed and stars in this action picture set throughout the city. It's fairly formulaic stuff—Yee's character gets out of prison as the movie starts, and when his former gang's members start dying, both the police and the boss of the gang accuse him of being responsible. Still, it's a respectable job, with more ambitious editing than you usually find in a low-budget film. Robert Patton-Spruill (*Squeeze*) is executive producer.

Dead Heat on a Merry-Go-Round (1966)

Bookended by its predominant California setting, this playful James Coburn caper comedy includes a half-hour of snowy Boston action in which the seductive con man he plays furthers his grand scheme of robbing a bank at Los Angeles' airport. Although few, if any, interiors were done here, Coburn appears in mid-winter scenes on Boston Common and the Comm. Ave. Mall. There's also a nice aerial shot of the city looking east from the South End (freeze-frame it and check out the cityscape) and a brief view looking out of the entrance at the Sheraton Hotel, though the interior action there (with young Harrison Ford as a bellboy) is obviously performed on a studio set.

Dead Silence (1998)

Writer-director Juliane Glantz shot her so-so black comedy in her native Berkshires, with Pittsfield, Dalton and Becket being the most prevalent locations (there are also a few Back Bay and South End exteriors during a brief Boston sequence). The story blends *Carrie* and *Twin Peaks* in its tale of teenage female revenge set against a wacky-small-town backdrop. The late Maureen Stapleton, then a Lenox resident, has a cameo. Also known as *Wilbur Falls*.

Dead Heat on a Merry-Go-Round: James Coburn and Joey Faye on Boston Common.

Dealing: Or the Berkeley-to-Boston Forty-Brick Lost-Bag Blues (1972)

A forgotten counterculture comedy worthy of rediscovery. It stars Robert F. Lyons and John Lithgow (in his film debut) as two drug-dealing Harvard students who scheme against a crooked detective (Charles Durning) who arrested the first's girlfriend (Barbara Hershey) and took the weed she was carrying in on a flight from California. It's hard to tell exactly how much of the movie was filmed here, as it's a widescreen picture that's not on video and not shown letterboxed on TV (in the ultra-rare instances it's ever on TV). The Harvard action may or may not be Cambridge and the wintry climax in the Walden Pond parking lot could be the real thing. But a sequence on the Ashmont-Mattapan streetcar and another in and around pre-renovation South Station are clearly legit, as are some of the driving shots, including one at Franklin and Washington Streets (notice the five-floor Woolworth's of old) and another on Route 128.

Defending Our Lives (1994)

Cambridge moviemakers Margaret Lazarus, Renner Wunderlich and Stacey Kabat's Oscar-winning 40-minute documentary is incredibly powerful. It's a totally unadorned succession of profiles of many of the "Framingham 8"—women serving time for killing the men who battered them—relating the horrors they survived and the steps they took to finally fight back.

The Deserter (2003)
Eric Bruno Borgman wrote, directed and stars in this Revolutionary War comedy about a wayward Redcoat drummer.

Dinner and a Movie (2001)
This little-seen indie comedy filmed in such Berkshires locations as Pittsfield and Stockbridge.

Dirt Boy (2001)
A New Yorker with a dark past (Jacob Lee Hedman) comes to fictional Atwater Commons to take a forensic criminology course, and discovers there's more truth to a local author's grisly bestselling novel than the townies want to admit. Jay Franco's nifty no-budget thriller, set and filmed on Cape Cod, weaves a little spell and, thanks to its stripped-down production—no Anthony Hopkins or Christopher Plummer chewing scenery as the imposing author—avoids many a cliché along the way.

Dirty Tricks (1981)
Although set locally, most of this long-forgotten comic thriller, involving a letter written by George Washington, a Harvard professor (Elliott Gould) and a reporter (Kate Jackson), was shot in Canada.

Dischord (2001)
As in *Dirt Boy*, wintry Cape Cod locations provide the backdrop for intrigue. But the plot and the characters in Mark Wilkinson's slow thriller about husband-and-wife musicians (Annunziata Gianzero,

Dirt Boy: Lonnie Farmer and Robert Rubin in Wellfleet.

Andrew Borba) and his estranged, murderous brother (Thomas Jay Ryan) never amount to much.

Distant Justice (1992)
This time it's personal! A Japanese cop (Bunta Sugawara) visiting Boston with his family unwittingly photographs a drug deal. Soon his wife is dead, his daughter's been kidnapped and he's gunning for revenge. George Kennedy plays a cop, David Carradine is here, too, and the movie offers glimpses of Bunker Hill Monument, Malden Hospital and Cambridge's Central Square, before its gentrified makeover.

Divine Intervention (2007)
A nutjob killer who thinks he's an agent of God—and definitely is a *Survivor* fanatic—interrupts the sex, drugs and rock 'n' roll of a group of friends in Ware in Rufus Chaffee's homegrown, comedy-tinged slasher picture. The plot isn't all that interesting, but Chaffee does a decent job of mixing his elements.

Domino One (2005)
Natalie Portman is among the cast in Harvard classmate Nick Louvel's digital-video drama produced over several years. It's unclear if this tale of Ivy League intrigue has ever had any public screenings, though.

Down Around Here (1996)
Long before he made such nationally aired documentary mini-series as *The Farmer's Wife*, Newton's David Sutherland shot this priceless non-fiction short. Filmed during the late 1970s in East Cambridge, when it was still a blue-collar neighborhood full of factories and greasy spoons, but not edited together until 20 years later, the film focuses on the long-gone Kitchenette Diner and its irrepressible counterman, Russ Young. One for the time capsule.

Down to the Sea in Ships (1922)
With its whale butchering and racist streak, this silent melodrama is about as politically incorrect as you can get. The 19th-century tale is also full of cardboard characters, but it's set against the backdrop of the New Bedford whaling community, and the action on and near the water, shot there, is very impressive. Land locations include New Bedford's Seamen's Bethel and South Dartmouth's Apponegansett Meeting House.

Dreamrider (1993)
This TV-style docudrama tells the story of a high school football star (Matthew Geriak) who loses a leg in an accident with a drunk driver, and then cycles from his native California to the Old North Church on

Down to the Sea in Ships: Raymond McKee in New Bedford.

a dare. The hero rides through the Public Garden (cue the swan boats), Copley Square and the North End during the Boston sequence.

Easy Listening (2002)

B.U. grad Pamela Corkey's 1967-set tale of a sad-sack trumpeter (David Ian) in an "instrumental pop" orchestra, whose life is brightened by the arrival of a sunny flutist (Traci Crouch), is sweet but slow. Call it *How I Learned to Stop Worrying and Love the Muzak*. Corkey split her shoot between Greater Boston and Providence, with such local spots as Allston's Model Café and Brookline's Larz Anderson Park prominently featured, as well as modernist architecture in the Coolidge Corner area. Cool 101 Strings Orchestra score.

The Eighteenth Angel (1999)

This schlocky thriller about a Boston family targeted by a group of Satanists—it takes place mostly in Rome—is generally the worst kind of offender during its early Boston action. Its "Boston" is almost entirely generic exteriors with shots of the cast presumably done elsewhere. But at least one big shot is the McCoy, with one character atop the

YWCA Building, showing a long stretch of Clarendon Street office buildings behind her.

Enough Already (1998)
It's set in Michigan, but Wellesley writer-director Tom Keenan's comedy was shot primarily in and around Waltham's Brandeis University, as well as in Wellesley and Newton. With a college slacker (David Wheir) saddled with a bossy, rich girlfriend (Alanna Ubach) he can't seem to break up with, the twist here is that it's a romantic comedy in which *losing* the girl is the triumph. Trouble is, Ubach (*Clockwatchers*, TV's *Beakman's World*) is such an amusing comic actress that you end up wondering why *she* doesn't dump *him*—not the intended effect.

The Europeans (1979)
James Ivory and Ismail Merchant's first locally shot Henry James adaptation precedes *The Bostonians* by five years. Filmed in preserved 19th-century houses in Salem, Waltham and southern New Hampshire, as well as at exteriors in the Route 2 area (Concord, Leominster), it's about the conflict of manners that brews when a family of repressed, suburban Boston WASPs hosts decadent cousins from abroad. Despite the homecoming for Quincy's Lee Remick, the movie is too much like a crafted trinket to succeed, with insufferably dainty music.

Everybody Wants to Be Italian (2007)
A group of area-college graduates return for a North End romantic comedy. Shooting half of its action locally, writer-director Jason Todd

Easy Listening: Traci Crouch and David Ian in the South End.

Ipson includes great local scenery (Hanover Street, Mike's Pastry, the Green Line) in his story of a fishmonger (Jay Jablonski) and a veterinarian (Cerina Vincent). But he fails to overcome the staleness of the ethnic romantic comedy, plus the ungentrified North End the movie touts no longer exists. But expectations of authenticity quickly plummet after one character refers to "the Commons."

Everyone's Got One (2000)
Needham's Garth Donovan funds movies by recycling deposit cans and scrap metal. Alas, that's not the only thing he recycles. This comedy in which Donovan plays a desperate aspiring moviemaker, an exaggerated version of himself (at least I hope it's exaggerated), is a low-rent knock-off of Martin Scorsese's *The King of Comedy.*

The Exchange (1999)
Writer-director Ed Nicoletti's crime drama, with an ensemble cast that includes familiar faces Robert Wahlberg and Don Gavin, is very amateurish. Among his locations are Brighton and City Hall Plaza.

Fade to Black (2007)
A passionate, but hyperactively edited and very scattered tale of violence in the streets of Boston (seen in a 2007 rough cut). It just tries to do too much, with the script's historical and sociological tangents about violence and racism being distractions (such ideas need to be

Everybody Wants to Be Italian: Jay Jablonski and Cerina Vincent on Boston Common.

better integrated into the story and its characters). Sometimes it's an interesting mess, but it's a mess, nonetheless.

Fear Strikes Out (1957)
The otherwise interesting movie biography of troubled 1950s Red Sox star Jimmy Piersall (Anthony Perkins)—whose relentless dad (Karl Malden) won't let him relax—does something a movie today would never do. It mixes in real Fenway Park game footage shot from a distance with tighter shots of Perkins and other actors shot in a ballpark that looks *nothing* like Fenway. There is also one non-game scene of Perkins on the Fenway field when the park is empty. But you have to make a big leap of faith to just accept the baseball action.

Federal Hill (1994)
The tradition of Fellini's *I Vitelloni* and Scorsese's *Mean Streets* comes to Providence in Michael Corrente's comedy-drama about a group of guys in the Italian-American neighborhood from which the movie draws its name. The central buddies are Nicky (Anthony DeSando), who's looking beyond the neighborhood (he's even dating a Brown student), and Ralph (Nick Turturro), an impetuous thief. Corrente covers familiar territory, but he avoids caricature and taps particularly well into Nicky's perspective.

Feelin' Good (1966)
Boston gets in on the 1960s pop-music movie craze with this local production by moonlighting industrial filmmaker James A. Pike (who'd had great success with the car crash short *Demo Derby*, filmed in Norwood). His son Travis stars, writing many of the songs in this story of young love and a battle of the bands. This teen film hasn't been seen in decades, so info on it is sketchy (there's a scene featuring the Public Garden's swan boats as well as plenty of tunes). Travis Pike has newsreel footage of the world premiere at Washington Street's Paramount Theater posted on his website.

Festival (1967)
It's a credit to Murray Lerner's documentary, filmed at the 1963-66 Newport Folk Festivals, that folk-averse people like me can enjoy it. Just fast-forward through Joan Baez and Judy Collins—to enjoy Pete Seeger, Buffy Sainte-Marie, Son House, the Swan Silvertones and Bob Dylan going electric—and you'll be fine.

Field of Dreams (1989)
In Kevin Costner's bad baseball movie—*Bull Durham* being his good baseball movie—his Midwesterner travels to Boston to find a reclusive writer (James Earl Jones) and drag him to a Sox game at Fenway Park,

where both see a message on the centerfield scoreboard only they can perceive. In addition to action at Fenway, there's a nice helicopter shot starting on Storrow Drive and then swooping up, as well as footage filmed on Huntington Avenue near the Museum of Fine Arts. But the Orthodox Jewish Boston neighborhood where the writer lives is actually a temporarily made-over section of Dubuque, Iowa.

The Firm (1993)

Director Sydney Pollack and star Tom Cruise spent a weekend in town shooting bits and pieces, mostly for the opening of their legal thriller, one of the better John Grisham adaptations. In addition to East Cambridge exteriors also featuring Jeanne Tripplehorn and Harvard University shots, Cruise filmed scenes inside the Copley Plaza Hotel. One such scene, with hotel owner Jim Daley playing a concierge who directs Cruise's law school grad to a job interview, doesn't appear in the finished film. Was there even film in the camera? Or was this scene just the Hollywood production's way of pretending to be nice to us small-town rubes?

Flowers in the Attic (1987)

Some exteriors (and maybe even a few interiors) for the cheesy dysfunctional-family chiller were done on the Crane Estate in Ipswich. But most of the action was filmed in California.

Follow the Broccoli (1999)

There's music and bingo in the air in Bob Coleman's absurd romantic comedy that includes many Boston and suburban locations.

For the Love of Movies: The Story of American Film Criticism (2008)

Real Paper and *Boston Phoenix* critic Gerald Peary's long-in-gestation documentary, which had a few work-in-progress screenings in 2007, looks at the tradition of movie reviewing in the U.S.

Freedom Park (2004)

Unlike most Hollywood family films, this independent production out of Worcester County actually feels as if it were made by real people. It's about a couple of twentysomething buddies (Tim Fields, Matt McDonald) who scurry home after chasing their dreams in Las Vegas and ending up in deep debt to the mob. Back home, they apply their gambling jones to youth sports and try to win back their high school sweethearts. Not everything works, particularly the generic mob comedy, but it feels genuine—plus there are cameos by Red Sox legends Jerry Remy and Luis Tiant. The same folks previously made 2002's *Rutland, USA.*

From the Hip (1987)

Although co-written by Boston-born future TV mogul David E. Kelley, most of this generally obnoxious legal comedy—hey, it stars Judd Nelson—was shot in North Carolina. There are perhaps only two moments filmed here with the cast, a brief shot of Nelson crossing Court Street to head into the Ames Building and an actual scene in the Public Garden.

The Game Plan (2007)

Dwayne "The Rock" Johnson's charisma elevated this formulaic family film into a surprise hit. He plays Joe Kingman, the star quarterback of the Boston Rebels and a confirmed bachelor whose playboy ways get sacked when the eight-year-old daughter (Madison Pettis) he never knew he had turns up on his swanky doorstep. There's an odd mix of fact and fiction here: although the implication is that the Rebels are an NFL team, there's no mention of the league and the climactic "championship game" is *not* the Super Bowl; Joe's big-game skills, model-dating lifestyle and unconventional fatherhood oddly mirror Tom Brady's; and, despite such locations as Gillette Stadium, The Barking Crab restaurant and the entryway to the upscale 1 Charles complex (as well as athlete cameos from the likes of Jo Jo White and Mike Eruzione), the movie could be set anywhere.

The Gate of Heavenly Peace (1995)

Boston-based Carma Hinton and Richard Gordon have made many documentaries about China, but this amazingly detailed, three-hour look at 1989's Tiananmen Square student protests is the most probing and powerful. Using little narration, and conveying its account primarily through interviews with those involved, this is an almost day-by-day peek into the seven-week attempt to bring democratic reforms to China. Definitive.

Gavin's Way (2001)

Dan Farquharson wrote, directed and stars in this North Shore comedy about three Irish-American cousins.

Getting Away with Murder (1996)

A D.O.A. comedy all too symptomatic of the 1990s craze of shooting U.S.-set stories in Canada. Aside from a few Boston exteriors, this tale of an ethics professor (Dan Aykroyd) who turns vigilante when his Brighton neighbor (Jack Lemmon) is exposed as a Nazi war criminal was shot north of the border in Ontario. It may have tried to compensate by using Channel 5's Heather "Heathah the Feathah" Kahn in its fake news footage, but the Canadian accents on the bit players say it all.

Getting Personal (1998)

Dedham-born writer-actor Michael Lewis' script was shot under the title *Somehow Scituate*. In addition to filming there, the movie also set up shop at Revere Beach, the Public Garden and the Pine Crest Motel on the Malden/Saugus line. Unfortunately, the romantic comedy, which never had a theatrical release and took two years to reach home video, turns out to be pretty amateurish.

Gift of the Game (2002)

Bill Haney follows former Red Sox pitcher Bill Lee and a team of middle-aged barnstormers as they travel Cuba, playing against local teams. An entertaining exercise in friendly international relations from the director of 2007's *The Price of Sugar*.

Glory (1989)

Harvard grad Edward Zwick's powerful drama about the Civil War's 54th Massachusetts Regiment of Volunteer Infantry, the black regiment led by white officer Robert Gould Shaw (Matthew Broderick), is a Boston story, all right. But only some of it takes place here and little of the finished film was shot here. There's the closing image of the Augustus Saint-Gaudens memorial to the 54th that faces the State House (a few doors away from Shaw's Beacon Street home), as well as close-up inserts shot on Union Park in the South End for the regiment's procession down Beacon Street, and more inserts at Ipswich's Appleton Farm for a battle scene. Zwick shot most of the Boston action in Savannah.

The Great Debaters (2007)

Denzel Washington received a rare OK to film on Harvard's campus, shooting inside Sanders Theater for his drama about Wiley College's debate team challenging Harvard in 1935. He also filmed inside the grand lobby of Citi Performing Arts Center, previously seen onscreen in *The Witches of Eastwick*, when it was supposed to be a mansion interior. This time it's made over to look like an old train station.

The Gypsy Years (2000)

Weston native Rebecca Bagley shot her tale of a college graduate (LG Taylor) who reluctantly returns to her hometown in the Waltham area. Matthew Del Negro of *The North End* is among the ensemble. Bagley has continued making films, though not locally.

Hanky Panky (1982)

This tired attempt at putting a comic twist on a Hitchcockian thriller—with Gene Wilder and Gilda Radner being chased by thugs led by *Coma* heavy Richard Widmark—includes a Boston sequence putting the two stars in Harvard Square, the New England Aquarium and Beacon Hill. Purely formulaic stuff.

Here on Earth (2000)
Shot in Minnesota, this silly fantasy about a girl (Leelee Sobieski) who falls for the new kid in town (Chris Klein) filmed a bit in western Massachusetts and includes a Boston aerial shot. It's like a cross between an after-school special and a romance novel. A bad cross.

Hiding Out (1987)
Like a lot of 1980s releases from the De Laurentiis Entertainment Group, this teen thriller—with Jon Cryer as a stock broker targeted by the mob who poses as a high school student—filmed mostly in North Carolina. But much of the Boston-set opening was actually shot here, with the Financial District and the South Station area appearing. A famous New England screenwriting team penned the original screenplay for this, but removed their names after they didn't like the changes made to it. My lips are sealed.

Hocus Pocus (1993)
Before the studio sets and special effects completely take over, this kiddie comedy starring Bette Midler, Kathy Najimy and Sarah Jessica Parker as Salem witches who return to life after 300 years features Salem and Marblehead exterior footage with the younger cast members who play foils to the stars.

The Hole Story (2005)
Newton-based writer-director Alex Karpovsky plays the obsessed hero of his clever faux-documentary, a filmmaker whose quest to capture a small-town phenomenon spirals out of control. He goes to wintry Minnesota, but the mysterious hole in a frozen lake he hopes to feature closes up as soon as he arrives. The quest not only tests the guy's filmmaking ethics, it also makes him question his relationship with the world around him. Karpovsky shot primarily in Minnesota, but also in Newton.

The Honeymoon Killers (1969)
A real indie classic, Leonard Kastle's mesmerizing true-crime thriller about the "Lonely Hearts Killers" (Tony Lo Bianco, Shirley Stoler) includes Berkshire County locations (in addition to upstate New York locales). Full of savage beauty.

House of Usher (2006)
Aussie director Hayley Cloake updates Edgar Allen Poe in this chiller shot on the North Shore.

Howard Zinn: You Can't Be Neutral on a Moving Train: Howard Zinn at Boston University.

Howard Zinn: You Can't Be Neutral on a Moving Train (2004)

A People's History of the United States author, former B.U. professor and local icon Zinn gets a documentary tribute in Deb Ellis and Dennis Mueller's movie. It's nothing special filmmaking-wise, but the guy certainly merits a movie. Matt Damon narrates. But, of course. (Boston filmmaker John Gianvito later paid tribute to Zinn's *A People's History of the United States* in his hour-long 2007 non-fiction film, *Profit motive and the whispering wind*.)

The Human Stain (2003)

Over 20 years after *A Change of Seasons*, Anthony Hopkins is back on the Williams College campus. It "plays" Athena College in Athena, Mass. in Robert (*Twilight*) Benton's adaptation of Philip Roth's novel, which shot mostly in Canada. The tale is unfocused and bursting with loose ends, which is unexpected for a Benton film, but most of this drama about a retired professor (Hopkins) with a secret and his emotionally wounded younger lover (Nicole Kidman) is very involving and certainly unformulaic.

The Imported Bridegroom (1990)

Boston College art history professor Pamela Berger, who'd written the 1987 French film *Sorceress*, turns writer-director with this adaptation of Abraham Cahan's novella about Jewish immigrants. Her own Cambridge house was used for scenes, as was Sanders Theater and locations in Beacon Hill, Chestnut Hill, Concord and the South Shore. The circa-1900 setting is the attraction here, as much of the staging is flat and the acting clunky. Berger later turned her movie into a musical that was produced on the community theater level in 1998.

In Dreams (1999)
Filmed mainly in the Northampton area, at such locations as Smith College and Northampton State Hospital, this psychological thriller is one of *The Crying Game* director Neil Jordan's lesser movies. Annette Bening plays a psychically attuned woman who descends into madness after a serial killer (Robert Downey, Jr.) possesses her dreams. But the script never pulls us deeply enough into the characters' heads to work up much suspense.

International Velvet (1978)
The follow-up to 1944's *National Velvet* takes place mostly in England. But the Tatum O'Neal coming-of-age story shot locally long enough to be one of the productions from which five Boston Teamsters were charged with extorting money.

In the Land of Merry Misfits (2007)
Years in the making, Boston native Kevin Undergaro's carny comedy features Medford's Maria Menounos, Fred "Rerun" Berry, former good-guy wrestling champ Bob Backlund and narration by *Hairspray* writer-director John Waters.

Jaws (1975)
Joseph Sylva State Beach and Menemsha Harbor are among the many Martha's Vineyard locations in Steven Spielberg's classic shark-scare popcorn movie. Still tense, still fun all these years later.

Jaws 2 (1978)
Civilization crumbles a bit, as the follow-up to Steven Spielberg's hit ushers in the age of rampant sequels with numbers in their title. Like its predecessor, this too was filmed mainly on Martha's Vineyard. But the drop-off in quality is precipitous. The later *Jaws: The Revenge* includes a little Vineyard action, too.

Joe & Joe (1996)
They mow lawns. They fish. They drink beer. The boyish title characters of David Wall's off-kilter Cape Cod comedy are amusingly dim and, as if in a Coen Brothers movie, they get pulled into intrigue by a mysterious woman (Tracy Griffith of *The Good Mother*). The

summery West Dennis locations, deadpan acting and genuinely sweet tone power this endearing low-budget comedy, which played at the 1996 Sundance Film Festival. Writer-director Wall later made another Cape film, *Mrs. Worthington's Party* (2006).

Johnny Slade's Greatest Hits (2005)
As a low-rent lounge singer hired by the mob to croon coded lyrics about all sorts of illegal activities, star-producer John Fiore (*Lift*, *The Autumn Heart*) surrounds himself with co-stars from *The Sopranos*. The mob comedy was filmed mostly at that hotspot of wiseguy activity, Tewskbury Country Club.

The Last Detail (1973)
Two members of the Navy Shore Patrol (Jack Nicholson, Otis Young) transport a prisoner (Randy Quaid) from Norfolk, Virginia to Portsmouth in Hal Ashby's essential 1970s dark comedy. The trio's journey includes a stop in Boston. There's a visit to the lower Washington Street area (the old, elevated Orange Line is visible) and to a park that's often assumed to be the Common, but clearly isn't.

Leaving Scars (1997)
Although set in Los Angeles, most of this ultra-low-budget drama about an actress (Lisa Boyle) who comes into possession of the 1990s' thriller default object of desire—a computer disc—was shot in Boston by Massachusetts native Brad Jacques.

The Legend of Lucy Keyes (2006)
It's separation anxiety times two in John Stimpson's thriller. Julie Delpy and Justin Theroux play parents who've just lost one daughter and move into a Princeton farmhouse where, local legend says, a colonial girl went out to pick blueberries and never returned. Not only does the ghost of the dead Lucy Keyes' mother roam the woods in search of her, but the new inhabitants' surviving daughter is also named Lucy. Much jeopardy ensues. Shot mostly in and around Princeton's Wachusett Mountain (with a bit of Waltham), the movie's intrigue over land deals can be a buzzkill, but it has its share of eerie moments.

Leona's Sister Gerri (1994)
Theme: Murder producer Jane Gillooly powerfully investigates the life of Geraldine Santoro, the woman whose grisly death photo—the result of a botched 1964 motel-room abortion—became an icon of the abortion-rights movement after its inclusion in a 1973 *Ms.* article. Through interviews with Gerri's sister, her best friend and two daughters, we learn of the circumstances that led to the abortion (including an abusive husband). But the movie, which aired on PBS, never stoops

to mere advocacy, offering a range of emotional perspectives on the politicized photo. Gillooly has more recently finished another probing documentary: *Today the Hawk Takes One Chick,* an impressively intimate, statistics-free look at the grandmothers of Swaziland who've been left to deal with the AIDS epidemic and to raise the children of their dead children.

Life's Too Good (1994)
Writer-director Hilary Weisman shot her comedy-drama in her family's Chelmsford home. Her story of the love lives of the women in one family is most remarkable for a professional polish that belies its low budget. She later made the 1999 semi-improvised road movie *I Love My Movie.*

Little Big League (1994)
This overachieving pre-teen sports fantasy about a 12-year-old boy (Luke Edwards) who inherits a big league team and installs himself as manager includes action at several real big-league ballparks, including—of course—Fenway Park. A sincere, dramatically convincing film from a gimmicky genre.

Little Erin Merryweather (2003)
Emerson grad David Morwick does a fine job as writer, director and star of this homegrown horror movie about a series of grisly murders on a college campus. It's a little flimsy towards the end, and might have used one more confrontation sequence, but other than that it's a well-told tale. For his fictional town of Willow Ridge, Morwick shot mostly in Bridgewater and Middleboro.

Little Erin Merryweather: Vigdis Anholt in Middleboro.

Little Shots of Happiness (1997)
There's meat in Todd Verow's premise about a bored Back Bay telemarketer (Bonnie Dickenson) who suddenly releases all the defense mechanisms keeping her life orderly. She leaves her husband and begins nights of binge drinking and scrounging for a bed. But the movie often fails to render her identity crisis (and the ripples it causes) in genuinely dramatic sequences. Too bad, too, since Verow's unconventional approach—shooting in handheld video, in sequence—might have resulted in something special.

Little Women (1994)
Director Gillian Armstrong's outstanding adaptation of the Louisa May Alcott novel has a splendid cast (including Susan Sarandon, Winona Ryder and Claire Danes) that filmed briefly in Historic Deerfield. Most of the movie was done in Canada, but it turned out to be a real boon to local tourism, luring visitors from all over the world to Orchard House, the Alcott home in Concord in which the author set the book.

Lola La Loca (1988)
Inspired by the early work of Spike Lee and *Alice in Wonderland*, Cuban-American Emerson grad Enrique Oliver's barrio comedy sends a social worker (Heidi Egloff) into a housing project to look for elusive title character Lola (Myrna Cruz). Unfortunately, the results aren't as amusing as Oliver's earlier short, *Photo Album*.

The Lonely Maiden (2008)
Boston-movie vets Morgan Freeman (*Gone Baby Gone*), William H. Macy (*State and Main, A Civil Action*) and Marcia Gay Harden (*Mystic River*) returned to the area in 2007 for this caper comedy. Christopher Walken joined them in The North End and South Boston.

Long Distance (2005)
The closed Mass. Mental Health Center on Francis Street "plays" an apartment building in this *Don't Answer the Phone* horror knock-off—revolving around a young woman (Monica Keena) who starts receiving calls from a killer. But there's an interesting twist at the end.

Made-Up (2002)
Writer and co-star Lynne Adams' comedy works better as a showcase for her Jamaica Plain Italianate Victorian house—its primary location—than it does as entertainment. Co-starring sister Brooke Adams and directed by brother-in-law Tony Shalhoub, this starts as a comedy targeting female self-image but morphs into feeble gags about documentary filmmaking, going from bad to worse. Lincoln's DeCordova Museum is the other noteworthy location.

Malice: Nicole Kidman at Beacon and Tremont Streets.

The Magic Stone (1995)

An improvement on writer-director Pamela Berger's previous *The Imported Bridegroom*, her follow-up (first released as *Kilian's Chronicle*) is a sort of medieval *Dances with Wolves*. Set in 10th century New England, with much of the dialogue in the native Passamaquoddy language, it tells of an Irish slave (Christopher Johnson) who escapes his Viking ship and befriends Native Americans. The B.C. professor shot her second feature in Gloucester and Andover's Harold Parker State Forest (as well as in Connecticut), and it's very ambitious, though Berger clutters the tale with subplots.

Malice (1993)

Set mainly in and around Westerly College, a fictional school "two hours from Boston," this enjoyably tawdry thriller stars Alec Baldwin's exuberantly lacquered hair. Director Harold Becker filmed mostly in the Amherst-Northampton area, including at Smith College, though the Victorian house in which Nicole Kidman's and Bill Pullman's characters live is actually on Cambridge's Arlington Street. The action occasionally creeps closer to Boston, including a scene at Beacon and Tremont Streets. As a Southie drunk, Anne Bancroft uncorks a particularly overdone Boston accent during her one scene.

Massholes (2000)

One of several low-budget movies that was filmed in the late 1990s, yet never made it much beyond cast-and-crew screenings. Hull is the main location for Reading native John Chase's 1980s-set teen comedy. Its cast includes such local favorites as Lenny Clarke (as a cop!), the Mighty Mighty Bosstones' Dicky Barrett and... Brooke Shields as herself. More recently, Chase made a police drama, *Interrogation*.

The Matchmaker (1997)
Janeane Garofalo and Denis Leary are well cast, but they fight a losing battle with a cliché-ridden script. She's a campaign worker for a Massachusetts senator who's sent to Ireland to find relatives of the pol for a campaign video; he's the senator's Machiavellian chief of staff. It's set mostly in Ireland, which it portrays as something out of a Lucky Charms commercial. You can spot a few landmarks during the Boston portions, including Faneuil Hall and Longfellow Bridge. But you're better off watching the stars in *When Stand Up Stood Out*.

Metal (2001)
Alice Cox's drama focuses on science and indie rock—perhaps not surprisingly, considering she's an M.I.T. grad and shot her film in Allston. It's about an aspiring singer-songwriter, but the catch is there are two of her: the real woman and her clone. In addition to Allston, Cox also filmed at The Abbey Lounge in Somerville. Not too shabby.

Mona Lisa Smile (2003)
It's too easy to spot the "good guys" and the "bad guys" in this simplistic early-1950s tale of the new Wellesley College art teacher (Julia Roberts) who—gasp—expects her groomed-for-marriage female students to think for themselves. The movie shot in a number of locations nationally, though it did spend a week at Wellesley in October 2002 and returned later for a few wintry shots.

The Mouse (1997)
Cape Cod writer-director Daniel Adams filmed much of his unimpressive biography of boxer Bruce "The Mouse" Strauss (John Savage of *The Little Sister*) close to home. But human punching bag Strauss, who makes a career of being knocked out in the ring, never becomes the lovable loser the movie thinks he is.

My Best Friend's Girl (2008)
Arlington's Dane Cook returns to Greater Boston for a romantic comedy opposite Kate Hudson (*Alex & Emma*). It shot (as *Bachelor No. 2*) at a variety of area locations in late summer of 2007, among them an apartment on Comm. Ave., Copley Plaza Hotel, Suffolk University Law School, the "gentlemen's club" Centerfolds and such restaurants as The Daily Catch in the Seaport District and The Beehive in the South End.

Naughty or Nice (2005)
Director Chris Tyrrell shot his Christmas ensemble comedy on weekends in such cities as Saugus, Lynn, Revere and Stoughton. It's unclear whether it ever played anywhere beyond one-off showings in Randolph and Arlington.

Neighborhoods (1997)
While still an up-and-coming novelist, years before Hollywood filmed his *Mystic River*, Dennis Lehane made his own low-budget drama. He shot it for $35,000 in the Back Bay, Dorchester, Somerville and Watertown, and showed it around town here and there. But if, like me, you didn't see it then, you're out of luck, as it has never resurfaced.

Never Met Picasso (1997)
Despite a solid cast including Alexis Arquette, Margot Kidder, Don McKellar and Keith David, and a score by Throwing Muses' Kristin Hersh, this Bay-State-filmed story of a struggling gay painter (Arquette) comes and goes without making much of an impression. The shots often feels as if the camera is in the wrong place, the plot just sits there and the movie lacks personality.

Night School (1981)
The Boston slasher movie. Well, sort of. Although this formulaic low-budget picture tries to cash in on the success of *Halloween* and *Friday the 13th*, it concentrates on the police investigation into a series of murders so much that it plays like a bland TV pilot about a Harvard-educated detective (Leonard Mann) and his blue-collar, Armenian-American partner (Joseph R. Sicar). For a while, this gained notoriety when Rachel Ward went on to such bigger things as *Dead Men Don't Wear Plaid* and *The Thorn Birds* after her shower scene here.

Oleanna (1994)
David Mamet shot the adaptation of his hot-button 1990s play in Waltham's Metropolitan State Hospital. But whatever made his sexual-harassment drama a sensation doesn't really translate in this flat film.

Oliver's Story (1978)
Like *International Velvet*, this too is a belated sequel (to *Love Story*) that takes place almost entirely elsewhere—but its brief local visit was long enough for it to also be one of the productions from which five Boston Teamsters were charged with extorting money.

On Broadway (2007)
Southie co-writer Dave McLaughlin turns writer-director in this

middling drama. It's one of those movies that's independent more because of its low budget than a desire to be unconventional. There's much heart-tugging in its tale of a construction worker (Joey McIntire) who feels compelled to drop everything and write a play about the day of a beloved uncle's wake, which he eventually stages in the back room of an Irish pub (Waltham's Skellig, though much of the movie was shot in Jamaica Plain). But the multiple happy endings might click better if we saw more of the actual play than a montage heavy on audience reaction shots. It's as if *The Commitments*—similar premise, better movie—ended without ever showing us its band can actually play.

One Crazy Summer (1986)
Better Off Dead director Savage Steve Holland and star John Cusack team up for another fun underdog comedy, this one set and shot on Nantucket and Cape Cod. While their previous collaboration is a cult film in some circles, this one is generally forgotten, unjustly. It's an often hilarious smart dumb-comedy with a deep cast that also includes Curtis Armstrong, Bob Goldthwait, Mark Metcalf, Rich Little, William Hickey, Joe Flaherty, Jeremy Piven, Taylor Negron and Demi Moore before her overhyped-star period. Buried treasure.

The Opposite Sex and How to Live with Them (1993)
A labored battle-of-the-sexes comedy about a romantic couple (Courteney Cox, Arye Gross)—she's a WASP, he's a Jew—and their

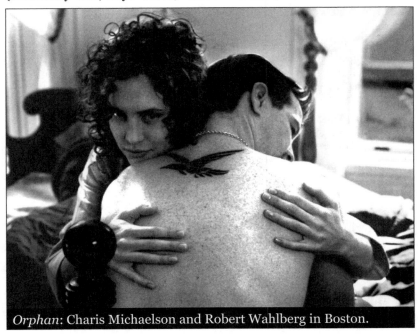

Orphan: Charis Michaelson and Robert Wahlberg in Boston.

wisecracking best friends (Julie Brown, Kevin Pollak). It visits a number of locations, including Fenway Park, the Public Garden and the Central Square Red Line station. Filming took place in the summer of 1990, yet this wasn't released in theaters until March 1993.

Orphan (2001)

Squeeze cinematographer-editor Richard Moos shot his $25,000 drama over two years in Boston, Watertown, Concord and Somerville. Writer Richard Murtaugh's premise is solid—a hit man (Marty Maguire) fulfills a vow to secretly watch over the daughter (Charis Michaelson) of a man he killed, while she is actually trying to find him and exact revenge. But the movie's scenes range from compelling to unconvincing. It's like a no-frills demo version of a catchy song that, with more resources and oomph behind it, would come across better.

Osmosis Jones (2001)

Peter and Bobby Farrelly battled a patch of bad weather during the summer of 2000 while shooting the live-action portions of their mostly-animated Bill Murray comedy. That's why the footage at such locations as the Nathaniel Morton School and Myles Standish State Forest in Plymouth looks so drab. But the movie—with the animated bulk taking place within the body of Murray's character—is very funny, and it spawned a TV spin-off.

Our Time (1974)

There is a mix of Boston and California locations in the 1950s-set coming-of-age tale set at a boarding school and focusing on two friends (Pamela Sue Martin, Betsy Slade). Later shown on TV as *The Death of Her Innocence*.

The Out of Towners (1970)

Jack Lemmon gives one of his more annoying worry-wart performances in this Neil Simon travel comedy in which *everything* goes wrong—including his and Sandy Dennis' New York plane being diverted to Boston. Scenes were shot at Logan Airport and South Station, featuring the two stars as well as Ron Carey and Billy Dee Williams. Director Arthur Hiller's next picture would be *Love Story*.

Outside Providence (1999)

Michael Corrente's fun adaptation of Peter Farrelly's 1988 coming-of-age novel about a Pawtucket townie (Shawn Hatosy) shipped off to an upper-class prep school shot scenes in Attleboro and Foxboro. But, fittingly, it shot mostly in Ocean State locations such as Pawtucket, the University of Rhode Island in Kingston and a soundstage inside a Providence armory.

Overserved (2004)
Writer-director Joe Gallo filmed his ensemble workplace comedy, set in a bar, at such locations as the Samuel Adams Brewery in Jamaica Plain and Redbones in Somerville, as well as on Boston Common. *Cheers* with hormones and tattoos.

The Paper Chase (1973)
The hit Harvard Law School drama spawned a TV series and an acting career for former producer John Houseman, whose imposing professor dominates the movie. But, a decade before it became a Hollywood trend to use Canadian locations to double for U.S. cities, this was shot almost entirely in Toronto. The original plan was to do it all in Boston and Cambridge, but in a 1985 *Globe* article director James Bridges lamented that he got "no cooperation" from locals when he tried to put together the production here. Ultimately, only a shot of stars Timothy Bottoms and Lindsay Wagner in Harvard Square and another scene at Harvard Stadium were filmed here.

Passionada (2003)
Set among New Bedford's Portuguese-American community, and filmed there, this romantic comedy plugs New Bedford into the ethnic romantic-comedy formula, and the results are, well, formulaic—right down to the multiple happy endings you can see coming from a mile away. This often amateurish tale of three generations of lovelorn women (Emmy Rossum, Sofia Milos, Lupe Ontiveros) is full of ethnic and local color, including the Shawmut Diner, but it's no *Moonstruck*.

Payoff (1998)
Kaylyn Thornal's documentary follows Jen Trynin, Kay Hanley and Laurie Geltman on each's quest to make music and succeed in the music business. A reminder of the mid-1990s alternative music boom, when record companies actually sought new voices.

Physical Evidence (1989)
Fuzz star Burt Reynolds is back, for one of the unconvincing crime thrillers he made in the late 1980s. Here, he's a cop on the edge, framed for murder and defended by a pouty public defender trying to prove herself (Theresa Russell). Despite the touristy opening montage and a few scenes filmed locally, particularly in Government Center and in Chelsea, most of it was done in Toronto and Montreal.

Pony Trouble! (2005)
It's only fun until someone gets hurt in Warren Lynch's Newton-shot comedy, spoofing role-playing games by giving its action (involving toy ponies) a creepy-kinky aspect. Bizarre.

A Pound of Flesh (1994)

Catherine Burns, later producer of such homegrown indies as *All the Rage* and *Starving Artists*, directed this flimsy but funny comedy in which a black market human liver is the center of everyone's attention. Its best parts are definitely those with Sandi Carroll and Ian Lithgow (son of John) as an irreverent couple looking for unconventional good times. This movie not only led to *Starving Artists* (its director, Allan Piper, is the assistant director here), but also to Brad Anderson's *The Darien Gap* (he's sound recordist and assistant camera); charismatic Carroll co-stars in both subsequent movies.

Possessions (2008)

Longtime local theater projectionist David Kornfeld directed this supernatural thriller—about a terminally ill girl who claims a benevolent spirit has healed her—in such locations as Somerville, Waltham and Jamaica Plain.

The Pool (1987)

Waltham was a location for this Tina Louise picture. There's no sign it was ever released, though.

Pray for Power (2001)

Leaving Scars director Brad Jacques, star Lisa Boyle and much of the supporting cast reteam for another direct-to-video erotic thriller. This was filmed in 1996, presumably just after the earlier movie, and includes glimpses of Copley Square, Chinatown, Charles Circle and the North Station area.

Pretty Poison (1968)

With Berkshires locations—particularly Great Barrington (look for its Mahaiwe Theater)—forming the fictional town of Winslow, this dark comedy is late-1960s buried treasure and a contender for the best movie ever shot in western Massachusetts. Anthony Perkins taps into his creepy *Psycho* weirdness as an unstable schemer with a rich imagination, but he meets his match in an All-American girl gone wrong, so devilishly played by Tuesday Weld. It's his best post-*Psycho* role, and her best movie role, period.

Pride of the Clan (1917)

Mary Pickford's Scottish-set drama uses some Marblehead exteriors.

Primary Motive (1992)

With Judd Nelson starring as a Harvard grad who becomes press secretary to a senator, this very obscure, locally set drama somehow meshes locations in Boston and, I kid you not, Luxembourg.

Prozac Nation (2001)

Norton's Wheaton College doubles for Harvard Yard in this hard-to-take adaptation of Elizabeth Wurtzel's best-selling memoir (as it did in *Soul Man*). Chronicling her mid-1980s breakdown while a student at Harvard, it includes a few moments shot in Harvard Square, most notably one involving Christina Ricci (who plays Wurtzel) and Michelle Williams walking through the area, which has been filled with 1980s cars. Canada was the primary filming location for the movie, which sat on Miramax' shelf for four years before premiering on cable.

Ratchet (1996)

Little-seen neo-noir about a Manhattan screenwriter (Tom Gilroy) suffering from writer's block who heads to Nantucket and encounters much intrigue there.

Real Men Cry (2008)

South Boston native Brian Goodman's former life of crime inspired his autobiographical script, which filmed locally in the early winter of 2007-08. His "neighborhood movie" stars Mark Ruffalo and Ethan Hawke, as well as Amanda Peet, years after she co-starred in *Southie*.

The Reincarnation of Peter Proud (1975)

Springfield-area locations highlight this supernatural thriller. Long out of print on VHS and not yet on DVD, it stars early-1970s leading man Michael Sarrazin as a guy having weird dreams who travels to Massachusetts to investigate them.

Return (1986)

Partially shot in central Massachusetts, director Andrew Silver's drama follows a young woman (Karlene Crockett) who discovers a man (John Walcutt) who can hypnotically regress into her late grandfather, who died under mysterious circumstances. Also starring Frederic Forrest and Anne Francis, it plays like a solid *Twilight Zone* episode. More recently, Silver made the documentary *Profiles in Aspiration*, and shot *Cape Cod Radio* in the late summer of 2007.

The Return of the Secaucus 7 (1980)

John Sayles' New Hampshire-shot comedy about counterculture pals reuniting—a premise later co-opted by *The Big Chill*—isn't just a well-written, character-driven comedy. Its success also helped to trigger the rise of American independent film as we know it today. Although only tangentially a Boston movie in content, many involved had ties to the area: Sayles and his producer-actress partner, Maggie Renzi, had lived in East Boston for a time, while fellow cast members Gordon Clapp, Adam LeFevre and David Strathairn had gone to Williams

College with them. And any Bostonian old enough to remember will surely get a kick out of several characters' spoof of the frantic stock car racing radio commercials for events in Epping, N.H. ("*Sunday*!!!").

The River Wild (1994)
Meryl Streep sculls down the Charles at the start of the Curtis Hanson thriller, as a river guide whose family tangles with a pair of armed robbers once the action heads west.

Rough Road (1992)
Instead of asking her parents to pay for film school, Lisa Faircloth convinced them to put up the seed money for her road movie, which started filming in 1989 but didn't finish until 1992. Her tale of a young couple whose desire to hit the open road is thwarted by meddling relatives is technically scruffy, but boasts endearing leads.

Rowing Through (1996)
Based on David Halberstam's book *The Amateurs*, this docudrama about Olympic rowers includes action shot on the Charles and at the Harvard Boat House in Cambridge.

Run (1991)
Patrick Dempsey can be seen briefly in the city at the start of this ludicrous thriller in which he plays a law student who goes on the lam after a run-in with the mob.

Sabrina (1995)
There are a few Martha's Vineyard locations, including Main Street in

Salesman: Paul Brennan in Boston.

Edgartown, among the many locales in the remake of Billy Wilder's 1950s romantic drama.

Salesman (1968)

Documentary innovators Albert and David Maysles, who grew up in Dorchester and Brookline, return home for much of their documentary about Boston-based Bible salesmen. When it's not showing us the Bible hawkers trying to push overpriced merchandise on working-class customers who could put the money to better use, it's focusing on Paul "The Rabbit" Brennan, the most dramatic of the four Boston men, a real-life Willy Loman whose confidence is fading fast. Brennan's luck doesn't get any better when the salesmen leave Dorchester and central Massachusetts and head to sunny Florida to ply their wares.

The Same Side of Rejection Street (2000)

Clunky moments aside, S.G. Collins' hi-def feature has one of the more ambitious scripts of any homegrown indie film. Set over one action-packed day, it's about the uneasy friendship that develops between a philosophical homeless man (Micheal Henderson) and an unemployed woman (Karen Ball). As the two walk from Downtown Crossing and the Financial District to South Boston and Dorchester, the movie mixes in heartache, laughs, the obstacle of racism and even gospel music. It's an all-encompassing mix that usually works.

The Sandpiper (2006)

After giving up on Hollywood, Cape Cod native Claudia Carey returned home to write and direct this love triangle about two teen friends (John Lavelle, Tom Mazur) who fall for the same girl (Vanessa Daniels).

The Same Side of Rejection Street: Karen Ball and Micheal Henderson in South Boston.

Screamplay (1984)

The Boston Movie Company, whose many shorts were a favorite at local alternative venues in the early 1980s, made this clever feature mostly within a South End loft, even though the comic thriller is set in Hollywood. Writer-director-star Rufus Butler Seder's movie is about a scriptwriter whose life begins imitating his murder-filled art; it's a sort of resourcefully lo-fi *Barton Fink* (which it pre-dates). It actually played at Copley Place Cinema, back when local chain Sack Theaters opened the since-shuttered concrete-bunker-filled multiplex as its flagship and let the Institute of Contemporary Art program one screen. But such ambition didn't last long there.

Second Sight (1989)

An embarrassing *Ghostbusters* wannabe about a psychic detective agency run by an irritable ex-cop (John Larroquette), a scientist (Stuart Pankin) and a "wacky" psychic (Bronson Pinchot). Someone thought it was a smart idea to set this special-effects comedy here since "our heroes" are trying to find a missing Cardinal. Production closed one of the harbor tunnels for one night for filming, while the Public Garden, Chinatown, the Naked I Cabaret and the original Blue Diner can be seen, as well as passing shots of Beacon Hill, the South End and Comm. Ave.

Serial Intentions (2001)

Director Brad Jacques (*Pray for Power*, *Leaving Scars*) makes another low-budget thriller, this time about the investigation of a serial killer. Locations include Burlington, Newton, Andover and Saugus' since-leveled club The Palace, and among its stars is Christy Scott Cashman (*The Strangler's Wife*, *What's the Worst That Could Happen?*). Showings of this were few and far between.

The Serpent and the Rainbow (1988)

Among director Wes (*A Nightmare on Elm Street*) Craven's best movies that aren't straight horror. This chiller about a Boston anthropologist (Bill Pullman) exploring voodoo and "zombie powder" in Haiti includes a few quick shots of the city, one with the star walking through Copley Square. Rob Cohen, Harvard grad and director of *A Small Circle of Friends*, is one of the producers of this adaptation of Harvard scientist Wade Davis' non-fiction book.

Sex, Drugs, Rock & Roll (1991)

Director John (*Henry: Portrait of a Serial Killer*) McNaughton shot Woburn-born monologist Eric Bogosian's character-filled performance film over several nights at Boston's Wilbur Theater. A provocative document of Bogosian's many one-man shows from the period.

Shallow Hal (2001)
A skiing sequence in Peter and Bobby Farrelly's Jack Black-Gwyneth Paltrow comedy was done at Wachusett Mountain Ski Area in Princeton; the wintry sequence was cut from the movie, though it survives in footage during the end credits.

She Lives to Ride (1995)
South End resident Alice Stone made this fun look at several female motorcyclists, including a few unassuming elderly ladies who, in their own way, blazed a feminist trail on their bikes.

Shuttle (2008)
The supernatural thriller filmed in Everett, Chelsea, Lynn and Revere, among other places, and was in post-production as this book was being readied.

Soul Man (1986)
There are a handful of Cambridge locations, but Norton's Wheaton College stands in for Harvard in this dud combination of 1980s campus comedy and *Black Like Me* social commentary. C. Thomas Howell plays the white student who nabs a scholarship to Harvard Law by, essentially, putting on blackface. The story isn't the only weird combination—how about Lou Reed replacing Dave Prater and singing, with Sam Moore, a cover version of the Sam & Dave song that provides the title?

The Spanish Prisoner (1997)
One of writer-director David (*State and Main*) Mamet's most ingenious movies. His drama about a naïve New York inventor (Campbell Scott) who's duped into giving up his top-secret "process" by a slick con man (Steve Martin) climaxes in Boston, during scenes set on Route 1A, at Logan Airport, on a water shuttle and at Rowes Wharf. Mamet also shot at Boylston Street's Tennis and Racquet Club.

Spartan (2004)
Another nifty thriller from writer-director David Mamet, this one partially set and shot in Greater Boston. Val Kilmer stars as a military covert operations specialist trying to retrieve the kidnapped daughter (Kristen Bell) of the president. She happens to be a Harvard student, and early action was filmed in such locales as Copley Square, Beacon Hill, Framingham, Cape Ann and on the expressway, including what was then the only partially open Zakim Bridge. When the action switches to the West and the Middle East, Los Angeles locations take over, though the under-construction Granite Links Golf Course on the Milton-Quincy line stands in for some desert action.

Starving Artists: Bess Wohl and Allan Piper in Harvard Square.

Starving Artists (1997)
The absurdity in Allan Piper's Harvard Square comedy is hit or miss. Its funniest action involves his playwright character's uncomfortable courtship of neighbor Mildred (Bess Wohl), whom he almost always manages to unwittingly insult. The production came up with a fun way to raise part of its $50,000 budget: everyone who donated at least $1 got his or her name in the movie, whether it was as graffiti, in a newspaper headline or on a note on someone's wall.

Steps (1980)
Eric Neudel's hour-long documentary is about friends Pamela Daly and Margaret Powell, the first of whom lost use of her legs in a car accident as a teenager. After impressing at the First Boston Independent Film Festival at the Coolidge Corner in 1980, it had a short run there.

Stiffs (2007)
The North End brothers Frank and Joseph Ciota's funeral-parlor comedy starring Danny Aiello—shot in the North End, Beacon Hill, Everett, Somerville, Watertown and Randolph in early 2006— underwent a lengthy editing process before debuting at 2007's Boston Film Festival.

Stuck on You (2003)
Peter and Bobby Farrelly's tale of conjoined twins (Matt Damon, Greg Kinnear) who move from Martha's Vineyard to Hollywood so one can pursue an acting career is very amusing and very good-

Stuck on You: Matt Damon and Greg Kinnear in Rockport.

natured (Kinnear is especially entertaining). Although only partially set locally—with Rockport and Gloucester usually doubling for the Vineyard—New England flavors the entire movie. Because of the Farrellys' penchant for casting their buddies in supporting parts, it seems half of Hollywood has a Boston accent in this one. But not Cher, though she's appealing as a fictionalized version of herself, nor Meryl Streep, who relishes the comic possibilities of her cameo.

Summer Catch (2001)
This irredeemably dumb combination of baseball and hormones—*Bull Durham for Dummies*, perhaps—is set on Cape Cod, but was shot mostly in the Carolinas. This fact gives the Freddie Prinze, Jr. Cape Cod Baseball League action one of *the* great botched local moments in all of movies—when someone even slips a "y'all" into the dialogue. Well, at least it wasn't "Pissa, y'all!"

Summer Wishes, Winter Dreams (1973)
There is rural Berkshires action in this drab drama about a disillusioned Manhattan couple played by Joanne Woodward and Martin Balsam.

Tax Day (1999)
Harvard grad Laura Colella's delightful film has a great fondness for serendipity. Set on April 15, it starts with Irene (Kathleen Monteleone) asking friend Paula (Donna Sorbello) to walk to the post office with

her so she can mail her tax return. But so much happens on that encounter-filled journey, and the unpredictable tale is like a road movie on foot, with canoe and bus rides thrown in. Perhaps the best homegrown Providence movie.

Tea Cakes or Cannoli (2002)
Abe Vigoda comes to the North End. Too bad it's only for this *Moonstruck* wannabe. The *Barney Miller* and *Fish* star plays the oldest in three generations of characters looking for love, but writer/co-director/co-star Francine Pellegrino and co-director Nino Pepicelli's romantic comedy battles credibility problems almost from the opening credits. The movie is so cartoonish it actually includes a stereotypical Italian woman walking into a North End butcher's shop while singing "O Sole Mio." So even the local color is iffy.

Temps (1999)
Director Maria Burton came to town to make her movie with her four sisters, because the city suited the story of college grads and because two of those sisters lived here at the time. Area locations include Brighton, Central Square's Liberty Café (R.I.P.) and the West Newton Cinema, while veteran actors Seymour Cassell (*Stuck on You*) and Jerry Orbach (*Law & Order*) have small roles—the latter in voice only. Despite a few festival showings years after its 1996 shoot, the movie never came out in theaters (and only just recently resurfaced on DVD), most likely because its tale of temping grads, one of whom is a moviemaker who films her friends, plays like a *Reality Bites* retread. The sisters have continued to collaborate on movies elsewhere.

There's Something About Mary (1998)
Although Peter and Bobby Farrelly's comedy classic takes place mainly in Miami, it starts in Providence, home to some of its characters. The brothers shot four days there with Ben Stiller, Chris Elliott (son of Winchester-born radio-comedy icon Bob Elliott) and Hillary Matthews. The neo-Colonial house where this early action takes place overlooks the city at the corner of Congdon and Bowen Streets. A little closer to Boston, Drew Bledsoe turned down the cameo role that went to Brett Favre.

This Town (2002)
Like its hero Rick (Barlow Adamson), Chris Engles' romantic comedy is kinda dorky, kinda charming. The comedy runs hot and cold as lovelorn Rick tries to find a girlfriend, and its surreal moments only sometimes click. But it definitely evokes the Cambridge-Somerville of its day, with scenes shot in such hot spots as the Green Street Grill, Lizard Lounge and the long-gone Record Hog.

Title to Murder (2001)

Step into the wayback machine as Maureen McCormack (*The Brady Brunch*) and Christopher Atkins (*The Blue Lagoon*) star in this thriller directed by Stephen Furst (*Animal House*). Shot entirely in Massachusetts; locations include Charlestown and Salisbury Beach.

To Gillian on Her 37th Birthday (1996)

With a script by former Boston lawyer and current TV mogul David E. Kelley, this ensemble romantic drama mixes Nantucket shooting with its predominant North Carolina locations.

Tough Guys Don't Dance (1987)

You'll never forget Norman Mailer's hilariously nutso thriller, shot in and around Provincetown. With dialogue like "Deep six the heads!" (from *Reservoir Dogs'* hard-boiled Lawrence Tierney) and "Oh God! Oh man! Oh God! Oh man!" (from overmatched star Ryan O'Neal), this really should have become a *Plan 9 from Outer Space* for the 1980s. It's not too late for its special charms to be appreciated, I suppose.

The Tourist (1992)

You'll find Robb Moss' name in the credits of most significant Boston documentaries—he's been a teacher or colleague of most of their directors. This may be his best work, an hour-long my-life-as-art movie that's a pleasing stew of melancholy and mirth as it balances Moss' globetrotting camera work (on other people's documentaries) with his and his wife's struggle to conceive a child. Sad ironies abound, and the balancing act somehow succeeds tremendously. Moss later made *The Same River Twice* and co-directed *Secrecy*.

Treading Water (2001)

B.U. grad Lauren Himmel's drama about a fisherwoman (Angela Redman) cautiously bringing her girlfriend (Nina Landey) to her family's Christmas gathering features plenty of chilly scenes of Cape Cod winter.

Tupperware! (2003)

Boston documentarian Laurie Kahn-Leavitt's fun movie zips us back to the 1950s. That's when Massachusetts inventor Earl Tupper and go-getter Brownie Wise (one of the country's first powerful female executives) rally a legion of housewives selling the plastic containers that ruled the world. Through interviews with Tupperware ladies and distributors (some of them local), amazing clips from company films and a heavy dose of vintage songs, Kahn-Leavitt recalls the country's post-war materialism and the opportunities Tupperware presented to thousands of working-class women.

Turntable (2006)

Robert (*Squeeze*) Patton-Spruill's return to directing—after several years spent establishing his Film Shack production house—is another French-New-Wave-inspired attempt at an urban tale broadened by artsy textures. This time, though, his story of a DJ (Russell G. Jones) caught up in the criminal schemes of his brothers (including Tyrone Burton of *Squeeze*) sinks under the weight of its hero's mopey, nearly incessant "deep" voice-overs. Patton-Spruill shot his reworking of François Truffaut's *Shoot the Piano Player* at such locations as Slades Bar & Grill in Roxbury and The Breakfast Club in Allston.

12 (2008)

Filmed throughout 2007, this is a thematically-linked anthology of twelve short films, each made by a different director and shot during a different month.

21 (2008)

M.I.T. math wizzes take on the Vegas casinos in the movie adapted from Ben Mezrich's *Bringing Down the House*, shot in the spring of 2007. Locations include Chinatown, Harvard Medical School, Boston University, the Fenway near Simmons College, the People's Republik bar and, for some casino action, the made-over interior of the Boston Convention and Exposition Center. The production also had the *cajones* to close down the Mass. Ave. Bridge for an entire Sunday. That's the closest it got to M.I.T., which denied it permission to shoot on campus.

Two if By Sea (1996)

Denis Leary was only able to get minimal location shooting on the romantic comedy he co-wrote and stars in with Sandra Bullock. It's set on the Cape and islands but shot mostly in Nova Scotia. What's worse, Leary and director Bill Bennett clashed creatively and the comedy about a thief, his girlfriend and a stolen painting fizzled.

Vendetta (2002)

Filmed as *Irish Eyes* and beset by last-minute cast changes and a host of production upheavals, Milton native Daniel McCarthy's Boston-set action-drama about two Bulger-like brothers—one a crook (Daniel Baldwin), one in politics (John Novak)—shot four days' worth of Boston exteriors. But, like *Blue Hill Avenue*, its primary location is Saint John, New Brunswick, with some shooting done in Los Angeles, too. The name change came for its DVD release.

Victor's Big Score (1992)

Although Brian Anthony's scruffy dark comedy failed to receive much exposure, it has enough laughs to overcome its no-budget production values. This story of an inept barber (Seth Barrish) who must choose between the affections of a rich widow (Elaine Wood) and a sexy but poor nurse (Eve Annenberg) has a lot of kismet behind it, too. It's based on a self-published novel that a friend of Anthony's found in a garbage can (one of only 500 copies printed). When Anthony didn't have $2,000 to purchase an option on the book's movie rights, he went outside and discovered that a tree had fallen on his car. The insurance settlement paid for the option, and the subsequent movie was filmed at such locations as Somerville Hospital, a Swampscott inn and a Bedford home.

Warlock (1989)
Footage shot at Plimouth Plantation enhances the early action in this fun supernatural horror film about a son-of-Satan villain (Julian Sands) who's about to be hanged in 1691 Boston. But he's saved when the Prince of Darkness whisks him to contemporary Los Angeles—with the demon-fighter who captured him (Richard E. Grant) in pursuit.

Whose Life is it Anyway?: Richard Dreyfuss and Kaki Hunter at Christopher Columbus Waterfront Park.

What I Did When I Was Away (1997)

Ted Cormey's black-and-white romantic drama, often set within the music clubs of the city (and featuring music by several local Goth bands), shot in Boston and Cambridge and on the South Shore.

Who's Afraid of Virginia Woolf? (1966)

The knockdown, drag-out Richard Burton-Liz Taylor slugfest includes Northampton and Southampton exteriors. The contentious couple they play is as misanthropic and riveting as ever.

Whose Life is it Anyway? (1981)

Set in Boston, most of this adaptation of Brian Clark's thought-provoking play was filmed on sets in California. There are exteriors of Faulkner Hospital and, most notably, an opening sequence in which sculptor Ken Harrison (Richard Dreyfuss) erects an abstract installation in Christopher Columbus Waterfront Park on the edge of the North End.

Working Stiff (2001)

Writer-director Greg Joyce labored for years on his workplace comedy about a debt-ridden guy making a sexual harassment training video who uses his company's equipment to make a porn version of the same video on the sly.

Yes, Giorgio (1982)

In his first (and last) Hollywood romantic comedy, Luciano Pavarotti plays an opera superstar on the prowl for a "fling" during an American tour (sample pickup line: "You are a thirsty plant. Fini can water you."). One of the more notorious and gimmicky flops of the early 1980s, this leaves few ethnic caricatures unturned and sometimes makes the Spice Girls' movie look like *A Hard Day's Night*. At least Bostonians got a free Pavarotti concert on the Esplanade out of it for the local sequence, while the Copley Plaza Hotel also appears.

Yidl in the Middle: Growing Up Jewish in Iowa (1998)

Veteran Boston filmmaker Marlene Booth's hour-long memoir of her childhood in the heartland is a warm and amusing look at the tug of war between heritage and assimilation. Booth had earlier co-directed *The Forward*, an evocative look at the Jewish newspaper.

Young Goodman Brown (1993)

Surf Nazis Must Die director Peter George tackles Nathaniel Hawthorne in this low-budget drama shot in Salem, Danvers and Topsfield. Called "hokey" and "static" by a *Variety* reviewer, this may not have ever actually been released, though.

The Great Boston Movie Quiz

1-Name the 2002 Hong Kong movie *The Departed* remakes.

2-Match the singer to the locally shot movie to which he or she sings the theme song:

1-Mary Kaye   A-*Six Bridges to Cross*
2-Sammy Davis, Jr.   B-*Never Too Late*
3-Vic Damone   C-*Home Before Dark* (1958)

3-Behind which fictional bar does Sean Penn's character murder the childhood friend played by Tim Robbins in *Mystic River*?

4-Which future two-time Oscar winner plays *The Next Karate Kid*?

5-Two directors parted ways with *Mermaids* before Richard Benjamin took over the helm. Name them, as well as the movies each later returned to Massachusetts to film.

6-Match each movie with the closed mental hospital in which it filmed action:

1-*The Cider House Rules*   A-Metropolitan State Hospital
2-*Session 9*   B-Mass. Mental Health Center
3-*Long Distance*   C-Northampton State Hospital
4-*Oleanna*   D-Danvers State Hospital

7-Name the boat that explodes in *Blown Away*.

8-In which locally produced movie were Matt Damon and Ben Affleck ready to play small roles, had they not landed pre-*Good Will Hunting* leads elsewhere in the fall of 1996?

9-To what Boston hotel does Tom Cruise's character go for a job interview in *The Firm*?

10-Which movie contains each of the following—*The Good Son* or *The Good Mother*?:

A-Divorced mother
B-Dead mother
C-Child-star deathmatch
D-Child custody battle
E-Sexual scandal
F-Vandalism

11-On which MBTA bus route do Burt Reynolds' and Jill Clayburgh's characters travel in *Starting Over*?

12-The lobby of which grand Boston theater provides the interior of the mansion belonging to Jack Nicholson's character in *The Witches of Eastwick*?

13-Ryan O'Neal was only the third choice to play Oliver Barrett in *Love Story*. Name the two actors who turned down the role.

14-Which local police force does Matt Damon's character infiltrate in *The Departed*?

15-Which locally born character actor was Tony Curtis' dialect coach for *The Boston Strangler*?

16-On which remote coastal island did *The Crucible* recreate 1690s Salem Village?

17-Match the fictional town with the movie:

1-Dobb's Mill	A-*The Love Letter*
2-Cape Ann	B-*Mermaids*
3-Eastport	C-*Housesitter*
4-Loblolly-by-the-Sea	D-*Moonlight Mile*
5-Cape Marble	E-*Never Too Late*
6-Calvertown	F-*Home Before Dark* (1958)

18-Which future TV and movie star is an extra in the courtroom scenes in *The Verdict*?

19-Who is told to "walk east on Beacon" in the 1952 movie of the same name, and who has instructed him to do so?

20-Whom did Goldie Hawn replace at the last minute as the female lead in *Housesitter*?

21-In which city were most of the scenes in *Good Will Hunting* and *Fever Pitch* filmed?

22-What is the name of the Gloucester swordfishing boat that rode into *The Perfect Storm*?

23-Which Boston sports hero does Robert Mitchum's title character root on in *The Friends of Eddie Coyle*?:

A-John Havlicek
B-Carl Yastrzemski
C-Bobby Orr
D-Norm Siebern

24-What is the real name of Jimmy Dove, the Boston Bomb Squad member Jeff Bridges plays in *Blown Away*?

25-Match the working title each movie was shot under to the name with which it was eventually released:

1-*Snitch*	A-*Getting Personal*
2-*Somehow Scituate*	B-*Moonlight Mile*
3-*Baby's in Black*	C-*Southie*
4-*Shakespeare's Sister*	D-*Monument Ave.*
5-*Brass Ring*	E-*The Proposition*

26-At what since-closed Harvard Square landmark do both Matt Damon and Minnie Driver in *Good Will Hunting* and Ali MacGraw and Ryan O'Neal in *Love Story* eat?

27-Name the veteran film director who plays a supporting role in *A Civil Action*, and name the legal thriller he shot partially in Boston and Cambridge.

28-Which Boston comic plays each of the following roles—Steve Sweeney or Lenny Clarke?:

A-Gabby cabbie in *Next Stop Wonderland*
B-A guy named Skunk in *Monument Ave.*
C-Unshaven landlord in *Celtic Pride*
D-Wacky uncle in *Fever Pitch*
E-Drunk wedding guest in *Southie*
F-Gadget-handy thief in *What's the Worst That Could Happen?*
G-Donut-downing mobster in *Southie*

29-The baseball romance *Fever Pitch* is an Americanized version of Nick Hornby's novel, in which the hero is a soccer fan. Which English football team does the book's hero support?

30-What is the title of the movie being filmed by the characters in *State and Main*?

31-Where does Robin Williams' character teach psychology in *Good Will Hunting*?

32-Which *Love Story* co-star and Oscar winner was the first house manager at Cambridge's legendary Orson Welles Cinema?

33-What is the name of the fictional alternative weekly newspaper in *Between the Lines*?

34-Name at least four movies that filmed inside Fenway Park.

35-Why was director Otto Preminger taken to court during the filming of *Tell Me That You Love Me, Junie Moon* in 1969?

36-Which three movies comprise director Jan Egleson's 1970s-1980s Boston trilogy?

37-Which Massachusetts college's quadrangle doubles for Harvard Yard in *Soul Man* and *Prozac Nation*?

38-Match each *The North End* actor with the role he later played on *The Sopranos*:

1-Frank Vincent   A-Brian Cammarata
2-Matthew Del Negro   B-Phil Leotardo
3-Tony Darrow   C-"Larry Boy" Barese

39-Which Red Sox superfan profiled in the documentary *Still, We Believe* bagged a speaking role in Peter and Bobby Farrelly's *Fever Pitch*—as a Red Sox superfan?

40-Name the locally shot movie Tony Curtis starred in over a decade *before* he made *The Boston Strangler*.

41-In which of the following Massachusetts cities did *A Civil Action* NOT film any scenes?

A-Dedham
B-Waltham
C-Woburn
D-Palmer

42-Which player hits the foul ball that konks Drew Barrymore's character in the head in *Fever Pitch*?

43-Robin Williams introduced Matt Damon to Steven Spielberg—resulting in Damon's casting in *Saving Private Ryan*—during a visit to the set of which Spielberg movie shooting at the State House?

44-What kind of store does Kate Capshaw's character own in *The Love Letter*?

45-What is the nickname of the high school sports team in the small town where *State and Main* is set?

46-Celtics fans played by Dan Aykroyd and Daniel Stern kidnap an opposing player in *Celtic Pride*. For which team does that Damon Wayans character play?

47-Which future Oscar winner plays the slacker activist who dumps heroine Erin (Hope Davis) at the start of *Next Stop Wonderland*?

48-Which movie do Karen Allen's and Brad Davis' characters see at The Orson Welles Cinema in *A Small Circle of Friends*?

49-Three movies feature scenes in The North End's Copp's Hill Burying Ground. Name them. (Hint: Two have character actor Jack Weston in their cast.)

50-Which under-construction complex was the site of much of the action in 1986's *Billy Galvin*?

51-Which Boston independent drama won a Grand Prize at Park City, Utah's 4th U.S. Film & Video Festival—the film fest later renamed Sundance?

52-From what does Joe Pesci's character in *With Honors* die?

53-Danny Aiello characters have daughters named Renata in *two* Bay State movies. What are they?

54-Name every Wahlberg that appears in each of the following:

A-*The Perfect Storm*
B-*Mystic River*
C-*Southie*
D-*Orphan*
E-*On Broadway*
F-*The Departed*
G-*Gone Baby Gone*

Answers:

1-*Infernal Affairs*.
2-1-C; 2-A; 3-B.
3-*The Black Emerald*.
4-Hilary Swank.
5-Lasse Hallström, who later made *The Cider House Rules*, and Frank Oz, who returned to direct *Housesitter*.
6-1-C; 2-D; 3-B; 4-A.
7-The Dolphin.
8-*Floating*. They were ready to join Casey Affleck as a trio of pot-purchasing preppies.
9-Copley Plaza.
10-*Good Mother*: A, D, E; *Good Son*: B, C, F.
11-#57 to Watertown.
12-The Wang Center (now Citi Performing Arts Center).
13-Beau Bridges and Michael York.
14-The Massachusetts State Police.
15-Alex Rocco, born Alexander Petricone.
16-Hog Island.
17-1-C; 2-D; 3-B; 4-A; 5-F; 6-E.
18-Bruce Willis.
19-A scientist being strong-armed by Soviet spies.
20-Meg Ryan.
21-Toronto.
22-Andrea Gail.
23-C.
24-Liam McGivney.
25-1-D; 2-A; 3-B; 4-E; 5-C.
26-The Tasty.
27-Sydney Pollack, who had directed *The Firm*.
28-Sweeney: A, C, E; Clarke: B, D, F, G.
29-Arsenal.
30-*The Old Mill*, though it's eventually changed to *Fires of Home*.
31-Bunker Hill Community College.
32-Tommy Lee Jones.
33-Back Bay Maritime.
34-Any of these: *Blown Away, Little Big League, Fever Pitch, Field of Dreams, Fear Strikes Out, The Opposite Sex and How to Live with Them, A Civil Action* (cut scene).
35-For desecration, after filming a scene in which Liza Minnelli's character does a striptease in Braintree's Blue Hill Cemetery. The actress was wearing a body stocking, and Preminger beat the rap.
36-*Billy in the Lowlands, The Dark End of the Street* and *The Little Sister* (a/k/a *The Tender Age*).
37-Wheaton College in Norton.
38-1-B; 2-A; 3-C.
39-Jessamy Finet.
40-*Six Bridges to Cross*.
41-C.
42-Miguel Tejada, then of the Baltimore Orioles.
43-*Amistad*.
44-Bookstore.
45-Huskies ("Go, you Huskies!").
46-The Utah Jazz.
47-Philip Seymour Hoffman.
48-*The Graduate*.
49-*The Thomas Crown Affair, Fuzz* and *The Proposition*. Jack Weston is in the first two.
50-Marketplace Center.
51-*The Dozens*.
52-Lung failure due to asbestos exposure.
53-*Once Around* and *Dead Silence* (a/k/a *Wilbur Falls*).
54-A-Mark; B-Robert; C-Donnie, Robert; D-Robert; E-Robert; F-Mark, Robert; G-Robert.

Index

Myles Standish State Forest, 215.
My Life as a Dog, 127.
Myopia Hunt Club, 161, 162.
Mystery Street, iii, 113-115, 140, 172, 174, 175.
Mystic River, ii, viii, ix, 50, 57, 62, 69, 94, 115-118, 210, 213, 233, 237.
Mystic Valley Parkway, 127.

Nader, George, 140, 141.
Nahant, 35.
Najimy, Kathy, 205.
Naked City, The, 172.
Naked I Cabaret, 221.
Nanstad, Erin, 57, 153.
Nantucket, 214, 218, 226.
Narragansett Race Track, 30.
Nashawtuc Road, 119.
Natale, Alan, 2.
Nathaniel Morton School, 215.
Natick, 13, 188.
National Baseball Hall of Fame and Museum, 100.
National Velvet, 207.
Natural, The, 27.
Naughton, James, 73, 74.
Naughty or Nice, 213.
NBC, ix, 31, 177.
Near Dark, 46.
Near Death, 164.
Needham, 190, 200.
Neely, Cam, 109, 177.
Neeson, Liam, 73, 74, 190.
Negron, Taylor, 214.
Neighborhoods, 213.
Nelson, Don, 51.
Nelson, Judd, 203, 217.
Nelson, Ralph, 33, 35.
Nepomniaschy, Alex, 102.
Nervous Eaters, 179.
Neudel, Eric, 223.
Neuman, David, 51.
Never Met Picasso, 213.
Never Too Late, iii, 118-120, 233, 234.
New Bedford, iii, 117, 197, 198, 216.
New Brunswick, 150, 191, 227.
Newbury Street, 23, 57, 62, 67, 89, 90, 131, 142, 157.
New England Aquarium, 122, 123, 205.
New England Casket Company, 21.
New England Patriots, 7, 62, 119, 120.
New Hampshire, 3, 22, 60, 83, 128, 150, 175, 177, 199, 218.
New Jersey, 57, 104, 126, 193.
"New Jersey," 193.
Newman, Paul, 169, 170, 171.
New, Nancy, 27.
New Orleans, 71.
Newport Folk Festival, 201.
Newsreel, iv.
Newton, 86, 90, 121, 123, 152, 165, 176, 177, 197, 199, 205, 216, 221, 225.
New York, ii, iii, 4, 5, 18, 26, 27, 30, 32, 36, 37, 47, 50, 66, 82, 97, 102, 104, 106, 123, 126, 127, 128, 134, 143, 144, 145, 148, 150, 158, 161, 169, 171, 172, 173, 175, 177, 178, 192, 205, 215, 222.
New York, New York, 167.

New York Yankees, 152, 153.
Next Karate Kid, The, 120–121, 233.
Next Stop Wonderland, ix, 121-124, 136, 194, 235, 237.
Nicholson, Jack, 47, 49, 50, 179, 180, 181, 208, 234.
Nicholson, Julianne, 94, 95, 96.
Nick's Comedy Stop, 143, 177, 178.
Nicoletti, Ed, 200.
Nietzsche, Friedrich, 75.
Nightmare on Elm Street, A, 221.
Night School, 213.
Night Shift, 143.
Nightstage, 93.
Nilsson, Rob, vi.
Nimoy, Leonard, 73, 74.
No Cure for Cancer, 108.
No Expectations, 106.
Nolan, Lloyd, 118.
No Man of Her Own, 102.
Norfolk, 208.
Norfolk County Jail, 169.
Norris, Bruce, 36, 37.
North, Alan, 6.
Northampton, 37, 86, 193, 207, 211, 229, 233.
Northampton State Hospital, 207, 233.
Northampton Station, 106.
Northbridge, 38, 40.
North Carolina, ii, 128, 138, 203, 205, 226.
Northeastern University, 39.
North End, i, x, 1, 12, 13, 14, 29, 30, 33, 35, 57, 62, 66, 98, 104, 106, 122, 124, 125, 126, 132, 140, 141, 142, 161, 190, 198, 199, 200, 204, 210, 223, 225, 229, 237.
North End, The, x, 1, 98, 122, 124-126, 204, 223, 236.
Northern Avenue, 23.
Northern Lights, vi.
Northfield, 193.
North Margin Street, 14.
North Station, 188, 217.
North Terminal Garage Building, 30.
North Washington Street, 30, 142.
Norton, 218, 222, 238.
Norwood, 190, 201.
"Not Another Face in the Crowd," 179.
Nova, 133.
Novak, John, 227.
Nova Scotia, 227.
Nubian Notion, 191.
Nuñez, Victor, vi.
Nykvist, Sven, 148, 149, 181.

Oakland Athletics, 152, 153.
Oates, Warren, 28, 29, 30.
O'Brien, Madeline, 70.
Occidental College, 136.
O'Connor, Kevin, 29.
O'Donnell, Chris, 134, 136.
Office, The, 152.
O'Grady, Gail, 31.
O'Hara, Maureen, ii.
O'Herlihy, Dan, 83, 84.
Old Burial Hill, 75.
Oldman, Gary, 44.
Old North Church, 197.
Oleanna, 213, 233.

Acknowledgments

Special thanks must go to all the filmmakers, location managers and others who helped me with copies of their films, photographs to use and answers to my many questions. The time and support these people offered helped to make this book more comprehensive than I ever imagined: David Kleiler, Jan Egleson, Dorothy Aufiero, Dick Bartlett, Aaron Schmidt at the Boston Public Library, Jaime Ipson Burke, Catherine Burns, Maria Burton, Frank Ciota, David Collins, S.G. Collins, Randall Conrad, Jeff Coveney, Stephen Croke, Christine Dall, Garen Daly, Kate Davis, Mark Donadio, Garth Donovan, Cheryl Eagan-Donovan, Chris Engles, Mary Feuer, Mark Fitzgerald, Maureen Foley, Jay Franco, Brad Gann, John Gates, Jane Gillooly, Ellen Gitelman, Tim Grafft, Mark Hankey, Kelly Hargreaves at First Run, Beth Harrington, Charlie Harrington, Jack Hynes, Norman Jewison, Robert Jones, Alex Karpovsky, Ray Loring, Jeff Maclean, Tanja Meding at Maysles Films, Dave McLaughlin, Doug Miller, Richard Moos, Patti Moreno, David Morwick, Nick Paleologos, Rob Patton-Spruill, Gerald Peary, Carolyn Pickman, Ed Pincus, Allan Piper, Adam Roffman, Jessica Rosner at Kino, Roger Saquet, Lindsay Shah at Beanywood, Andrew Silver, Joan Micklin Silver, Ray Silver, Lucia Small, Fran Solomita, John Stimpson, Zack Stratis, Martha Swetzoff, Paul Tritter and Karen Kocinek and Anna Moore at Fred Wiseman's Zipporah Films.

Great thanks to my sister, Betsy Sherman (a fine reviewer in her own right), for copy editing my manuscript, and for David Yount for his cool cover design. More thanks to Dave and to Angelynn Grant, as well, for design and layout advice. I am also grateful to the crew at Photofest for digging up photos that served both the movies and the pictured locations at which those movies shot.

I'm also indebted to colleagues who've supported me over the years— among them Jim Verniere, Erin Graham, Rochelle O'Gorman, Nat Segaloff, Joyce Kulhawik and Black Bars Publishing's Arch Stanton. And I can't begin to explain my gratitude for the unflagging support of my wife, Susan.

■ □ ■ □ ■

About the Author

PAUL SHERMAN has been writing about movies for over 20 years. His articles and reviews have appeared in *The Boston Herald*, *The Improper Bostonian*, the Turner Classic Movies website, *Salon*, *The Chicago Sun-Times*, *Video Eyeball*, *The Boston Phoenix*, *Filmfax*, *Film Threat* and *The Dallas Observer*. He is a past president of the Boston Society of Film Critics.

Photo Credits

All Kindsa Girls: *Courtesy of Controversy Films; photo by Patrick Mathe.* • **American Wake**: *Courtesy of Hazelwood Films; photo by Claire Folger.* • **Between the Lines**: *Courtesy of Silverfilm Productions, Inc.* • **Billy in the Lowlands**: *Courtesy of Jan Egleson.* • **The Blinking Madonna and Other Miracles**: *Courtesy of Beth Harrington Productions; photo by Catherine McDermott-Tingle.* • **Blown Away**: *Courtesy of MGM/Photofest; ©MGM.* • **The Blue Diner**: *Courtesy of Jan Egleson.* • **The Brink's Job**: *Courtesy of Universal Pictures/Photofest; ©Universal Pictures.* • **Charly**: *Courtesy of ABC Pictures/Photofest; ©ABC Pictures.* • **A Civil Action**: *Courtesy of Touchstone Pictures/ Photofest; ©Touchstone Pictures.* • **Could Be Worse!**: *Courtesy of Zack Stratis; photo by Mary Kocol.* • **The Dark End of the Street**: *Courtesy of Jan Egleson.* • **Dead Heat on a Merry-Go-Round**: *Courtesy of Columbia Pictures/Photofest; ©Columbia Pictures.* • **The Departed**: *Courtesy of Warner Bros./Photofest; ©Warner Bros.; Photographer: Andrew Cooper.* • **Dirt Boy**: *Courtesy of Cool Blue Pictures; photo by Christina Morassi.* • **Down to the Sea in Ships**: *Courtesy of Kino International.* • **The Dozens**: *Courtesy of Calliope, Inc.; ©1980 Calliope Film Resources.* • **Easy Listening**: *Courtesy of Buttersnack Films; photo by Steve Calitri.* • **Everybody Wants to Be Italian**: *Courtesy of Asgaard Entertainment.* • **Fever Pitch**: *Courtesy of 20th Century Fox/Photofest; ©20th Century Fox; Photographer: Darren Michaels.* • **The Friends of Eddie Coyle**: *Courtesy of Paramount Pictures/Photofest; ©Paramount Pictures.* • **Fuzz**: *Courtesy of United Artists/Photofest; ©United Artists.* • **Girltalk**: *Courtesy of Kate Davis.* • **Gone Baby Gone**: *Courtesy of Miramax/ Photofest; ©Miramax.* • **Good Will Hunting**: *Courtesy of Miramax/Photofest; ©Miramax Films; Photographer: George Kraychyk.* • **Housesitter**: *Courtesy of Universal Pictures/Photofest; ©Universal Pictures.* • **Howard Zinn: You Can't Be Neutral on a Moving Train**: *Courtesy of First Run Features.* • **Little Erin Merryweather**: *Courtesy of Three Stone Pictures/Indican Pictures.* • **The Little Sister**: *Courtesy of Jan Egleson.* • **Malice**: *Courtesy of Columbia Pictures/Photofest; ©Columbia Pictures.* • **Mission Hill**: *Courtesy of Robert Jones; photo by Teresa Metcalf.* • **Monument Ave.**: *Courtesy of Lions Gate/Photofest; ©Lions Gate.* • **Mystery Street**: *Courtesy of Metro-Goldwyn-Mayer/Photofest; ©Metro-Goldwyn-Mayer; Photographer: Otto Dyar.* • **Mystic River**: *Courtesy of Warner Bros./ Photofest; ©Warner Bros.* • **Next Stop Wonderland**: *Courtesy of Miramax Films/ Photofest; ©Miramax Films; Photographer: Claire Folger.* • **Orphan**: *©Cathartic Film-works; photo by Eric Levenson.* • **Salesman**: *Courtesy of Maysles Films. Photo by Bruce Davidson.* • **The Same Side of Rejection Street**: *Courtesy of S.G. Collins.* • **Six Bridges to Cross**: *Courtesy of Universal Pictures/Photofest; ©Universal Pictures.* • **Squeeze**: *Courtesy of Miramax/Photofest; ©Miramax.* • **Starving Artists**: *Courtesy of Feste Films; ©1997 Joshua Lavine.* • **Stuck on You**: *Courtesy of 20th Century Fox/ Photofest; ©20th Century Fox.* • **Theme: Murder**: *Courtesy of Martha Swetzoff.* • **The Thomas Crown Affair**: *Courtesy of United Artists/Photofest; ©United Artists.* • **Titicut Follies**: *Courtesy of Zipporah Films. ©1967 Bridgewater Film Company.* • **Urban Relics**: *Courtesy of Roger Saquet.* • **The Verdict**: *Courtesy of 20th Century Fox/Photofest; ©20th Century Fox.* • **Walk East on Beacon!**: *Courtesy of Columbia Pictures/Photofest; ©Columbia Pictures.* • **Whose Life is it Anyway?**: *Courtesy of MGM/Photofest; ©MGM.* • **The Witches of Eastwick**: *Courtesy of Warner Bros./ Photofest; ©Warner Bros.*

www.BigScreenBoston.com
Get updates and news.
Post **your** favorite Boston movies.